Big Fish

45'

Also by Ken Grissom

Drop-Off

Big Fish

A John Rodrigue Novel by Ken Grissom

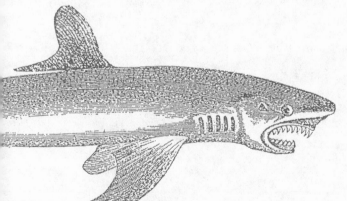

St. Martin's Press · New York

HOUSTON PUBLIC LIBRARY

R0139735145
humca

This novel is a work of fiction. All of the events, characters, names, and places depicted in this novel are entirely fictitious or are used fictitiously. No representation that any statement made in this novel is true or that any incident depicted in this novel actually occurred is intended or should be inferred by the reader.

"Guiltiness" by Bob Marley © 1977 Bob Marley Music Ltd. All rights for the United States administered by Ackee Music Inc., c/o Polygram International Publishing Inc. (ASCAP). All rights reserved. Reprinted by permission.

BIG FISH. Copyright © 1991 by Ken Grissom. All rights reserved. Printed in the United States of America. No part of this book may be used or reproduced in any manner whatsoever without written permission except in the case of brief quotations embodied in critical articles or reviews. For information, address St. Martin's Press, 175 Fifth Avenue, New York, N.Y. 10010.

Editor: Jared Kieling

Design by Judith Dannecker

Library of Congress Cataloging-in-Publication Data

Grissom, Ken.
    Big fish / Ken Grissom.
        p.   cm.
    ISBN 0-312-05385-1
    I. Title.
PS3557.R5366B5   1991
813'.54—dc20   90-48947
                                                                         CIP

First Edition: February 1991

10   9   8   7   6   5   4   3   2   1

For Scotty

"As a rule of thumb, should a shark accelerate unexpectedly, or assume an unnatural posture, an attack may be imminent."

—*U.S. Navy Diving Manual*, Vol. 1,
NAVSEA 0994–LP001–9019

Big Fish

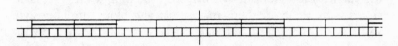

Chapter 1

Leigh Kindler's bikini bottom just missed covering the cleft of her firm, round butt. Rodrigue's one good eye locked on the top edge of the suit, where the edge of the flimsy white material spanned a breathtaking gap of bronze skin that glistened with a fine sheen of sweat. From there, his gaze took a leisurely journey downward—a tiny triangle of suspended cloth narrowed into a crease that was etched just as clearly as if she was naked. The cloth bonded to her firm buttocks without making the slightest impression on the flare of her hips. It might have been painted on except that when she shifted her weight to her other leg, a small ripple ran up the cleft.

She was standing on a high counter in the cockpit of her husband's custom-built sportfishing yacht. The counter had a small stainless sink in it and cabinets below, and it served as a work area for rigging trolling baits. It was high enough so that Mrs. Kindler—who was a good five seven, Rodrigue judged—had to stoop slightly to feed a wire through a hole in the eavelike overhang of the flying bridge.

Rodrigue was struck dumb. He stood on the smooth concrete wharf of A Row and stared at her. He had never even seen Mrs.

1

Kindler in a swimsuit, let alone a teeny-weeny bikini. Around the yacht basin, she usually wore crisp yachting whites—pleated shorts with plenty of room in the seat and blousy military-style shirts with epaulettes and flap pockets. Over the left pocket would be embroidered the name of the yacht, *Abaris*, and a leaping blue marlin. Always cool and correct, she was the perfect rich man's wife.

What in the world was she doing working on the boat like a hired hand?

Rodrigue had come from the back room of the bait camp, where the tangy mist from the aerated tanks took the sting out of the suffocating June afternoon. Over beers, he and a few of the other regulars had been considering one of the ironies of living on the Texas coast in the late seventies: being surrounded by refineries and paying $1.89 a gallon for gasoline. Then the bait camp's owner came back from lunch and leafed through his messages and found one for Rodrigue: Mrs. Kindler wanted to see him.

He had often fantasized about Leigh Kindler, but he never dreamed of actually touching her. She seemed too blond and creamy and, well . . . untouchable. Besides, any prudent male would've thought twice about strapping on the wife of a man like Garrett Kindler.

His family's money had come first from cotton, with an early and very profitable detour into oil, and Kindler—a land developer himself—still exuded the genteel loftiness of the old Houston cotton barons. Yet people were afraid of him.

Everyone had heard the story about Fred Gower, who had owned a gas station on Broadway, not far from the marina complex. Many of the people who kept boats at the yacht basin had their cars serviced at Gower's station. It was even handier for the Kindlers, since they had a condo within an easy stroll of their boat slip and didn't really need a car when they were down. For whatever reason—maybe because inflation was eating him alive as it was most people—Gower started cheating Kindler, changing parts that didn't need changing at first, then eventually charging him for things he hadn't done at all.

Kindler caught him by accident. Something finally broke that was supposed to have just been fixed, and the mechanic in Houston, probably anxious to have a billionaire for a steady customer, put together a list of new parts on the car to be compared to the invoices from Gower.

Kindler acquired the property on that corner and had Gower evicted. Gower's wife left him for a while and he nearly lost his home, but he finally got on as a roustabout offshore and, Rodrigue had heard, was piecing his life back together.

Kindler had the station razed, along with the one-hour dry cleaners next door, and he built a new station with a four-bay garage and a convenience store. But no one had ever heard him say an unkind word about Fred Gower.

Up on the flying bridge of the *Abaris*, a serviceman in blue work clothes was installing a new radio antenna. Rodrigue realized he had been flattering himself. All the possibilities he had entertained on the walk over to A Row now collapsed into one neat category: some kind of job.

"Hello," he called.

At the sound of the voice, Leigh came out from under the overhead and looked around. Her hair was tied mammy-style in a white scarf.

"Cap-tan Rod-*reeg*!" she called, exuberantly attempting a Cajun accent. *"Comment allez-vous?"*

"Bien, bien," he replied tentatively, puzzled by her sudden chumminess. *"Et vous?"*

"Fine, thank you," she said, either running out of French or tiring of it. "We're getting her shipshape for a run down to Jamaica."

"So I see." He stepped to one side and peeked down the yacht's side, the better to admire her lines. He didn't imagine *Abaris* required much to be put shipshape. She was at least as pampered as Mrs. Kindler. Designed by an Italian naval architect, she was fifty-eight feet in length and had a trim, rakish hull blacker than midnight at the bottom of the sea. The gleaming white superstructure was low and swept-back, and the flying bridge was completely open, adding to her low, sleek profile. She would've looked more at home running scotch to Saudi Ara-

3

bia than out fishing for marlin alongside fat white boats piled high with remote-steering towers.

Abaris was reputed to have a fully stocked bar on board that would rival the lounge at the Bob Smith Yacht Club. With a laundry room, full-size galley—even a special restaurant-style griddle for preparing Garrett Kindler's favorite seafood dishes— she had all the comforts of a very comfortable home.

Leigh patted the fixture above her head. "This darned cockpit light shorted out."

"You couldn't get someone to fix it?" he asked absently.

Rodrigue found himself staring at the delicate crease of her groin where it emerged from the tiny triangle of white cloth. "Forgive me my impertinence," he added quickly, breaking into a wide grin that gleamed menacingly in his dark face, "but you tan beautifully."

She eased down from her perch, demurely shielding her loins but almost at the expense of spilling her breasts. "It just so happens I *like* to work on the boat. Thank you, by the way." She gave him a strange, almost fearful smile.

Rodrigue decided he was on the verge of shoving a size-twelve Hush Puppy down his own throat. He waited silently for her to say why she had sent for him.

"Garrett assures me that there's nothing wrong." She wiped her hands on a scrap of towel. "And Harry agrees. But it sure seems to me that she's vibrating in an odd way just below cruising speed. With all that distance to travel, I would rest easier if you could go down and maybe take a look at the props and the shafts."

The old inspection dive—it was a bauble God often dangled before him, probably to see whether the generations had cleansed the Rodrigue blood any. All he had to do was suit up and get wet and it was an automatic one hundred dollars. (At the age of forty-one, he refused to get into the water for less than a C note.)

Rodrigue stepped onto the finger pier that extended out alongside the boat, and he peeked down into the water as if it would tell him something. Should he or shouldn't he? He didn't really need the money, but then neither did the Kindlers. On the other hand, how could he cheat such a gorgeous creature?

"I wouldn't be able to tell much in this murky water, Mrs. Kindler. Why don't you have her hauled?"

"Harry just spent two weeks up at Kemah having her hauled," she said. Harry was Harry Morgan, the *Abaris*'s captain. "Can't you feel around the props and tell if a blade is bent?" she asked.

"Maybe, but you can feel that on the helm just as easily."

She gave him a delicious pout and he reconsidered. What the heck—he already had arranged to make a dive that afternoon anyway, a job on another boat out on the flat outside the breakwater, where the incoming tide hopefully would bring in three or four feet of visibility.

"I'll tell you what," he said. "If Harry doesn't mind moving her outside the marina, I'll go down and take a look."

"Harry does what Garrett tells him," she said. She smiled then, but it was a fragile one. Rodrigue thought she had sounded almost angry.

"In that case, maybe Mr. Kindler will lend me Bones for the rest of the day," Rodrigue said. "I need someone to tend my air hose."

"Oh, certainly. That's no problem, I'm sure." Without taking her eyes off him, she called out, *"Harry!"*

The steps to the saloon rose, pivoting on hinges below the saloon door, and Harry Morgan emerged from the well leading to the engine room, wiping his hands on a red mechanic's rag. He settled his wraparound polarized shades into place and unwrapped one of those skinny cigars with the plastic mouthpiece, lighting it with a hissing disposable butane lighter.

Morgan was a cocky Australian with over a 100,000-pound-plus black marlin to his credit. Garrett Kindler had imported him in the spring, setting the Atlantic billfish circuit buzzing. The way people were talking, Rodrigue had wondered aloud whether Kindler intended to breed him. Morgan inspired a lot of jealousy around the yacht basin, and Rodrigue had to admit he wasn't immune.

5

"Harry," she said in a flat tone, "do you know where Bones has gotten off to?"

"Ah, Bones. He's over on Pier D, visiting with some of his cobbers up from South Padre." Morgan broke his inscrutable stare with a sudden grin, something he did now and then to reveal the core of humanity around which the legend had grown.

"Be a dear and go fetch him, will you? Captain Rodrigue needs his help."

"All right," Morgan drawled. He made a show of brawny quickness, leaping from the cockpit sole to the gunwale to the cement wharf in one fluid motion and striding off without a rearward glance.

She ignored the display, looking at Rodrigue with a mouth that was no longer smiling yet looked somehow satisfied.

"Mrs. Kindler, I've never seen you in a bathing suit before," Rodrigue blurted. He was sorry he had begun it but he was in too deep to back out now. "How did you ever get that gorgeous tan?"

She laughed, a polite tinkle. "Normally just wear one when we're out, but we're out a lot." She pulled the suit away from her flat stomach to inspect her tan line. ". . . been so hot this year," she was saying.

Rodrigue looked, too. From where he stood on the wharf, he glimpsed the stark transition from caramel to snowy white skin, and lower, a wisp of amber curls like spun honey, and his mouth went dry.

"Come on in, Rod," she said, letting the suit snap back into place. "Let me buy you a beer. Or fix you a drink, maybe?"

He followed her through the saloon door, which gushed refrigerated air. She slid the door closed behind them.

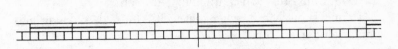

Chapter 2

They stepped into a saloon (more often than not called a salon on hoity-toity vessels such as this) with a stark black-and-white motif. The free-form bar was black marble. Behind the racked wineglasses and cabinet doors of frosted glass, etched with the leaping marlin logo, were black lacquer cabinets. The carpet, side curtains, and long suede divan were blinding white.

Rodrigue tasted the Cuba libre she had mixed. "You and, ah, Mr. Kindler taking her down yourselves?" He didn't know what he was doing there but he suspected it didn't have anything to do with propeller shafts.

"No, Harry and Bones are. We'll fly down and meet them. But we are bringing her back. I'm looking forward to that."

"So. You going down there to fish?" He was curious; American boats were steering clear of Jamaica these days. They went to Bimini, the Caymans, Cozumel.

She shook her head reflexively as she sipped a light scotch and soda. "Uh-uh," she said, brushing the moisture from her lips with the ball of her thumb, daintily. "Some business of Garrett's. Really just going to be there for a few days. We'll have her back in plenty of time for the tournament. You don't think Garrett would miss his own tournament, do you?"

"I don't know Mr. Kindler that well," he said, suddenly uncomfortable in the chilly saloon.

"No, he wants to do some entertaining down there, in connection with Trenchtown—you know, buttering up some of the local officials-to-be. The way things are now, that's difficult to do in Jamaica . . . ashore, anyway. So we'll just do it aboard *Abaris*."

Rodrigue had no idea what connection Kindler could have with a Kingston slum, but he decided it was none of his business.

Mrs. Kindler found a more comfortable position on the stool. "But when the whistle blows in the Islands Invitational, it's every man for himself. Do you ever fish tournaments, Rod?"

"Nope." He left it at that—anything else would've been impolite.

"Pity. I'll bet you'd be awfully handy in the cockpit." She smiled that funny nonsmile again. "You look strong enough."

"You're not being cruel, are you, Mrs. Kindler? I'm a little too old and way too stove-up for that kind of work."

"The limp . . . I've noticed that. You don't do it all the time, though. Was it the same, er, accident that took your eye?"

Everyone knew about his artificial eye, although he was good at hiding the lack of motor control by cocking his head instead of shifting his gaze. He also made frequent use of the one-eyed squint he copied from his boyhood hero, the Long John Silver of the 1950 Disney movie. It was the difference in colors that eventually gave him away. His own eye was hazel. The left one was off-the-shelf brown from Oakland Naval Hospital.

"No, I got the bends a few years ago and I've developed arthritis in my right knee. It's okay as long as I'm good to it. Had to quit running marathons."

"You used to—?"

"I'm kidding you, Mrs. Kindler. How about you? Tournaments, I mean. Do you actually get back there and crank in those monsters?"

"Of course. But I'm afraid I'm going to be beached during the

Islands Invitational. Garrett insists that I play hostess to the wives and girlfriends—mostly girlfriends—who prefer to stay ashore. I'd rather fish, but who knows, maybe I'll have some interesting company."

She watched him, clearly expecting a comment. Instead, he merely stared back at her, studying the frank sky-blue eyes in the flawless oval face, the faint dimple in her chin he hadn't noticed before, the way her soft lips were set between determined lines. . . .

"Rod?"

"Forgive me. I didn't mean to stare. You have such a beautiful face."

"*Rod!*" She laughed nervously.

Footfalls thudded down in the cockpit, startling her.

"Hello inside," called a man's voice—flat, almost monotone. "Anyone home?"

Leigh switched on a too-broad smile. "It's Al Ahlmark." She slid off the stool to open the door. "Associate of Garrett's," she added over her shoulder, in a tone that carried a hint of warning.

A big man in a straw cowboy hat and a loud Hawaiian shirt strode confidently into the saloon. He was as big as Rodrigue, a little older but in better shape, it looked. His handsome face was sneering, and he was chewing gum almost contemptuously. He looked coldly at Rodrigue for an instant, then lifted his lips and continued to gnash the gum with all his teeth showing.

"I'll be damned," the man said, "if it isn't Petty Officer Rodrigue."

Rodrigue felt a chill, as though he were looking at a ghost. The face was familiar and it evoked a feeling of dread or regret or revulsion—or maybe all three. He couldn't pin it down.

"You don't remember me, do you?" asked Ahlmark.

"Not sure I want to. Nam, right?"

"Could be." Ahlmark turned and gleefully smacked his gum at Leigh. "Garrett below?" he asked. It sounded to Rodrigue like an accusation.

"He's in Houston, or on his way down. Fix you a drink?"

"Yeah, thanks. Gin and tonic. Or, no—make it rum. Might as well acclimate myself. With soda."

9

The accent was Boston or thereabouts, but that wasn't enough of a clue. He was definitely of the officer class, which meant their relationship probably hadn't been cordial. Maybe that was all there was to it.

Maybe it was the air conditioner making him feel as if someone had clamped an ice pack on his neck.

Suddenly, the saloon door slid open. Harry Morgan was there, followed by Bones McKenzie, a good-time Charlie who just naturally fell into company with Rodrigue from time to time. Morgan regarded Ahlmark with a blank stare for an instant, then turned his sudden grin on Rodrigue.

"Here he is, mate. Just a loan, now. I want him back."

"Once he gets a glimpse of how the other half lives, I don't think there's much danger in him wanting to stay around the shrimp boats," said Rodrigue.

He led the way out, grateful to be back in the hot sunshine.

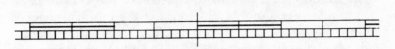

Chapter 3

Rodrigue's six-year-old black Coupe de Ville was like a kiln, only humid. Bones McKenzie shifted uncomfortably on the worn pile seat.

"Ain't this motherfucker air-conditioned?"

"You hot?" Rodrigue asked absently.

Bones shook his head and chuckled. He was tall and skinny, while most mates were built like bulldogs. They came that way for good reason, too. A low center of gravity and arms like a weight lifter helped tremendously when you had to lean out of a boat in sloppy seas and grab an angry four-hundred-pound fish by the nose. But Bones was good, everyone agreed. He looked as if he couldn't walk down the street without tripping over himself, but somehow he kept on his feet in a heaving cockpit and used his leverage like a crowbar. He was both good and a little bit goofy and everybody liked him.

Rodrigue drove slowly with his elbow out the window, sniffing the humid air appreciatively. Galveston had come to feel like home to him. The old part of the city had tall houses with high verandas and louvered French windows surrounded by explo-

11

sions of lush vegetation, very similar to the Garden District of New Orleans. There were narrow streets and lots of black faces.

And there was also a beach—not like the sugar-and-emerald strips of Alabama and Florida, but still a beach, where teenage girls went bounding in pursuit of sailing Frisbees, their hard little butts covered more with sand than cloth.

Best of all, there was the Galveston yacht basin, hub of all waterborne fun on the island. It was like a big marine amusement park, with Yacht Club Land, Charterboat Land, Trailerboat Land, Sailboat Land. . . .

Rodrigue liked to think of himself as retired, doing these little jobs just to keep busy and make some drinking money. He had done two and a half hitches—ten years—in the navy, but he had intended to do thirty, winding up a potbellied senior chief passing out from the local beer every night in some backwater of the world. Both of the times he reupped, he had been on a diving team out on the fringes of the fleet, where the flow of military chickenshit wasn't quite so strong. It had been challenging work—just dangerous enough to get his attention and usually uncomfortable enough to make him appreciate the little things in life, like dry socks and a hot cup of coffee.

Then came orders to Vietnam and a transfer to the brownwater navy. Because of his experience in shrimp boats and oilfield crew boats before he enlisted, he was given command of one of the small shallow-water craft used for patrolling the maze of inland waterways. One night on the Co Chien River in Kien Hoa Province, he walked astern to piss and the seaman at the helm ran over a mine. Rodrigue was pitched overboard. He landed on a raft of logs and debris that took his eye but saved his life. In six months, he was out on a medical discharge with a pension.

Having but one eye didn't hinder him a bit diving in the oil fields of the Gulf of Mexico. He free-lanced successfully for a while and then went to work for Peg Thompson, another chewed-up former navy diver, so named because of his prosthetic right leg. The North Sea was opening up and divers were becoming less like underwater roustabouts and more like astronauts—breathing exotic gas mixtures and working out of bells that resembled Apollo capsules. The pay was excellent, the work was very dangerous, and Rodrigue thought he had died and gone to heaven.

Then on a job in Africa, he and a crazy Frenchman named Jean-Marc Delmas got the bends—Jean-Marc seriously, with no relief immediately available—and suddenly life grew ugly.

The year before, Peg had sold out to a multinational with almost as many tentacles as Beatrice. The old "worldwide head-quarters" at Harvey, across the river from New Orleans, was nothing more than a yard and warehouse to store the equipment while the show was being run from a sprawling business park in the woods of Connecticut.

At least Thompson Diving International now had some deep, deep pockets. A jury in New Orleans, piqued by the classic confrontation between the haves and a have-not, awarded punitive damages in the staggering sum of $750,000.

After the laywers sauntered off to the shade to rest, Rodrigue still had over $300,000. And even after he had split it down the middle with poor Jean-Marc—who lay wasting away in France, thinking God knows what thoughts but certainly none about suing his former employer—Rodrigue figured he was set for life. He already had saved a lot of money, and he had no bills beyond the monthly ones that terminated the day he drove out of New Orleans.

What he couldn't cram into his car, he had tossed in with the diving equipment in a purloined U-Haul trailer, repainted gray, that he had used back when the jobs had taken him to Louisiana backwaters like Leesville and Intracoastal City—to lonely wharves with the sweet-sour smells of tarred pilings and salt marsh. In later years, much of the work had been overseas, and it had been more common for him to leave his Garden District apartment carrying only what would fit beneath the seat and in the overhead compartment of a 747. Now this loading up like the Beverly Hillbillies brought a new sensation with it—of rootlessness, aimlessness.

He had taken his time crossing the river that day. He knew he would miss the jungly tangle of bougainvillea, wrought iron, and neon. But eventually he wound up on U.S. 90 headed west across the swamps. When he reached Morgan City, he left the highway and drove to the levee for old time's sake. And it was there he first saw the *Miss Colinda*.

She was a sixty-four-foot cypress-hull trawler with a spacious trunk cabin and twin outriggers, the classic Gulf shrimp boat. It reminded him of his childhood, when all the men in his family had been shrimp fishermen, before they all succumbed to the lure of the steady paychecks and benefits of the oil fields.

The boat was in good shape, solidly built and well maintained, but the sign in the pilothouse window said DIRT-CHEAP! Shrimp prices were down, while the costs of fuel and wire rope and nets and ice and everything else it took to catch shrimp were way up. It wasn't hard for Rodrigue to convince himself she was just what he needed.

He had called the number on the sign and the boat's owner was there in less than ten minutes. Rodrigue listened to the engine and probed around in the bilges, feeling for rot in the frames with his pocketknife. Satisfied, he followed the owner to the bank and they completed the transaction.

It was getting late. He knew he ought to find a seafood restaurant and a motel. Instead, he phoned a high school chum whose Christmas cards had doggedly followed him around the world for years.

His old friend was gray and balding and had an enormous potbelly—all of which was mildly gratifying to Rodrigue, who still had a headful of curly black hair, and if not exactly a flat stomach, at least not one threatening avalanche.

Overall, though, it had been a melancholy reunion. Not only had his friend grown fat, the little fishing village had turned into a muddy boom town, with chain restaurants and discos glimmering in the midst of huge reclining towers of gray steel, acres of stacked drilling pipe, and cavernous warehouses. Rodrigue felt like Rip Van Winkle.

The friend had a plump, cheerful wife who cracked bawdy jokes while she stirred the shrimp sauce piquante, and five stairstep kids nudged around the table after Papa's affection.

The oldest boy was just right—seventeen years old, licensed to drive, and saving his money for a new pump shotgun. Rodrigue put a hundred-dollar bill in the father's hand for safekeeping, and gave the kid enough money for gas, hamburgers, and a bus ticket back from Galveston. He told him to leave the Cadillac wherever the shrimpers tied up in Galveston. Then after the sauce piquante, they gave Rodrigue a ride back to the levee to where the *Miss Colinda* was waiting.

It was a clear night, filled with the rattle of big diesels on the river and the clatter of raw steel from the shipyards. The orange glare of the yards was pierced with the more intense pinpoints of welding arcs, sputtering and flickering like lightning bugs. Their acrid smell spoiled the musty aroma of the swamp.

Rodrigue had decided to move on. There was plenty of fuel on board, so he fired up the single Detroit 8-71, loosed the dock lines, and set off down the Atchafalaya on a sentimental journey that would take him across the old fishing grounds offshore.

Arriving in Galveston, he had found a berth for the *Miss Colinda* down at the commercial docks, among the seafood houses and ice plants. He lived aboard for a while, and it was a nice dose of nostalgia, but then he had found himself a two-bedroom house on the other end of the island, right on the Gulf beach. It was a new life, rising early with nothing to do but watch the sun slowly scatter the clouds over the sea every morning. He began to adjust.

Rodrigue parked and he and Bones boarded the *Miss Colinda*. Rodrigue dropped down into the engine room and checked oil and water levels, inspected hoses connected to through-hull fittings, tested the automatic bilge pump, and generally tried to divine trouble. She was an old boat, and old boats wanted badly to sink. Satisfied, he climbed up on deck and signaled Bones to start throwing off lines while he started her up.

At the peak of the high, upswept bow, Bones was having a devil of a time flipping the eye splice of the heavy bow line off the postlike bollard on the wharf. This was a different world for him. High-toned sportfishermen like *Abaris* had dock lines waiting wherever they went. He finally shook it loose, coiled the line in a pile, and stomped back to the wheelhouse, grinning angrily.

"And that's the easy part," Rodrigue teased. "Lassoing the bollard in the first place is what's tough."

"What the fuck you want a big ol' piece of shit like this for, anyway? You *shrimp?*"

"Nah, the price was right."

She was clearly wrong for him, though—too big and not fast enough. In order to properly enjoy retirement, Rodrigue still had to do a little work, which was why he had moved to Galveston in the first place. Galveston Bay and adjacent Clear Lake contained the largest concentration of pleasure craft between Fort Lauderdale and San Diego. He found he was doing far more recoveries and out-and-out rescues than light salvage, however. What he needed was a faster boat.

And one that was a little smaller, too, so he could keep it at the yacht basin, where he could always find somebody to drink beer with and where—as he had just begun to appreciate—anything was possible.

Once the anchor was out and he began to prepare for the dive, Rodrigue was able to put Leigh Kindler out of his mind. From long habit, he concentrated on one small task at a time. He lashed a wooden ladder to the stern so that it stuck down in the water several feet. He was faking down his lifeline in a figure eight when the VHF began crackling in the wheelhouse.

"It's the *Wahoo Too,*" said Bones, after grabbing the mike and answering the hail.

"Yeah, tell him to back up to our stern and hang off."

"What're you doin', running a special?"

"Two birds with one stone, eh?" He attached a diving mask to the canvas-sheathed end of the lifeline and started the big ten-horse Desco compressor, squinting suspiciously at the bank of filters.

If he went to a smaller boat, one thing he'd have to get would be a smaller compressor—this brute weighed nearly a half a ton. It would supply two divers well beyond the depth where they ought to be using air, with enough pressure left over for a pneumatic jack. But its capacity became a liability in shallow water, because when a compressor was working light, it was harder to keep its lubricants filtered out of the diver's air. He'd have to buy

16

himself a little five-horse painting compressor at Sears and convert it for diving.

Mickey Aimes was running the *Wahoo Too*, a fifty-foot Hatteras, on one engine; he made a wide circle and backed squarely against the *Miss Colinda*'s stern instead of pivoting sharply on her props the way such a crackerjack skipper would've liked. She had a wad of heavy monofilament fishing line wrapped around her starboard prop and Aimes had engaged his old friend to cut it out—for the usual fee, of course.

"Okay, Mick, shut her down," Rodrigue ordered as he weaved the other boat's stern line onto a cleat on his own deck. Idling engines made him nervous when he was diving around propellers.

He pulled on the mechanic's coveralls he used to protect himself against barnacles and jellyfish, strapped on six pounds of weight, grabbed up his fins, and eased down the ladder with Bones feeding the lifeline behind him.

As the water buoyed his arms and legs and lapped at the Lexan face port, he switched on the constant air supply. Although the mask had a demand regulator that supplied air upon inhaling, like a scuba regulator, Rodrigue liked a steady blast whenever he felt he was exerting himself—which he was almost anytime he went in the water. Also, it kept the mask free of residual carbon dioxide, too much of which could cause a diver to black out.

The nest of monofilament glowed eerily in the yellowish-green water. The serrated edge of his old navy knife cut through individual strands easily enough, but there was a lot of it that was tightly wound, tough to get the blade under. So he sawed away methodically at the thick bundle.

Over the hiss of his air, he could hear the *Abaris* coming, a high-pitched whine that seemed to be locked on to him like fire-control radar.

17

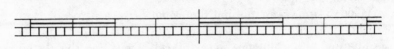

Chapter 4

He couldn't hide from her forever. Leigh Kindler found him in the dim olive shade under *Wahoo Too*, still sawing at the bundle of monofilament, and she teased him with a glimpse of golden pubic hair, and with the dimple in her chin.

Was there ever a woman so perfect? Those cool blue eyes and that calm, sexy voice . . .

Then what the hell was wrong? Was it Ahlmark? Whatever Ahlmark had been was in another life on another planet. It wasn't even history; it was myth. Gone away.

Maybe it was Kindler, but if it was, it was Kindler's power, pure and simple. Sad to say, the sanctity of marriage had never stopped Rodrigue before.

Maybe—he liked the feel of this one—just maybe it was because she was *so* goddamned perfect, so beautiful and built like something out of *Playboy*—no, better than that, the Sears catalogue. The lingerie section. Showing it off, but innocently somehow. Too goddamned good to be true—that's what was setting off the alarm. . . .

And well it should. When had she ever managed more than a cool nod of recognition before this? So why the sudden interest?

It took something of a free spirit to be attracted to a vagabond like Rodrigue, with his wild dashikis and even wilder reputation, but God knows, there were plenty of them out there—especially around beaches and marinas. But why the *sudden* interest? Or was he flattering himself? Maybe it was just her way of being nice to the help.

Finally, the last wrap of mono came off the shaft. Rodrigue sank beneath the *Wahoo Too* and swam on his back over to the motionless propellers of the other boat. He shut off the steady air supply. The hissing free-flow was too noisy when the radio was used.

"Bones! If my hose is free, Mickey can take off!"

Underwater, Rodrigue heard Bones reply, "That's a roger!" The words sounded tinny against the faint buzzing of the busy channel nearby.

First one engine roared to life, then the other. Rodrigue noticed that both engines were put into gear simultaneously, that there was no tentative testing of the starboard one to see whether the problem had indeed been solved. A lot of people in Galveston were inclined to distrust Rodrigue, but Mickey knew better—at least when it came to underwater work.

To Rodrigue, there was a clear difference between faking a job and leaving a job undone. The latter was unthinkable. The former was just business.

He did the best he could for Leigh Kindler in spite of it. The props—"wheels," they were called colloquially—looked fine. Rudders, shafts, struts—all seemed in perfect order. He kicked over to the bottom rung of his ladder and pulled himself to the surface.

Leigh was at the gunwale, peering down at him, wearing a terry bathrobe. He threw his fins on the *Miss Colinda*, climbed up a step, and pulled off the hooded mask, careful to wipe the mucus from his nose before he turned around.

"Well?" she called.

"Nothing that I can tell." He squinted up at the figure on the flying bridge. "If you really think you've got a problem, Harry, you'd better have her hauled again."

Morgan shrugged.

19

"Come by the boat and I'll write you a check," said Leigh. "And pour you another rum'n Coke." She wheeled around with a saucy swish of the robe about her perfect hips and stepped up into the saloon.

By the time Rodrigue got his anchor up, the *Abaris* was already turning into the yacht basin breakwater—and he had decided that Leigh was worth it . . . whatever. It was nearly an hour later when he and Bones drove back into the yacht basin parking lot. But in case she needed more time to shoo Morgan out of the way, Rodrigue called on Mickey Aimes first. Bones tagged along. When they walked into the saloon of the *Wahoo Too*, Mickey opened the boat's big checkbook, wrote out a check, and handed it to Rodrigue.

"I thank you from me heart but me liver's pissed," said Rodrigue in his playful pirate growl. "You know Bones McKenzie here?"

"Sure, heard of you," Mickey said, offering the mate his hand and a friendly grin.

"Fishing the Islands Invitational?" Bones asked.

"Can't be left out of that. This may be the first-ever million-dollar pot on the Gulf Coast."

"Jesus!" said Rodrigue, suddenly interested in sportfishing. "How much does first place pay?"

"The whole enchilada."

Bones nodded excitedly.

"Winner take all? A million bucks?" asked Rodrigue.

"Yeah, if he managed to buy his own boat, the winner could walk away with around a million dollars—before taxes, of course," said Mickey. "Biggest crapshoot this side of Vegas."

"Wait a minute, what do you mean, 'buy his own boat?' Don't these guys who enter these high-dollar fishing tournaments own their own goddamned boats?"

Bones laughed and Mickey grinned. "I mean in the Calcutta bidding," Mickey said. "Before the tournament, they hold a sort of an auction where anyone with enough money can try to place a bet on any boat in the tournament. They announce the name of each boat, talk some shit about the reputation of the captain and crew, then people bid on the right to bet on that particular boat. The winning bid becomes the bet, in effect."

"And all the money from the bidding, that's the prize money, eh?"

"Yep. And whichever boat wins the tournament, half of its winnings goes to the boat, to be split between the owner, captain, crew, however. And the other half goes to whoever 'bought' that boat in the Calcutta. If he has a winning record, an owner might have to spend a lot of money to buy his own boat."

Rodrigue's mind was reeling with the vision of a room crowded with fat men, hundred-dollar bills in their fists, more bills spilling out of every pocket, bills floating above the commotion as they shouldered each other aside for the opportunity to throw money into a big cast-iron pot. Not *that* big a pot, though—not that heavy-looking . . .

"So how does a person win one of these tournaments?" he asked slyly. What he was really wondering was how a person could rig a tournament—not that *he* would do such a thing. It was a thought bred into him centuries ago.

"There'll be the usual point system—hundred for a blue, fifty for a white, and twenty-five for a sail, plus a point a pound for each fish's weight. But instead of first, second, and third—or even best blue, best white, and so on—the boat with the most points wins it all. This is an unusual tournament, to say the least. Most of the non-Arab billionaires in the world are going to be here."

"And, boy, will they be wagging their wallets," said Bones. "The way the bids ran down at Poco and the Veal Brothers last summer, I wouldn't be surprised to see *over* a million bucks in the pot. Kindler'll bid that much himself if he has to."

"I thought Kindler was sponsoring the tournament," said Rodrigue. "You mean he gets to bid, too?"

"Why not?" asked Bones. "We're fishing it."

Rodrigue made a conspiratorial Long John Silver look.

"Nothing wrong with that," said Mickey. "It's done all the time. It's like a kid taking his ball and bat to the park and inviting all the other kids to play. He gets to play, too."

21

"Yeah, but wouldn't it look bad if he won?"

"Why? There's an independent weighmaster whose word is law. There are certified scales, and the fish are weighed in public. Texas A&M even has someone there to certify that each fish is fresh, or at least wasn't caught over at Cabo San Lucas or somewhere and frozen."

"Actually, the fact that he *is* fishing it himself has taken some of the heat off about the lay day," said Bones.

"Lay day?"

Mickey nodded. "The way the tournament is scheduled, we fish on a Friday, and we have to be back at the dock by eight that night, whether we have fish to weigh or not. The Saturday we're not even allowed out—that's called a lay day because we lay off. Then we fish again on Sunday. That means we've got to run ninety, a hundred miles out to where the water is deep enough for billfish, and then turn around and run back in again before dark. Doesn't leave much time for raising fish. It's not going to take a whole boatload to win, that's for sure."

"Why did he set it up that way?" asked Rodrigue.

Mickey shrugged. "Maybe he's a conservationist."

Bones snorted a laugh. "You know why they call it the *Islands* Invitational?" he asked Mickey.

"Ah, the 'twinning of the islands,'" Mickey said with a wry grin. "Some tourist-bureau crap Kindler has tied in with the tournament. Already got posters up everywhere."

"He wants to sell shares in a damn marina he's gonna build down in Jamaica. Trenchtown, he calls it, 'cause it's right off the Cayman Trench. Be west of Port Antonio somewhere on that north coast. Fuckin' great fishing."

"Sell shares to the people in the tournament?" asked Rodrigue. His mind flashed on the imaginary scene around the cast-iron pot again.

Bones granted him a exaggerated *eureka!* look. "He's going to have a big model of the marina in the hotel lobby during the tournament, with little tiny palm trees an' the whole bit. Then he'll have all these fuckin' billionaires running around, drinking imported rum and rubbing elbows with his Jamaican pals.

There'll be a lot more than a million dollars raised here, I'd be willing to bet."

"Why do they go along with it, then, if it's just a come-on?" Rodrigue asked. "I mean the people in the tournament."

Mickey's face turned serious—almost angry, Rodrigue thought.

"A lot of these owners, they figure it's pure luck anytime you catch a fish," he said. "It's prestige, being here—hell, just being invited. And there's something macho about spending money, you know? Hell, I don't know. *You* figure it out."

Earlier, Rodrigue had planned to ditch Bones before going around to collect his money and the promised Cuba libre and God only knew what else from Leigh Kindler. Now he was glad to have a chaperon to keep him from making a fool of himself— or worse.

Garrett Kindler was spooky. Too many motives. Too many friends with motives. Man like that had trip wires all around him.

The saloon door on the *Abaris* was locked. Bones rattled it a few times, then shrugged at Rodrigue. They turned and stepped back onto the finger pier, but then the door opened and Morgan stuck his head out. His hair was mussed slightly and an unlit cigar jutted from his mouth.

"Hey, Rod, here's your check, mate." He stoked the cigar with a hissing lighter. "Mrs. Kindler said sorry about the drink but she had to get back to Houston." The way Morgan held on to the door was not an invitation to come in.

Rodrigue stepped back down into the cockpit and took the check. "No problem and thanks."

Another tousled blond head appeared over Morgan's shoulder. For a brutal instant, Rodrigue thought it was Leigh, but it was a teenager with a lot of blue eyeshadow.

"C'mon, Harry," she said drowsily. She wrapped her arms around his bare torso.

Morgan winked at Rodrigue and clicked the door shut.

Rodrigue stroked his jaw and squinted up at Bones in his Long John impression, and Bones laughed.

"Who's the lucky lady?" Rodrigue asked as they walked to the bait camp for a beer.

"No idea. Never seen him bring a woman on the boat before. Hope t'hell Kindler don't find out."

"Why? I thought laying dock groupies was part of the benefits package for you hotshot billfish crews."

Bones grinned sheepishly. "Depends on the boat. Some owners just turn it over to you, and act more like guests themselves. But to Kindler, his boat's his castle. I don't think he'd like Morgan using it like some kinda cheap motel."

Rodrigue sighed. That was the trouble with nice things—so hard to keep nice.

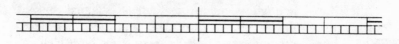

Chapter 5

That night, Rodrigue had an erotic dream about Leigh. He couldn't remember much, just that he was with her, and the next thing he knew the darkness around him was growing pale and beneath the limp bed sheet he throbbed with a familiar, pleasurable pain. He ripped the sheet aside and glanced down.

"Help," he said aloud in the empty house. His head dropped wearily back to the pillow. "Help. They've laid a pipeline over me."

He fantasized about her for a moment, teasing himself, but then he remembered all the complications, all that money being piled up—and Ahlmark, the mystery man from the past. He got up and went naked into the kitchen to put the coffee on.

Out of habit, he wandered into the living room to check the weather. The Gulf outside his window was calm and pale gray-blue, but dull gray clouds with rose-colored shafts of sunlight stabbing over them were gathering on the horizon. Rain, he thought absently.

His reflection in the plate glass reminded him of his condition. He turned sideways to admire the angle, but then he remembered all those nasty impediments again. He went in and lingered under the shower while the rich coffee aroma filled the house.

After Mass, Rodrigue went to the Kettle Restaurant and sat down with an omelet, chilled fruit plate, and the *Daily News*. The door opened and the first of the rain-smelling gusts blew in, ruffling the pages of the paper. He looked up and found Leigh Kindler approaching. She sat down and looked around to see whether anyone else had noticed her.

Rodrigue hastily daubed at his mouth with his napkin. All of his caution had left on the wind. Leigh's face—now happy and maybe even a little excited—was to die for.

"You want a job, Rod?" she asked, almost whispering.

"This is my day off, Mrs. Kindler." He was unable to hide his disappointment. A screaming headlong fuck, yes, but not another chance to exchange longing looks while he wallowed around in the fucking bilge or something.

"Not today. Middle of the week sometime. Take *Abaris* to Jamaica. And please, it's Leigh."

"Take—?" He had to stop and think this one over: The Kindlers, he remembered her saying, were going to fly over and meet the boat in Jamaica. . . . He and Leigh Kindler in Jamaica . . . No, he and Leigh and Garrett Kindler in Jamaica . . . Worse, he and Leigh and Garrett Kindler and Bones fucking McKenzie in a fifty-eight-foot boat anchored *off* Jamaica . . . Not a promising situation. Still, it was nice of her to offer.

"What happened to Morgan?" he asked suddenly.

She stared at him for a moment—hotly or coldly, it was impossible to tell. "Garrett let him go. This morning."

"Why?"

"He had a little honey on board with him last night. Garrett found out." She leaned forward and touched his hand. "Listen, don't tell him I told you—about the job, I mean. Just say you heard he needs someone in a hurry. He does, too. Of course he'll be wanting someone with marlin-fishing experience when we get back. But for this trip . . ." She let it hang.

"It's tempting, Leigh, but I don't think so."

"But why not?" Now it was her turn to look disappointed.

"Yacht deliveries are just not what I do. Besides, if I ran off and left my boat unattended for two weeks, she'd sink."

"That's not the real reason, is it, Rod?"

"Let's just say I *have* a reason and let it go at that." Explaining himself was not something Rodrigue did graciously.

"Okay." Her eyes flitted down at the table, then up again. "But we are still friends, aren't we?"

"That we are."

"And you won't tell Garrett I spoke to you."

"Of course not."

She smiled sadly, patted him on the hand, and left.

Black clouds loomed close overhead and a swirl of shell dust rose from the Liberty Seafood docks. After Rodrigue checked the *Colinda*'s engine room thoroughly, he ducked inside the cabin. Rain clattered suddenly on the tarred roof. And from the shadows of the galley, a dark figure stirred. Rodrigue was set to charge when Morgan spoke up.

"A bit edgy aren't we, mate?"

"Aye," said Rodrigue, uncoiling. "Must be the weather. Cold beer? Or ain't this a friendly visit?"

"Don't mind if I do. I was bumped today. Kindler caught me in mid-stroke last night."

"Since when is fucking a firing offense for a boatman?" He reached into the cooler and fetched icy Budweisers for them both.

"Kindler's a bit more fastidious than most." Morgan took a long drink of the beer. "Hah!" he said, wiping his mouth with the back of his hand. "I'm better off. The bastard won't fish. He wants to *catch* fish, all right enough, but he won't get out and balls-to-the-wall fish for 'em. Gets rough, he wants to come in. He thinks you ought to be able to buy the damn things with a bonzer boat and good salaries for the crew—and then he wouldn't let me put a tower and decent outriggers on *Abaris*. Said it'd spoil the bleedin' *profile*. Of course you don't really need a tower here, but some shade would've been nice."

Morgan unwrapped a cigar and put it in his mouth. "He

27

nearly passed out when he walked in and found me pounding that little twit. I think he thought it was his wife for a second there. Bleedin' good thing she jumped up and started yabbering at him like he'd come with a pizza. Bastard might've had me killed. He just turned around and was off without a word. Until this morning, that is."

"Uh-huh," murmured Rodrigue, waiting for Morgan to get around to why he was there.

"I don't hold any hard feelings against Bones—didn't think he had the stuff for it, though, that's for sure. But all's fair in love, war, and tournament fishing." He flicked his lighter and sucked on the cigar, but the flame was a full inch away from the cigar's tip.

"I just want you to tell him for me that he wouldn't make a pimple on a fisherman's ass," he said, giving up on the cigar. "Just runnin' a boat and keepin' it clean might make you a captain, but to be a fisherman, you've gotta catch fish . . . an' bigger fish than the rest of everyone else on top of it."

Rodrigue realized that Morgan was drunk, but that didn't excuse anything. "Listen, Morgan, I don't know that Bones blew the whistle on you and I don't fucking care," he said roughly. "Deliver your own goddamned messages. Take the beer with you."

There was a moment in which both men were poised, but then Morgan set the bottle on the dinette and let himself out of the cabin.

"You're better off staying away from those people," he warned. He threw his unlit cigar overboard and disappeared into the gray curtain of the rain.

As soon as the thunderstorm let up, Rodrigue drove to the yacht basin. He parked on A Row, walked over to the *Abaris*, and called out.

He had made up his mind: He was going to have her, no matter what. She was the Golden Fleece and no amount of one-eyed monsters was going to keep him from diving headlong into it.

The saloon door slid open and a tall man with white hair and clothes to match looked out.

"I'm sorry, there's no one here but me."

"It's you I've come to see, Mr. Kindler. I'm John Rodrigue."

"Yes, of course, Rod. Won't you come in? Fix you a drink?"

Naturally, Rodrigue took the offer. As his host carefully measured out a jigger of coffee-colored Bacardi—then added an extra dollop—Rodrigue studied him. He had seen Kindler numerous times before, but never with any sense of what the man was about. Now what he saw didn't jibe with what he knew. Kindler was polite almost to the point of being humble.

Rodrigue felt a pang of jealousy as he realized that, despite his age, Kindler was handsome and even a little imposing. He was sort of regal—or maybe even saintly, but with a bit of machismo somehow. Rodrigue found to his disgust that he was impressed.

"Now," said Kindler as he handed over the Cuba libre, "was there some problem with the check Harry gave you?"

"I wouldn't think so, Mr. Kindler. I didn't deposit it yet. I didn't come to complain about anything; I came to offer you my services."

Kindler's eyebrows arched curiously, as though he thought it might be a good idea, whatever it was. "In what way?"

"Well, I know that you fired Morgan, and I know you were planning to have him take *Abaris* to Jamaica this week, so I thought maybe I could help you. I have a hundred-ton license and I know the way to Jamaica."

"That *would've* been the solution," said Kindler, slapping the bar lightly. "I wish I would've known this morning. Unfortunately, I've already hired a new captain. He's an older fellow—" He smiled. "About like me. I certainly couldn't renege on him at this point. I hope you understand."

"Of course." Rodrigue downed the drink. "It means you are a gentleman, and I'm glad to know you." He offered his hand.

Rodrigue's head buzzed a little from the quick jolt of rum. The rain-washed air, cooler than it had been at midnight, quickly erased the effects.

Just great, he thought, stalking back to his car. She's got a wall

29

of money around her. Then there's this grinning baboon Ahlmark, who reeks of Vietnam. . . . And now this fucking Civil War statue for a husband!

No problem.

It was just a matter of time before the right set of circumstances tumbled into place and they would get together. She probably had something in mind for Jamaica. Him turning her down was actually a pretty good move; it would heat her up all the more.

The next move was hers. Maybe she would figure a way to stay behind when Kindler went to Jamaica. Maybe . . . Well, there was no use in trying to anticipate her. All he had to do was be ready—and, God, was he ready!

He drove hurriedly back home, where he could sit out on the deck with a stiff rum and enjoy the rain-freckled beach.

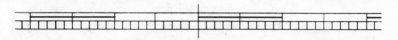

Chapter 6

Islamorada, Florida, three weeks later . . .

Hayato Shokaito had been captain of a Japanese tuna boat. He fished off the East Coast until the United States established the two-hundred-mile Fishery Conservation Zone and ejected foreign competition. The boat he ran was too decrepit to be shifted elsewhere, so it was sold at Islamorada to a Boston firm, and the crew was transferred to other fishing vessels in the company's fleet.

During the weeks it had taken the deal to unfold, Shokaito had fallen in love with the land that had loomed so enticingly just over the horizon all those years—or at least with what he had seen of it thus far, which was the casual, sandy world of the Keys. He took a job at the yard and quickly rose over the ever-shifting tide of itinerants and sluggish local "conches" that flowed through the place.

When the representatives of the Boston firm had revealed their intention to scrap the longline gear—thirty miles of monofilament line to be strung out on the ocean with baited hooks dangling and radio buoys at each end to help find it again—

Shokaito salvaged it and stored it at the back of the yard for . . . well, who could say?

The answer finally came in the person of a rich Texan who accidentally ran his yacht, a beautiful black-hulled craft called *Abaris*, over a coral mass and damaged a prop and shaft. His name was Garrett Kindler, and he and his wife and their crew were on their way home from a vacation in Jamaica.

When Kindler wandered idly around to the back of the yard as the work on *Abaris* progressed in dry dock, Shokaito watched him carefully. He considered it his duty to do so anyway, but in this case, he was fascinated with the tall, stately, white-haired gentleman from the Deep South.

He didn't have to be told that the man was fabulously rich—everyone around Islamorda was fabulously rich. Everyone had a big fine boat and a young beautiful wife and a big gold watch. But this man was . . . *courteous*, that's what he was. Almost Oriental-like. And then when someone told him just how rich Kindler really was, it put Shokaito in awe of him. So he watched him.

Thus when Kindler paused beneath one freshly painted boat and examined a new propeller-shaft strut, Shokaito was immediately on hand to explain that it was of monel, a tough alloy of nickel, copper, iron, manganese, silicon, and carbon. The alloy got along nicely with a stainless-steel shaft and bronze prop, he said earnestly, providing, of course, that there was adequate protection from galvanic corrosion with the use of standard sacrificial anodes.

Kindler listened with rapt attention, his spacious brow furrowed with concentration. He was elegant in his crisp whites. His hair grew back from a widow's peak that made him resemble the film star Stewart Granger, but even more dignified, or . . . yes, *placid*—that was the word. The man who truly had it all.

Then Kindler's calm gray eyes wandered to the back fence, to the huge spool of monofilament line and the neat stack of buoys—the long-lining gear—and Shokaito winced.

"Well!" Kindler said. "How did you ever come by those?"

Shokaito had to tell him the truth, that he had once been a long-liner.

32

"Tell me, Hayato," said Kindler (he could use the yard foreman's first name and not seem the least condescending), "is it true that lots of big marlin are caught on longlines?"

The expression on his face as he waited for an answer was one of mere curiosity.

Shokaito had heard the question before. After all, the blue marlin was an icon in Islamorada, home port of a fleet of luxurious sportfishing yachts. Marlin were revered. They were reproduced in gold miniatures to be hung around the necks of the rich men and their beautiful young wives.

"Very, very occasionally," he said. "Even then it is a simple matter to release the fish alive. We fish for tuna, you see."

"Hayato—" Kindler stroked his long, smooth chin between thumb and forefinger, brow wrinkled in thought again. "Hayato, what if you were fishing *for* marlin? Could you catch them—on purpose, I mean?"

His expression now was clearly hopeful. Shokaito might have exaggerated to please him, but he didn't have to.

"No problem whatsoever. I would shorten the main line—it's fifty kilometers and I would cut it to sixteen or so—and shorten the drops and bait them with live bonito. Also, I would fashion flags on the buoys to pop up when there is a fish on. In that way, you see, we don't have to run the entire line to find the fish. We go straight to it."

"That's remarkable, Hayato. Truly remarkable." There was a gleam in his gray eyes that was a reward in itself.

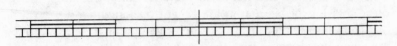

Chapter 7

While the Kindlers were down in Jamaica, Rodrigue finally decided to put the *Miss Colinda* up for sale—and the boat instantly took on a shabby appearance. In particular, the tiny utilitarian galley suddenly blossomed with a coat of grease he hadn't noticed before. He wore out one Brillo pad and was halfway through another when Bones came calling.

They went aft, to get away from the sour Brillo smell, and relaxed with beers from Rodrigue's ice chest. Bones was mysteriously quiet. But he had a peculiar gleam in his eyes, Rodrigue thought.

"Well, how was the trip?" Rodrigue prompted.

"Aw, hell, I ran over a big coral in the Keys and we had to have her hauled at Islamorada to straighten the port shaft. Other'n that, fine. Vandegriff's okay."

"Who's Vandegriff?"

"New captain. Been around forever. Hell of a fisherman." The gleam was joined by a grin.

"Bones, what the fuck are you grinning at?"

"Kindler wants to charter *Miss Colinda* for a week. Pay you five thousand dollars. Bare-boat."

"What? What the fuck for?"

"Ah, to know that, you've got to get in deeper. But then the payback's a lot better. A *whole* lot better—like maybe as much as a hundred grand. I'm supposed to give it to you like there's two options, but there ain't but one as far as I'm concerned."

Rodrigue was getting tired of the game Bones was playing. He got up for two more beers, opened them, and sat back down. "Okay, lay it out. And don't be pausing for my fucking reaction, hear?"

"Option number one: You charter the *Miss Colinda* to Kindler for a week, no questions asked. You stay on the beach and collect five thousand bucks, guaranteed." The sly grin crossed his face again as he waited for a reply.

Rodrigue sighed. "You want me to wring it out of you?"

"Okay, option number two: You come in on a slightly crooked scheme, the details of which I ain't supposed to tell you. But let's say this is a million-dollar tournament, sure enough, and we take the whole enchilada. Kindler gets half for the boat, and then he and you and me and Vandegriff and one other guy split the other half. Your cut could be as much as a hundred thousand dollars. And of course it could be zip if we don't win."

"What do I have to do?"

"Nothing. Same thing. Let Kindler use the boat."

"Well what kind of fucking choice is *that*?"

"That's just what *I* said."

"He's going to rig the tournament, isn't he?" Rodrigue knew it. There was no contest in the world that could stay honest with that much money involved.

Bones nodded.

"But how? You can't exactly buy a blue marlin at a seafood market."

"No, but you can go out with a longline and a gook to run it and catch you one in advance. That's what they need your boat for."

"To run a longline? So why not just hire the boat, why cut me into it?"

Bones grinned again. "Tell you what *I* think, I think Mrs. Kindler's got the hots for you. It was her idea—to bring you in, I

35

mean. Said a big, tough guy like you might come in handy for security purposes, whatever that means. Also said you'd probably jump at a chance to stiff all the fat cats."

"All but the fattest. What *about* Kindler? How'd he act?" If he were Kindler, he'd be afraid of being blackmailed by so unsavory a character as Rodrigue the Pirate.

"Like it was the best idea since toilet paper. You know Kindler."

"Not really."

Nor did he care to.

But *Mrs.* Kindler—that was something else altogether.

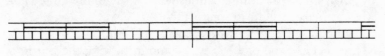

Chapter 8

Shokaito's eyes met Rodrigue's in parries and thrusts. The two men had just been introduced. Kindler, perhaps sensing something, spread his long arms and put a hand on each man's shoulder as he ushered them into his suite at the Lake Charles Hilton.

Leigh, mixing the drinks, also caught Rodrigue's eye and held it, but that was different.

The Japanese long-liner didn't have much love of money, and he thought anyone who did was dangerous. With Kindler, it clearly wasn't the money. It was a prank, a joke on other wealthy men. Money was just their means of keeping tally and had about as much intrinsic worth to them as the wooden matches the poor conches used to keep score when they played poker.

To Shokaito, it was a chance to fish again. He was tired of going to the same sweltering, echoing, corrugated-metal shop day after day, the same predictable unrolling of events. Life wasn't meant to creep by in measured steps. It was a race—or, no, a *chase*, a noble quest. Win or lose, it didn't matter as long as there was the chase.

But a man like this modern-day pirate cared only for the winnings. He would not be very loyal.

Rodrigue read the distrust in the Asian's flat, impassive eyes. In Leigh's, he read amused curiosity, as if she didn't quite know what to make of him in long pants.

"I should have at least two good men," Shokaito was saying. "Three better. The problem will come in moving the fish from the slush tank to the ice bin."

The meeting was being held in Louisiana to be far from the prying eyes of Galveston. Rodrigue's boat was nearby at the fishing village of Cameron, waiting to be outfitted for long-lining. He had drawn a floor plan of the *Miss Colinda*'s ice hold and explained how the bins were formed along both sides by walls of two-by-six planks slid into steel tracks that restrained the ice and shrimp. The starboard bin would be filled with crushed ice. The port bin would be half-filled with ice. The marlin would be placed on the ice in the port bin, and ice from the full starboard bin shoveled in on top of it.

First, though, Shokaito had said, the fish must be cooled down in slush—a mixture of ice and brine. Shokaito would build the slush tank himself, down in the center of the ice hold, where it would be hidden from view and where its considerable weight wouldn't cause the *Miss Colinda* to become unstable in sloppy seas. A block and tackle could easily be rigged to lower the marlin into the ice hold, but shifting it laterally into the ice bin could present a problem if it was a big one. So he needed manpower.

"Illegal aliens," Rodrigue said. "I'll find you some who don't have any English. That way, there'll be no problem with loose lips." He grinned evilly at the Japanese.

"Where will you find illegal aliens?" asked Kindler.

Rodrigue cocked his head and squinted at him. That was like asking where to find broken glass at the dump.

"Anywhere there are shrimp boats, there are illegals," he said. "They pick a lot of them up when they're shrimping down around Aransas, Mansfield, or Port Isabel. They're good hands, most of them, and they don't stray far from the boat. I imagine I'll find what we need down in Cameron."

"But I don't speak Spanish," Shokaito protested.

"It won't matter. I'll get you some experienced fishermen. You point and they'll know what to do."

Shokaito nodded. It was true; their jobs would require very little explanation.

"But how are you going to determine which ones are the experienced ones if they can't speak English?" asked Leigh.

"I have enough Spanish."

In fact, Rodrigue could pass for a South American. He had lived four years in Maracaibo as a schoolboy while his dad was working in the oil fields there. Years later, he returned to Venezuela with Peg Thompson to spend six months in a company town of identical concrete-block houses on the Orinoco.

He also had served two tours in Panama when he was in the navy and later had his winter sojourns through Mexico and Central America, so his Spanish was well practiced.

"But I thought you were French," Leigh said.

"Creole, my dear," said Kindler, holding a long, elegant finger aloft. "Isn't that right, Rod? A widely dispersed race, when you think about it. Almost like the Jews."

Widely dispersed, yes, but not a race. A class—possibly the very first middle class, although Rodrigue couldn't say about ancient times.

Originally, Creoles were Frenchmen and Spaniards who chanced to be born in the Americas at the time when their nations were exploring and conquering the new lands. French Creoles beat the Cajuns to Louisiana by seventy to seventy-five years. Spanish Creoles invented the Latin American revolution. Caribbean blacks were considered Creoles, too, probably inheriting the label from the white masters of yore.

In Mexico City today, a Creole might be considered an aristocratic relic, someone whose family had somehow kept the skin blanched and the Spanish pure, like a delicate orchid surviving in a tangle of more hardy growth.

In Belize, everybody was considered Creole except for Mexicans, Guatemalans, and of course the British.

In New Orleans, few people had any idea what a Creole was

39

anymore except that he was apt to use a lot of cayenne in his cooking.

At some point in the hovering past, however, all Creoles everywhere were considered a whole lot better than the local Indians and mestizos, and nowhere near as good as the nobles back home in Europe. They were a people in the middle—both oppressors and the oppressed.

"Everybody," Rodrigue said to her, "who grew up where I did speaks French, whether they're German or Italian or whatever. Not anymore, of course, not now that the oil brought down all those Texans and Okies. But when I was growing up, you spoke French. I learned my Spanish later. English, too, for that matter."

"Interesting," Leigh said, and her tone blatantly said more. Rodrigue watched Kindler for a reaction and saw none. He really began to believe then that anything was possible.

The young men with Rodrigue—Baldemar, Ignacio, and Chuy—were definitely mestizos, mostly Indian with an ancient tinge of Spanish.

The four of them were sitting in a sour-smelling bar in Cameron, jammed into a booth, Rodrigue and Ignacio facing Baldemar and Chuy. They were all drinking beer, although it was just nine-thirty in the morning and the barmaid was still sweeping out the cigarette butts from the night before. Breakfast was pickled eggs that looked like cactus apples, stained with beet juice.

Chuy said he and Ignacio were from Champotón and Baldemar was from Paraíso. Chuy was a bright-eyed, handsome, white-toothed lad and Rodrigue liked him, but he didn't believe what he was hearing—at least not about the brooding, shovel-faced Baldemar. Baldemar had the disposition of a Salvadoran.

Ignacio seemed friendly enough. But he was either drunk or stupid. He was skinny and rat-nosed, with a drooping mustache composed of no more than a dozen hairs on each side.

"Will we also share in the fish?" Ignacio was asking. "That is to say, will we get a share when they sell it?" They were speaking Spanish.

40

"You pubic hair!" barked Chuy. "Don't you understand that the money we will each get is the same as two thousand five hundred pesos?"

Ignacio clapped both hands over his mouth and looked at Rodrigue with rounded eyes.

"He doesn't yet comprehend the rate of exhange," Chuy told Rodrigue.

"Yes, but what does become of the fish?" asked Baldemar casually, tipping his mug and watching the amber liquid slide away from the bottom. Baldemar was the kind who wouldn't be working for wages long.

"It will be studied by scientists."

"Ah!" said Chuy, delighted.

Ignacio shrugged; Baldemar just stared, postponing for the time being a decision on Rodrigue's veracity.

"The boat is green and white, the one being prepared at the yard just over there. The *Miss Colinda* is how it is called. It will be ready to leave tonight, so you can go aboard this morning. The captain is called Shokaito—Captain Shokaito." He said it slowly this time. "A Japanese. He doesn't have Spanish, so it will be necessary to talk with your hands and listen with your eyes, true?"

"There is no problem," assured Chuy, flashing the white grin.

"I know it," said Rodrigue. He elbowed Ignacio and gave him a wink.

41

Chapter 9

The morning of the day when the Islands Invitational Billfish Tournament was scheduled to begin with a cocktail party and Calcutta bidding, a delegation of Jamaicans flew into Houston Intercontinental via Miami and were whisked to Galveston in a convoy of limousines. There were three bankers (one of whom actually lived on Grand Cayman but had controlling interest in a Port Antonio bank), the owner of several Port Antonio office buildings, the former mayor of Montego Bay, and a rum magnate who was his own best customer—plus a half a dozen young women with Spanish accents, thought to be of Cuban origin, in undisclosed roles. It was an unofficial delegation, picked by Garrett Kindler from the supporters of Trenchtown, his Jamaican marina project, and representing neither the Manley government nor its opposition in the upcoming election.

The travelers entered Galveston as unobtrusively as it was possible to do in three fast-moving stretch limos, and they went straight to the Flagship Hotel, a solid concrete-decked structure built over the gentle breakers that rushed like spilled suds to the seawall. They had six of the nine suites, and immediately put room service to work hustling nachos and margaritas.

42

There was some ugliness when an assistant manager asserted that Texas law forbade him to deliver mixed drinks to the rooms. Al Ahlmark, who was standing in for Kindler as host, bought a temporary repeal of the law, then soothed ruffled feathers by having six new electric blenders, six gallons of Cuervo Gold, six fifths of Triple Sec, six containers of cocktail salt, and a two-pound bag of limes delivered to the rooms. At the same time, he made arrangements for fully stocked bars, complete with bowls of pretzels and Goldfish, to be set up in each of the suites.

Meanwhile, over at the yacht basin, the temporary floating piers installed along the bulkhead had filled up with gleaming sportfishermen, a dazzling clutter of chrome and brass, rich oiled teak, and gel coats as white as the heart of the sun. Multicolored wind socks hung limply from the outriggers for decoration.

On several of the boats, the crews were busy setting the drags on the huge fishing reels. A man stood on the pier behind each boat, taking line in long, sweeping pulls while another standing at the fighting chair in the cockpit cranked it back in again and again, cheered on by the lazy crooning of Jerry Jeff Walker blasting from someone's deck speakers.

The drag on a big sportfishing reel worked like disk brakes in a car except they were only supposed to slow the reel's spool, not stop it. The man on the pier was a marlin surrogate, tugging repeatedly on the lines until the drag washers grew as hot as they would in a real battle, then attaching a hand scale and calling out the pounds of resistance as he pulled. The man in the cockpit would adjust the drag accordingly and reel in line for another pull. The ritual was necessary to ensure that the drag would be set just right (it varied from boat to boat, but about a third of the line's breaking strength was about average) if and when the real thing happened.

It was also a golden opportunity for crewmen to flex their muscles before throngs of admiring women—except that in the midday heat in Galveston, most of the women were behind the smoked glass doors of the boats' saloons, partying with the soft-bellied owners in chilly sophistication.

Rodrigue was relaxing with a beer in the misty gloom of the

43

bait camp when Leigh Kindler came looking for him dressed in a bathrobe and a garish cowboy hat, turquoise felt with a wide band of pink and white feathers.

The prospect of being compared to so colorful a locale as Jamaica had prompted Galvestonians to scramble for some sort of culture of their own, and the *Urban Cowboy* shtick was the handiest. Suddenly, big hats and long-necked bottles of Lone Star beer were everywhere.

Leigh was obviously wearing the hat mockingly, however. And—Rodrigue guessed by the deliberateness of her speech— she was a little tipsy.

"Garrett asks if you'll move *Abaris* for him."

Everyone in the bait camp was looking at her—Leigh Kindler in a terry bathrobe and flip-flops.

"Of course," he said, hurrying to his feet. There was nothing unusual about a boat owner—or even a boat owner's wife— seeking out Rodrigue in public. But it was an arrogant move under the circumstances and it made him a little angry.

"Where's the new captain?" he asked, ushering her into the blinding sunlight.

"Garrett sent him in the Suburban to pick up the reggae band. They're flying into Intercontinental, which is, God, halfway to Dallas. Bones went to Clear Lake to find a new trap for the galley sink. And Garrett's still in Houston until later this afternoon . . . although I don't think he'd trust himself to move her, anyway."

Her hip brushed his leg as they walked.

"A boat's due in from Orange Beach and he's giving them our slip on A Row for the duration of the tournament. Mighty white of him, don't you think?" She smiled a little too broadly.

He expelled his anger with a sigh. "So where does he want me to move her?"

"To the anchorage outside the breakwater, where you went down for me that time."

"And how will I get back to the yacht basin?"

"What's your hurry? Garrett's fixing blackened redfish for the crew later. That includes you. I thought you might help me get things ready."

44

To appear too eager now, Rodrigue knew, would be the kiss of death.

"Blackened redfish? He's not going to cook that in the galley, is he?" A former habitué of the French Quarter, Rodrigue was familiar with Chef Paul Prudhomme's new dish, highly seasoned fillets pan-broiled almost to the point of incineration amid clouds of pungent smoke.

"There's a propane griddle back of the bar, with a powerful exhaust. Garrett loves blackened redfish." She stretched her mouth flat in the first sign of disapproval of her husband Rodrigue thought he had seen.

"I kinda like 'em charcoaled myself," Rodrigue said happily.

He hadn't operated a twin-screw boat in ages, but it was a piece of cake. The *Abaris* fairly leapt forward in idle and spun in a smart left face with the port engine in reverse. As they plodded between the long rows of boats, Leigh came up on the bridge wearing a hot-pink bikini that was the color of the cap on a bottle of 151-proof Bacardi, a genital pink, Rodrigue thought dizzily.

"*Jesus*, Leigh!"

"What's the matter, don't you like it? You were so complimentary before."

He sucked in a gulp of hot, moist air. "It's, ah . . ."

Crazy was what he thought it was. To be parading around with him practically naked just before they were about to commit a million-dollar fraud? But then money meant nothing to these people. The woman was plainly—and rather clumsily for one of her sophistication—on the make.

Tsk, tsk, he thought.

"Words fail me," he said.

She rubbed his head playfully. "Good ol' Rod. There's more to you than meets the eye, isn't there?" She colored suddenly. "Eyes, I mean. I meant eye, of course, but— Goodness, I'm getting tongue-tied."

He knew the source of her embarrassment. It happened all the time. People assumed he was sensitive about his missing eye.

"No problem," he said. "It's a badge of honor among us pirates."

45

"Like the Congressional *Medal* of Honor?" She pulled away and fixed him with a smile that said she knew.

"How'd you hear about that?"

"A little bird."

"Must've flown a long way," he said softly. Not even Mickey Aimes knew about that.

"A business associate of Garrett's," she said. "Al Ahlmark. He's acting as weighmaster in the Islands Invitational. You met him, don't you remember?"

"Yes and no." He remembered meeting Ahlmark aboard *Abaris* a month earlier, but he couldn't remember when and where he had met him before.

When he ran a PBR in Vietnam, Rodrigue had ferried dozens of nameless men into the jungle—navy SEALs, CIA operatives, even a few mercenaries—for quickie, one-time-only missions. Their faces blurred together, and Rodrigue felt Ahlmark's belonged there. It was an ugly time, of that he was sure. But all of that happened before he was awarded the medal.

"Where did Ahlmark say he knows me from?" he asked—casually, he hoped.

"He didn't." She took a sip of her scotch. "But why so grim? A Medal of Honor's nothing to be *ashamed* of, you know."

"I guess not."

It wasn't anything to be proud of, either. A down-home boy, career navy man, hard-hat diver-turned-warrior—he had been a perfect public-relations tool against the growing unpopularity of the war. What he had done was lead his crew to slaughter for a code book that was already compromised and a wounded sailor who died later, anyway. But he killed a lot of the enemy in the process, and that was what they gave medals for in those days.

"Look, there's our Zodiac right there," she said, leaning over the wheel to point, all scented softness. "See? Tied up on the end over there? Let's pick it up so we'll have a way back if we need it."

"Yeah? And how will your husband get aboard?"

She frowned for an instant, then smiled broadly. "I'll run back in in time to meet him. How about that?"

The inflatable dinghy with a twenty-five-horse outboard was

46

bobbing at the end of B Row. Rodrigue kicked the stern around and backed up to it while Leigh scrambled down the ladder.

"*Ow!*" she cried. Rodrigue went to the aft rail and looked down in time to see her wipe tears from her eyes with her bare forearm. She looked up with an embarrassed grin. "Ummm, stubbed my toe on the base of the ladder. Hurt like hell." She bent and unlimbered a boat hook from beneath the cockpit coaming, and then limped to the transom.

"Here, let me do that," called Rodrigue, abandoning the helm.

"Uh-uh." She waved him back. "I can handle it."

Sure enough, she neatly unhooked the eye splice from the pier cleat and pulled the inflatable behind the *Abaris*. She looped the eye on a stern cleat and climbed back to the flying bridge.

"Done that before, have you?" he asked.

"Well, there are so many ports where slips are unavailable at any price and an anchor buoy is the best you can get. You get to where you can handle a dinghy pretty well." She winced with pain.

Rodrigue looked down at her toe; it seemed to be swelling but the nail was okay and there was no blood.

"Just sort of doubled it up," she said.

"I'll take care of it in a minute."

They were on the flat now, which was glassy. Low, fluffy cumulus lined the horizon over the mainland, not near nor congested enough to make wind. The tide was running in but producing very little current that far off the channel. Rodrigue headed into it and backed the gear levers into neutral.

Leigh turned toward the ladder again. "Whoa." He grabbed her gently by the arm. "You just stay put."

He went down and forward and dropped anchor.

She killed the engines and climbed down into the cockpit as Rodrigue returned aft. She looked at him and little frown lines formed between her eyebrows.

"C'mon, let's put some ice on that," he said, sliding open the saloon door.

She bit her lower lip.

"C'mon," he said again, and led the way inside. She followed and sat on a bar stool.

Rodrigue went around the bar into the galley, nearly tripping on a green garden hose that snaked from beneath the sink forward across the snow-white carpet. He remembered she had said something about replacing the sink trap. "What are you doing here?" he called. "Draining the sink down below?"

"Uh-huh. With the trap out, there's not enough slack in the overboard line. So I bought a funnel and a garden hose and ran it into the forward bilge. The pump there'll take care of the drainage until Bones brings me a new trap."

He opened the ice maker and filled a bowl with ice. "Relax," he said, back kneeling on the thick carpet before her. "Give me your foot."

She extended her leg tentatively, like a pouting little girl daring him to kiss it and make it well. He put a piece of ice in his mouth and gently sucked on the sore toe.

"*Rod!*" She reflexively tried to jerk the foot away, but he had a firm grip on her heel. He removed his mouth, let the ice protrude from his lips, and drew a damp line with it along her instep to her ankle, then up the inside of her calf.

"Rod—I don't want to."

"I don't either," he lied. He crunched the ice in his teeth and nuzzled the inside hollow at her knee with his cold lips. "I can't help myself."

"Please," she said in a small voice. "I . . . I've had too much to drink. Please, I don't want to spoil it."

She reached down and took his head in her hands, gently, brushing back the curls from his forehead.

"Nor do I," he said. He fixed himself a stout Cuba libre and put another piece of ice on her toe.

He couldn't stay for the blackened redfish. She had rejected his clumsy advances and now he felt about the size of a double-A battery. He helped her prepare the complicated mix of spices—Kindler only did the actual spatula work—and then he made an excuse and took the Zodiac back to the yacht basin.

Knowing that he would have to return to the *Abaris* that evening to listen for Shokaito's radio call put him in a nasty mood. He felt he was getting into something he didn't fully understand—like boarding a sampan full of smiling peasants, every one of them with their hands out of sight.

It was Ahlmark who drew out these ugly memories. Ahlmark and some mean, unfinished business that was meaner yet for refusing to step out of the haze of all those years and all that booze. No fucking wonder he drank.

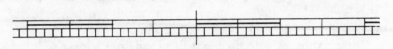

Chapter 10

When the sun fell into the clouds, it seemed as though all the refineries in Texas caught on fire. The reds and oranges and purples flickered like glowing coals, and with the same hypnotic attraction. The sizzling of the single-sideband radio added to the effect.

"I never thought I'd stoop to something like this," said Ed Vandegriff.

Physically, Vandegriff wasn't stooping; he was standing nervously erect beside the electronics console, hands clasped behind him and legs slightly apart in the time-honored stance of the mariner on his quarterdeck. He was at the age where his muscles were beginning to shrink and leave the skin loose. His sport coat was draped over the back of the helm seat and the short sleeves of his pale blue shirt were rolled even shorter, and there were muscles yet in his wrinkled arms.

"I wouldn't feel too bad," said Rodrigue, leaning against the back rail. "It's just theft."

Vandegriff glared at the dark, hulking figure against the flaming sky. "You're an asshole, aren't you? A regular asshole." They had just met.

"No, I'm a fucking peach. But nobody carried you aboard here. Least you can do is try to enjoy it."

Rodrigue didn't welcome the other man's misgivings. He had a few of his own. But they didn't prick at him nearly as much as the dwindling hope of bedding Leigh Kindler.

Vandegriff said nothing. He turned and studied the lighted dial on the radio, which was crackling with receptive juice but receiving nothing.

In graciously vacating his slip and anchoring outside the breakwater, Kindler was setting a sterling example for the other Galveston-based participants of the Islands Invitational. He was being a jolly good sport. He was also getting out from under the high steel-beamed roof over A Row, which sometimes interfered with radio reception.

No, Rodrigue didn't like it either, but it wasn't any of his business. Spending thousands of dollars and then betting thousands more to see who could catch the biggest fish only to let it rot off the bones at the weigh station wasn't his idea of recreation. Nailing Leigh to the khaki-colored beach in front of his house—just holding her there, motionless, until she squirmed for relief and begged him to get on with it—now *that* would be sport. So what was a little thievery among a bunch of fat cats?

Shokaito's voice came in so clearly, they both jumped. "Motor Vessel High Seas, Motor Vessel High Seas, this is Motor Vessel Bluebird, do you copy? Motor Vessel Bluebird calling Motor Vessel High Seas. I am heading for base number five-oh-oh, do you copy? Bluebird out."

Vandegriff switched off the set, quickly, as if to snuff out the evidence. Shokaito would be heading inshore. Later, when he dropped anchor, he would call again with his location.

"'Do you copy?' . . . out. You make a hell of a secret agent, Shokaito," said Rodrigue, laughing.

Shokaito's message was in a code—"Bluebird" for a blue marlin, "base five-oh-oh" for an estimated weight of five hundred pounds—intended to sound vaguely like traffic from a seismograph vessel, perhaps, or an oil-field supply boat. Signing off immediately after calling for an acknowledgment was a minor faux pas, however. Evidently, Shokaito was excited.

"Yeah, but damn, did you hear that?" said Vandegriff. "A five-hundred-pounder! Hell, that sews it up!" The old man's forehead was glistening with a fine sheen of sweat, and a grin deepened the lines in his cheeks.

Five hundred pounds was a respectable weight for a blue marlin caught in the northwestern Gulf. Given the terms of the contest—only two days of fishing with a mandatory lay day sandwiched in between—it was more than just a good head start.

"He's a hell of a fisherman, all right," said Rodrigue. "He might do better before it's over."

"He'll be wasting fuel. The way this fuckin' thing's being run, I'd be surprised to see another blue *entered*, let alone anything close to five hundred pounds. It is in the fuckin' bag," he said happily.

"See? Thieving ain't so bad when everything works out, is it?"

"You really *are* an asshole, Rodrigue," Vandegriff said, still grinning.

Some of the big-money tournaments had begun to employ lie detectors, but Kindler naturally had not made any provision for polygraphs. If anyone had asked why not, he would have smiled a patient smile and carefully—so as not to appear offended—explained that the moral characters of the sportsmen invited to fish the Islands Invitational did not warrant second-guessing. Rodrigue had to admit, it was a pretty slick plan.

The loose cannon was *why*. Kindler certainly didn't need the money.

"You been with Kindler long enough now to have the foggiest fucking notion why he would want to cheat on his own tournament?" Rodrigue asked.

Vandegriff put on his 1950s-era white sport coat and carefully smoothed the collar of his shirt outside. "'Course I know. Every owner I ever worked for woulda liked to done the same thing, if they'da known how to do it."

"Why, though?"

Vandegriff stared at him in the darkness. "You think Kindler knows how to catch marlin? Listen, if marlin fishing was easy, niggers'd do it. Kindler pays the bills, that's all. These owners, they slap themselves on the back a lot, but down deep they know who wins the tournaments. That's just the same as cheating as far as I'm concerned."

"I don't know, though. Kindler seems too laid-back for that kind of a dogfight."

Vandegriff looked at Rodrigue out of the corners of his eyes—openly, though, and stroking his lined jaw, as if sizing up the younger man.

"You want to fuck his old lady, don't you?" he said.

Rodrigue laughed and looked down at his crotch. "Does it show?"

"It figures, that's what. You're a goddamned babe in the woods when it comes to people like Garrett fuckin' Kindler. He don't have to think and act like a normal goddamned person. You think he'd let me put some tarps down in the fuckin' saloon when he was taking them big shots fishing in Jamaica? Think he'd at least tell them to take their fuckin' shoes off when they come inside? Fuck no. *White* fuckin' carpet in a fuckin' sport-fisherman—Jesus! Me and Bones like to never got the blood up. And that fuckin' propane cooker—what a genius to put something like that on a boat!"

The old man smoothed his jacket and said out of the side of his mouth, "Listen, let me tell you something else about fuckin' Garrett Kindler—and this is just between us girls, you understand?"

"Go ahead."

"You take this tournament—big public-relations bullshit, the goddamned twinning of Galveston and fuckin' Jamaica, huh? Just dangling a carrot for a bunch of big fuckin' investors—gonna treat 'em right and all?"

"It's obvious. Nobody seems to mind, though."

Vandegriff shook his head. "Tip of the fuckin' iceberg. Did you know that ten percent comes off the top of the Calcutta for the Jamaican Free Enterprise Foundation? You know who the Jamaican Free Enterprise Foundation is? Fuckin' Garrett Kindler. A hundred thousand dollars right into his pocket."

"I thought it was illegal to cut a Calcutta, no matter who gets it."

"It is. But the damn district attorney's on the board of directors of the fuckin' tournament and the fuckin' governor's the head speaker at the awards ceremony, so there ain't gonna be any state charges. And whoever wins will sign a federal gaming ticket, so the feds can't touch him—and wouldn't want to as long as the IRS gets theirs."

They heard the whine of an outboard motor. The sun was down now. White and yellow harbor lights lay in pale streaks over the black lacquer channel. Cutting across the streaks, stirring them like a runny watercolor, was the silhouette of the stubby inflatable boat with two people aboard.

"And that's just what I've been able to pick up," Vandegriff continued in a low voice. "Have you seen the fuckin' weighmaster? Guy looks like Don Meredith and talks like John F. fuckin' Kennedy?"

"Ahlmark? Yeah, I've seen him." Rodrigue's danger sensors twittered again.

"Well, that son of a bitch was in Jamaica when we were down there," Vandegriff continued. "And let me tell you what, he didn't take a backseat to Kindler or nobody else. I think he's fuckin' Mafia. I don't know what the hell they're up to, but it's big fuckin' stakes."

"Hey, *this* ain't exactly peanuts, you know? I just can't imagine Kindler scheming to pick their pockets for a hundred grand when he's going to steal the whole million, anyway."

Vandegriff shrugged. "He didn't come up with the idea to cheat on the tournament until we got to Islamorada and he met the nip. And it ain't the money, really. I mean a hundred grand really is peanuts to him. Guy like that, the only reason he's doing it is 'cause he can. That's all the reason he needs."

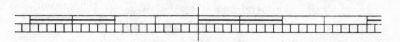

Chapter 11

The Kindlers had come to pick up Vandegriff and have a last drink in celebration before going ashore for the Calcutta. Rodrigue would stay aboard to listen for the second radio call, the one in which Shokaito would reveal the coordinates of the spot where the *Miss Colinda* and *Abaris* would rendezvous. The four of them stood in the saloon, which still smelled strongly enough of Prudhomme's spices to sting Rodrigue's eye.

"Poor Rod has to miss all the fun," said Leigh. She was in a dressy pants outfit, her hair pulled into a bun and tied with a flouncy silk scarf to mitigate its severity.

She stepped into the galley to put a quiche into the oven. It was a secret ritual that Bones had begged Rodrigue not to mention around the yacht basin. Quiche might be the perfect finger food for busy fishermen but it had an image problem on B Row.

"Poor me," agreed Rodrigue.

"We'll be thinking of you," said Kindler. "And of course make yourself at home. There's beer, liquor, whatever you like."

"It's rum, isn't it, Captain Rodrigue?" Leigh said teasingly. She walked around into the bar. "There's a bottle of Bacardi

Dark—no, two bottles. And plenty of limes in the fridge. I wish we could get those big Jamaican limes here, don't you?"

"God, yes," said Rodrigue. He got those in Belize. Huge, orange-melted, juicy—they were excellent.

"Coke, too, am I right?" asked Leigh.

"Uh-huh."

"There's Coke here, too," she said. "Listen, Rod, do you mind staying down here awhile to watch the quiche? Just take it out when it's ready and set it on the counter here to cool, and turn off the oven for me."

"I guess I can handle that."

He walked over to peek into the galley and see whether the controls of the oven might confound him. The green garden hose was still running into the cabinet beneath the sink. "Bones didn't put in the sink trap?"

"We haven't *seen* Bones since this morning. And *I* will put in the trap." She winked at Vandegriff.

"My chief engineer," Kindler said proudly.

"The timer will ding when the quiche is ready, Rod," she said.

"Yeah, but don't forget—ten o'clock," said Vandegriff, still grinning.

At ten o'clock, Shokaito would give the location for the next morning's rendezvous, and Rodrigue needed to be on the bridge to receive it.

"Don't worry. And quit grinning like that. You're going to wind up with your face in traction."

"Actually, Ed, I wish you wouldn't look *quite* so happy," Kindler said seriously. "People are going to think you know something."

"Hey, let me enjoy it while I can. You got any idea how many of these goddamned Calcuttas I've sweat out, watching the ante get higher and higher, and me all the time wondering where in the hell we're gonna fish, and what we're gonna drag, and whether the new wireman has enough grease on his ass to keep from losing right at the goddamned boat whatever fish we *do* manage to catch?"

Unexpectedly, he was angry. He was still sweating the Calcutta, literally. His shirt collar was soaked and his face had grown red as he spoke.

Kindler wore a look of fatherly kindness. "It'll look funny, of course, but if you want to stay here with Rod—"

"We can always tell people you're still upset after your run-in with the band," offered Leigh.

"Run in with the *band*?" said Rodrigue, laughing.

"Aw, that was nothing," said Vandegriff with a wave of his hand. "More fuckin' nigger shit. I'm just nervous, is all." He took a handkerchief from his breast pocket and mopped his face. "I ain't ever done nothing like this before. I guess it's about time."

It was a dolorous admission. Men like Vandegriff were artists of sorts. He and Bones were here because of their art—they could find and raise marlin. Bones could rig a blunt-nosed chunk of acrylic to dive and skip like a panicked dolphin; Vandegriff could make a forty-ton boat pirouette like a figure skater on mescaline. They each had mastered a myriad of basic skills from securing a boat to ride out a hurricane to whipping up a batch of ceviche in a heaving galley. Together they were a professional team, like the Astros.

And like John McMullen, Kindler was the Owner. The word was a title, a rank of nobility. He couldn't even put *Abaris* in the slip without banging her on the pilings, but he was the Owner. And his particular talent—the ability to produce money—was the one skill that couldn't be done without. Maybe—as Vandegriff was starting to see, and so late in life, too—maybe it was the *only* skill necessary.

"May I fix you another drink before we leave?" Leigh asked Rodrigue.

"No thanks, Mrs. Kindler. I can take care of myself."

"I'm quite certain, but here, let me. A good two fingers and fill the rest with Coke?"

"Aye, sez I." He took refuge in his gravelly pirate voice. "An' with a wee twist of lime if ye would be s'kind."

She gave him a good *three* fingers and went light on the Coke and stood watching coolly—Evita and Mo Dean and Marilyn Monroe all rolled into one—as he tasted.

Then they left to join Bones in the ballroom at the Holiday Inn for the Calcutta bidding, boozing, and jockeying for supremacy in the strange bifurcated contest, crew against crew and Owner against Owner.

Rodrigue didn't mind baby-sitting *Abaris*. Before dawn tomorrow, Kindler, Vandegriff, and Bones would be breaking the jetties. Mrs. Kindler would remain ashore, ostensibly to serve as hostess to those guests who would not be going to sea. Did that include him? There was always a lot of socializing around the pool bar while the men were fishing. Rodrigue knew from experience that a certain percentage of the women who hang around billfish tournaments get hornier when the boats go out. How the phenomenon would affect Leigh was thrilling to contemplate.

Besides, this wasn't exactly slumming. Like most boats campaigned in the Caribbean, *Abaris* had a full complement of reggae tapes—Rodrigue's favorite music—along with Henry Mancini and Willie Nelson for the stereo system. And there was the VCR, which Bones had shown him how to operate.

What he was wishing, now that they left him to combat the relentless air conditioner alone, was that someone had shown him the location of the thermostat. He searched in vain, then fixed himself another stout drink to compensate, and then turned his attention to the VCR.

One by one, Rodrigue sampled each videotape in the library, hoping to find more evidence of Leigh's rigorous tanning regimen. But the best he could come up with was her dressed in her dutiful whites, sitting in the fighting chair and grinding away on a big gold Fin-Nor while an inky blue sea bounded in the background. He wound it back to make sure he hadn't missed anything, and then he fixed himself another drink and prepared to study the tape in earnest.

As a showcase for her beauty, it wasn't very satisfactory. Bones kept getting in the way, standing behind the chair and swiveling it to keep the rod pointed toward the fish. Twice the scene panned dizzily to the sky and the overhang of the flying bridge to avoid a frothing wall of water as the *Abaris* backed down in the towering seas. Then the perspective changed, the cameraman evidently seeking a drier spot up on the flying bridge. There was a shot of her strong brown legs flexing prettily against the wide teak foot brace of the fighting chair, but then a voice intoned, "She's comin' up!" in a limey accent—no, Australian. Harry Morgan, of course. The camera zoomed just in time to catch the marlin leap, a metallic blue-black against the blinding glint of the sea's dimpled surface.

"Leap" doesn't quite describe it. Sculling with its powerful tail, the fish lifted itself into the air and hovered there, whipping its head back and forth with a rage that Rodrigue understood. When at last Morgan appeared in the cockpit and joined Bones in hauling the brilliantly hued monster over the transom, Rodrigue could watch no more.

He was rewinding the tape when the saloon door banged open and a man in a black diver's wet suit stepped past the galley. He wore a woman's nylon stocking over his head, and in his hand was a small chrome-plated pistol, pointed right at Rodrigue's face.

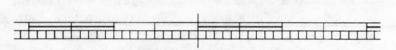

Chapter 12

Blood & Money was on the block at the hotel.

"Owner, Milo Perrin of Houston," the auctioneer was saying. "Captain is Howard Horton. Brand-new boat, a forty-six-foot Egg Harbor with GM T435Ds—she's fast. This is a new team but the captain made a good showing at Poco aboard Ted Gutierrez's *Marlin Teaser* with a four-hundred-thirty-three-and-a-half-pound second-place blue. This is a local boat, ladies and gentlemen. Who'll gimme two thousand—who'll gimme two—two—do I hear two. . . ?"

The Calcutta was being held in a large undecorated ballroom at the Holiday Inn. It was jam-packed, yet fully half of the chairs were empty, their owners milling around in the grid of narrow aisles around the tables, ganging up in knots of enthusiastic chatter. It was bedlam. The auctioneer's chant was amplified over the distinctive rhythm of a reggae band and the noise of the crowd. Down the center aisle, Bones was doing the marlin shuffle, left arm thrust in front of his face to symbolize the bill, right hand spread above his head like a dorsal fin. He bobbed and weaved through the navy blazers, tournament T-shirts, and low-cut sun dresses while onlookers grinned broadly and bumped

60

hips to the music. Bartenders at portable bars in each corner of the room poured the drinks a half a dozen glasses at a time, as though they were serving Gatorade at the Boston Marathon.

The Jamaican delegation had shed their Cuban honeys and were matched with Texas bottle blondes in Islands Invitational T-shirts that bobbled and swayed with each comic toast. The blondes were shed, too, temporarily, as the delegation scooted their chairs around to one side of the table for a photo.

Across the room, Morgan watched appreciatively as the photographer squatted to catch her subjects at a pleasing angle, her firm buttocks straining her silken jumpsuit. His eyes were hidden behind dark wraparounds, and his smile was a mere widening of his flat mouth. A slender raven-haired woman at her sexual peak caught his attention with a penetrating stare, then directed her gaze toward the side exit. Morgan stared back a full second, then flashed a wide grin. He waited another second, then eased toward the front door.

Leigh squinted into the automatic 35 mm camera, waiting for just the right combination of smiles from the Jamaicans. Her knees wavered and the smiles grew tense, but nothing happened.

"Drat," she said, straightening and frowning at the camera.

"What's the matter, dear?" asked Kindler. "Is it broken?"

"This is a roll of twenty-four. I thought it was a thirty-six. Is there a drugstore around here?"

". . . five—five—five, gimme five—willya gimme five . . . ?" the auctioneer sang.

The gunman's hand was shaking, but not enough to suit Rodrigue. If the pistol went off, there was a good chance the bullet would strike him somewhere in the face—and the fact that it would be a relatively small bullet didn't make him feel any better about it.

The intruder was pudgy and wheezing. His mouth made a small wet oval in the stocking that bowed inward like a diaphragm with each ragged breath. When he could speak, he gasped, "Drink!"

"Good idea!" said Rodrigue brightly. "What'll you have?"

"*You* drink! C'mon, goddamn it!" He jabbed the air with his pistol.

"Me? You want *me* to drink?"

"Get the fucking bottle and shut up!"

"Uh, any particular brand?"

"What's that there?" He stuck his chin out in the direction of Rodrigue's glass on the black lacquer coffee table.

"Cuba libre . . . Rum and Coke with a twist."

"Then get the rum, quick!"

Rodrigue did. "Sure you wouldn't care for a snort?" he asked affably, hoisting the Bacardi bottle.

"Don't be cute, motherfucker. *Drink!*"

"Aye-aye. *El hígado no existe!*" And with that base toast, he turned the bottle up.

The gunman frowned at the bubbles rising in the bottle as Rodrigue drank. A lot of it was spilling down his chin and darkening the front of his African-looking smock, but that was good, too. The more he stank of booze, the better.

Over the quiet hum of generator and air conditioner, they heard the sound of an approaching boat. Rodrigue lowered the bottle and the gunman whipped his eyes to the curtained windows and back to Rodrigue again. The tiny, ugly snout of the pistol quivered violently.

"Don't you make a fucking sound!" he warned, easing the door shut.

"I don't know who it is," Rodrigue said. "Nobody is supposed to be coming."

There was a thump against the *Abaris*'s hull and another thump as someone stepped heavily into the cockpit. "'Ta fuck?" came a quizzical exclamation. Rodrigue recognized Vandegriff's voice, growing louder as he stepped through the door. The gunman tensed and darted a panicky look at Rodrigue. Rodrigue shrugged and tipped the bottle again.

As soon as Vandegriff stepped into sight, the gunman wheeled and shot him. Rodrigue's monocular vision collapsed to a tight circle encompassing the old man's face. For an instant, he saw only the awful look of surprise.

He was already in action, reflexively, swinging the rum bottle

62

at the gunman's face with all his might. He misjudged and over-swung, catching the stranger in the throat with the clenched fist that held the neck of the bottle. Then it was over—the wet-suited stranger was writhing on the cabin sole, gurgling horribly, and Vandegriff stood looking with amazement at the spreading crimson stain on his white sport coat.

"Son of a bitch *shot* me!" he said, incredulous.

"No shit," said Rodrigue, snatching the little chrome pistol off the carpet. "Let's see how bad. Peel your shirt off. Where do you keep the goddamned first-aid kid?" He shoved the pistol into his back pocket.

"Galley. It's screwed on the inside of the lower cabinet door. Fartherest one. Goddamn, you slapped the *shit* out of him!"

The gunman had ceased to gasp and was kicking spas-modically. "Fuck!" Rodrigue barked, feeling the icy grip of panic for the first time in ages. He knelt and ripped the stocking from the man's head. He tried to open the man's airway. No luck. He tried again. It was like blowing into a closed fist. Gently, he felt the pulpy windpipe.

Vandegriff was examining himself under his loosed shirttail. There was a mere red spot on his skin. "It just punched into the blubber here. See? Ain't even hardly bleeding now. Just burns a little."

Rodrigue looked up from the gunman. "Listen, you ever done a tracheotomy?"

"Shit no."

"Find me something hollow, then!" He remembered a pen lying on the bar. "Ballpoint! Gimmie that ballpoint!"

Rodrigue clawed out his jackknife and jabbed a hole in the man's trachea just above the sternum. It bled a lot more than he had expected. Vandegriff unscrewed the barrel of the pen and handed it to him. In desperation, Rodrigue bit off the pointed end to make the hole larger, and he shoved the other end into the ragged, bloody opening. He took a big gulp of air and blew it through the plastic tube. In his excitement, he blew too hard and splattered his face with blood.

"Fuck!" He tried again, more gently. And again. And again.

"He's dead," came Vandegriff's voice. "Dead, Rod. Quit."

"Oh fuck," Rodrigue said, sitting back, tears streaming from his good eye.

"Wha—? Say, you *know* this son of a bitch?"

"No, but I didn't mean to kill him."

Vandegriff took a step and surveyed the saloon. "What, were y'all having a *party*? Smells like the backside of fuckin' Kingston in here. What'd he want?"

"No idea," said Rodrigue, wiping his face. "He busted in here—swam out from the looks of him—and put a gun on me. Fucking made me drink rum!"

"What?"

"Told me to drink that." He indicated the near-empty bottle lying in the dark stain on the white carpet. "You all right?"

"Ruined a goddamned good jacket," said Vandegriff. He examined his paltry gunshot wound again. "Ain't bleeding much at all now."

"Well, let's get a patch on you just the same. Then we'll get you over to the emergency room. You—hey, you hear that?"

"What?" Even as Vandegriff said it, he heard the outboard-motor noise that had crept into his consciousness plunge suddenly in pitch and then die.

"*Shhh!* Get down over there; someone else's coming aboard!"

A footfall thudded in the cockpit. Rodrigue waved Vandegriff to safety down the companionway to the staterooms, and he coiled up behind the galley counter. Let another cut-rate commando step inside and he'd find out what the fuck was going on.

A figure crept stealthily into the saloon, and Rodrigue caught himself in mid-spring—

Garrett Kindler—who was carrying a diving mask and fins as though they were a shedding cat—regarded him with bland surprise.

"What are you doing here?" he said as Vandegriff climbed out of the companionway. "And who the hell is *that*?"

"Getting my ass shot," said Vandegriff, answering the first question first. "And that's who done it."

"*Rod?*" The word had the sharp edge of accusation.

Rodrigue explained as best he could. Vandegriff added the part where Rodrigue had probably saved both their lives by smashing the intruder in the throat. Kindler stacked the diving gear neatly against the end of the white suede divan and sat, brow wrinkled.

"It *could* be just a simple hijacking," he said. "But why would they want to get you drink? Dump your body off someplace . . . make it look like you were involved . . . throw the police onto the wrong trail . . ." He was thinking aloud. Finally, he shrugged and rose from the divan. "In any case, there's plenty of time to worry about it."

Rodrigue hurried into the galley, jerked the cabinet open, and peered inside. He noticed, with admiration for her workmanship, where Leigh had puttied an aluminum funnel to the bottom of the sink, then attached the garden hose to the funnel with a plastic tie-wrap. The first-aid kit was mounted on the inside of the door.

"We've got to get Ed to the emergency room," he said, returning with the sterile compresses.

Kindler looked steadily into Vandegriff's eyes. "How is it?"

"Aw, I'm all right. I'm not fuckin' off this deal over a little pinprick like this."

Kindler turned to Rodrigue. "You see," he explained patiently, "the hospital will have to call in the police, and the police will want us to spend all morning explaining what went on here. I'm not sure our marlin will keep until Sunday, so what we'll do is just put off the police until tomorrow evening."

"Kindler, we've got a *stiff* here."

"Thanks to you," he said kindly. He waved aside the inconvenience. "We'll put him on ice and turn him in after we weigh in tomorrow."

"On ice?"

"Yes. The chest freezer's big enough. There's nothing in there but a few boxes of squid, and we can jettison those if need be. We'll curl him up and he'll fit fine. Now, let's dress that wound."

Rodrigue's head was buzzing. He wasn't sure whether Kindler's speech had made sense or not. He shook it off and helped Kindler carry the body down into the starboard stateroom, him grasping the man at the armpits and backing down the stairs while Kindler lifted at the knees.

Kindler had at some time removed the bunks from the starboard guest stateroom—or more likely had *Abaris* built without them—and turned the space into a tackle room. It was lined with racks of rods and reels and dangling lures the size of thermos bottles. The chest freezer was against the inside bulkhead, where it would be as close to the center line as possible and not have an appreciable influence on the boat's stability. Inside there were a couple of cardboard cartons of squid and a plastic-wrapped bill from a past conquest. Rodrigue was glad he didn't have to look at the gunman's face as they lowered him butt-first into the freezer. With the legs folded, the lid shut securely and Rodrigue breathed a grateful sigh. It wasn't the first man he had killed—it was *another* man he had killed. That was worse.

"You know, I knew something was wrong when I stumbled over that diving gear in the cockpit," Vandegriff said angrily as they ascended back to the saloon. His mind was starting to play it back now. "I told myself it was probably just some more of Bones's shit."

Rodrigue examined the mask and dangling snorkle, both black and substantial, military-looking.

"There's a plastic freezer bag out there, too," said Kindler. "Crumpled under the fighting chair. Probably how he kept his gun dry. Where is the gun, by the way?"

"I've got it in my pocket," said Rodrigue.

"Hang on to it. The police will want it, of course."

"Hey!" said Vandegriff urgently. "How in the hell're we going to explain Rodrigue being on board?"

Kindler looked at him blankly. "What is there to explain?"

"I mean what if somebody spots his boat out there and puts two and two together?"

"So what? Unless they actually see us transfer the marlin . . . and we're going to make sure *that* doesn't happen—"

"What are you guys doing back here, anyway?" Rodrigue asked, coming out of his daze. "The bidding over with already?"

"Oh, we got *Abaris* all right," said Kindler with a reassuring wave of his long fingers. "We were first up. The bidding will go on for a couple of hours yet, but we were already over two hundred thousand when I left. I'm sure we'll break the million-dollar mark."

He looked disgustedly at the rum-stained carpet. "Needed some more film. Nobody sells black and white film anymore except a camera store. If I would've known *you* were going to leave early, Ed, I'd have asked you to run us some back."

"I'd had enough," Vandegriff said simply.

"Whose boat is that tied up out there?" asked Kindler.

"Belongs to a fellow named Jerry Taylor," said Vandegriff. "Kind of a local hotshot in the small-boat tournaments. You know him, don't you?"

Rodrigue nodded distractedly. Was this something Kindler had anticipated? he was wondering. His surprise had seemed genuine enough, but now he was so blasé about it. . . . And why in the hell would the gunman make *him* drink rum, then so quickly and deliberately shoot Vandegriff? It was obvious Vandegriff didn't know him from Harry Truman.

"Put it back in his slip on B Row for me, okay? The key goes in the rope locker forward."

"What?"

"Taylor's boat," said Vandegriff, irritated. "Leave it where it belongs for me. I'll stay here and catch the nip's call."

"Yeah, sure."

Kindler fumbled in a drawer and came up with a box of Pan-X. "Well, there's no problem with Rod being on board," he said. "Rod gets around." He gave Rodrigue a good-natured wink.

And then his face turned to stone.

"But don't say anything about this to Leigh," he said. "Stay completely away from her."

A loud ding came from the galley. The quiche was ready.

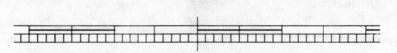

Chapter 13

Rodrigue woke up hungry. That was a good sign. He hadn't gotten drunk—he had let most of the rum run back out of his mouth—but he had gone to bed with a psychological hangover, a deep malaise. *Had he really killed that guy?*

It was like a bad dream. And what made it worse was the suspicion that he hadn't been saving their lives at all; he had merely struck out in frustration, the way someone in the complaint department might come home and kick the cat. He was already feeling dirty about the company he was keeping, and then the perfect scapegoat, with his ineffectual little gun and frantic vibes, had materialized like the Virgin of Guadalupe. Rodrigue had the ugly feeling that he would've throttled the man if he had come to fix the sink.

But why had he come? They might never know, thanks to him. If the blow had landed an inch higher, it only would've broken his jaw. Son of a bitch could've been made to *write* what the hell was going on.

Kindler's notion that the gunman intended to steal the *Abaris* seemed weak in the harsh light of day. He could've just popped Rodrigue between the eyes and gotten under way. And why did he turn right around and shoot Vandegriff so abruptly? He was nervous and simply might've panicked, but it sure seemed like he intended to kill the old fart all along. But why? Could it have anything to do with the cheating in the tournament? No, they would want to shoot Kindler for that.

Why didn't they at least *report* the shooting? He had been in shock, and Kindler—Kindler was used to doing whatever he wanted. It would look bad to the cops, but Kindler would have to take the heat for that.

Rodrigue had signed on to help fix the Islands Invitational and he would see it through. That was Rodrigue—stay cool, pay attention to the job at hand. But he knew he had better figure out what was going on and be quick about it. Otherwise, he might wind up squashed between a wall of money and God knows what other crushing force.

He needed some time to think. At least he was hungry again. He browned some Jimmy Dean pan sausage, put it aside, and fried cubed potatoes and onions in the grease. He scrambled in two eggs, added the sausage, and ate the mixture on flour tortillas with pico de gallo—sitting out on the sun deck of his beach house, reading the morning paper and washing down the taquitos with strong Cajun coffee.

Leigh called at exactly nine o'clock, as though she had forced herself to wait until a decent hour.

"What are you doing?" she asked. If it was meant to sound casual, it didn't quite make it.

"Washing dishes," he said truthfully. He was scrubbing the cast-iron skillet, cradling the phone on his shoulder.

"Somehow it's hard to visualize Rodrigue the Pirate washing dishes." The confidence was back in her voice. Rodrigue was reminded of how badly he wanted her.

"You should come over and watch. No, you shouldn't."

"No, I shouldn't. Maybe we, ah, could get together later this morning. Someplace else. You know, to talk about it."

"Talk about what?"

Hesitation. Rodrigue could hear long nails tapping on the receiver. "Are you interested in me, Rod?"

He thought he had taken charge. Why was his mouth dry?

"Lately, Mrs. Kindler, I've been interested in little else. But under the circumstances, I don't think we'd better as much as wink at each other."

"Circumstances?"

Her voice had a vulnerable warble in it. God, could she be *falling* for him? He had forseen a single lusty romp, with them parting as somewhat better acquaintances and keeping a polite distance from then on but regarding each other in secret awe. He was totally unprepared for any hint of true emotion from Leigh Kindler.

It almost made him break loose and tell her about the gunman—whether to somehow reciprocate with candor or just to get it off his chest, Rodrigue couldn't begin to guess. Soul-searching was not his long suit.

Neither, in the end, was candor. And he had other arrangements for making confession.

"Well," he said, "maybe you don't consider them circumstances. It's not that often I steal a million dollars."

"That was a hurtful thing to say. Are you *mad* at me? I mean—"

"No, of course not. I'm sorry. Frustrated is what I am. But business is business . . . and us taking a chance on being seen together would most definitely be bad for business."

"But everything's okay, then. I mean, so far. . . ?"

"How would *I* know? Aren't you bird-dogging tournament headquarters like an anxious wife? What *did* the Calcutta get up to?" He was curious in spite of himself. Money was never an overriding consideration to Rodrigue, but it was always a consideration.

"One million one hundred and sixty-eight thousand," she recited. "Garrett hasn't radioed in with the catch yet. I guess he's playing it cool. Nobody's radioed in, in fact."

He whistled. What a party there would be, he thought glumly. "Well, just keep playing your part, Mrs. Kindler. We'll see what happens. Maybe I'll see you at the weigh-in this evening."

Actually he had no intention of going anywhere near the weigh station, but he couldn't just sit around. He drove to the yacht basin to find Jerry Taylor, the fisherman who had lent his boat to Vandegriff. Maybe he would have some idea who would want to kill the old man.

Taylor's boat—a twenty-foot Shamrock, open inboard with a center helm console—was where Rodrigue had left it in its slip on B Row. But no Taylor. Rodrigue parked his car in the side lot and walked around to the bait camp, where Taylor could often be found anchoring a table.

At tournament headquarters, across the boat ramp from the bait camp, two teenage girls with glittering blue eyelids were hawking excess Islands Invitational T-shirts to the weekend fishermen. Most of the people associated with the tournament would be poolside at the nearby Holiday Inn, Rodrigue knew.

He was crossing the ramp when a flat, distinctive voice hailed him from the weigh station. It was Ahlmark, the smirking mystery man Kindler had tapped to be weighmaster. Beside him was a willowy brown girl.

"Hey, Rod! Get your butt over here, guy," he called good-naturedly. "Got someone here who wants to meet you."

Reluctantly, Rodrigue trudged back across the ramp. He stepped into the shade of the canopy and waited from them to come the rest of the way to him. Ahlmark was acting as though he and Rodrigue were old friends. It was unnerving.

"Susan, this is the famous John Rodrigue," Ahlmark said. She turned out to be a young woman in her twenties. "Rod, Susan Foch." He pronounced it *fak*.

"An honor, miss." Being evilly charming, Rodrigue planted a kiss on her fragile brown hand.

"Likewise," she said in a Deep South accent with a faint *shush* to her s. She turned to Ahlmark and said, "I can certainly see the resemblance."

"You might imagine some resemblance," said Rodrigue. "But I assure you this fellow and I are not related." He eyed Ahlmark coldly. "We're scarcely acquainted."

"Not you and Al," she said. "I mean Jean Lafitte. Al tells me you're a direct descendant of Jean Lafitte."

"Ah, but Al's wrong. I *ares* Jean Lafitte. Re-in-*car*-nated!"

People got it mixed up, but he was used to that. He was the descendant of a pirate, all right, one Dominique Rodrigue who captained a corsair under the Lafitte brothers' franchise. According to actual historical accounts, Dominique had served valiantly in the defense of New Orleans and was pardoned with the rest of the Baratarians. When Lafitte bolted for Galveston, Dominique stayed straight, founding a clan of shrimp fishermen in south Louisiana. The family took some pride in the ancient association with Lafitte, though, and pirate stories, some of them true, had been substituted for fairy tales for generations of young Rodrigues. Jean Dominique Rodrigue was named after both pirates, so he didn't mind when someone assumed he was related to the famous one.

Ahlmark grinned nastily. "Susan just flew in from Florida. She's a magazine writer, here to do a story on the tournament."

"Are there some skulduggery to be exposed, mayhap?" Rodrigue cast a furtive one-eyed squint across the parking lot in a faithful imitation of the actor Robert Newton. Never mind that Lafitte was probably a Frenchman and his own ancestor unquestionably a Spaniard. To Rodrigue, the only proper pirate was an Englishman.

"Yeah, mayhap. Do you ever fish tournaments?" she asked.

"I only fish for me supper. Say, how about a cold beer? I was just going over to the bait camp."

The last thing he needed was a curious writer on his tail, but before he could evade her, he needed to know how much she knew.

"Why, sure," said Susan Foch in her tough drawl. "Sure, don't mind if I do." She smiled broadly and Rodrigue noticed the thin dark gum line of a crown on one front tooth. With her sun-streaked brown hair and no-nonsense T-shirt and jeans, she was waiflike and almost cute.

"I'd join you but I have me duty," said Ahlmark, picking up on Rodrigue's pirate talk. "Take care."

Vandegriff was right—there was an air of authority about Ahlmark. He had a slow, hip-rolling stride, and he glanced casually along the roof of the bait camp as though making sure all the snipers were in place. And as Rodrigue turned and ushered the young woman across the ramp, he imagined he felt the tingle of Ahlmark's gaze on the back of his neck.

Taylor, a sandy-haired linebacker type in his late twenties, was sitting with the old man who sold the camp its bait shrimp. Rodrigue steered Susan to the table. "This is Pop Joiner and Jerry Taylor. Susan . . . Fuchs, was it?"

"Foch. Pleased to meetcha."

"Pleased to meet you," said Taylor with an embarrassed grin. He never knew what to think of a woman who showed up in Rodrigue's company, let alone one with the name of Fuck.

Pop Joiner just grunted. He had been married for fifty-one years and he had no truck with women of any kind.

Rodrigue pulled out a chair for Susan and went to the old-fashioned metal cooler. "What'll it be?"

"Oh, anything cold."

With one hand he pulled two Budweiser longnecks out of the ice for Susan and himself, and with the other pawed up two more of the canned beers Taylor and Joiner were drinking. For regulars like Rodrigue, payment was on the honor system.

"Where you from, honey?" asked Pop Joiner, coming to life.

"The Keys. Islamorada." She took a long pull on the beer.

"Naw, I mean where wuz you raised. Alabama, right?"

She looked startled for an instant. "That's right, Mobile. How on God's green earth did you ever guess that?"

Joiner's shrunken barrel chest heaved with a derisive chuckle. "I'd know that way of talkin' anywhere. Been fishin' with Alabamians all my life."

"That's *unbelievable!*"

"All talk like they got a mouthful of shit," Joiner confided in Taylor.

Susan choked on her beer laughing.

"Don't be ugly now, Pops," said Rodrigue.

"Coonass," pronounced the old man, hooking his thumb at Rodrigue. Pop Joiner tended to get rascally after several beers.

"So, Susan," said Rodrigue, turning his back to Joiner, "who do you write for?"

"*Marlin* magazine. Know it?"

"Can't say that I do," Rodrigue said. "I'm afraid you've fallen

73

in with a gang of meat fishermen here. Do you go out with them sometimes? The boats, I mean?"

"Oh, you bet. About two-thirds of what I do is take photos. There was a goddamned wreck on Highway One—up from the Keys?—and I missed my plane, or I'd be out with someone right now."

"So who're you going out with Sunday?"

"Oh, I don't know. I was hoping Mr. Kindler, but I haven't had a chance to talk to him about it. I asked Al if he could arrange it, but he was sorta noncommittal. Can you set it up?" She eyed him evenly.

"*Me?* I just do odd jobs for him occasionally."

"That's not what I heard."

"Yeah? What'd you hear?"

"Oh, I dunno . . ." She deliberately took a long swig of beer. A wicked smile appeared as she wiped the liquid from her lips. "Financial adviser?"

Pop Joiner choked on his beer and Rodrigue had to slap his back to stop him from coughing. Taylor was staring almost cross-eyed at Susan. But it was obvious to Rodrigue: She was playing with him. She didn't know shit.

"Well," he said, "I gotta get back to my advising. I hope I'll have the pleasure of seeing you again, Miss Foch." He kissed her hand once more and wheeled toward the door. "Oh, and Jerry," he said, turning, "about that leak in your boat—the pump seems to be handling it okay. I wouldn't worry about it as long as the battery holds out."

When he turned back to leave, he held a vision of Susan looking at him with a curious mixture of attraction and animosity in her dark eyes.

Taylor, on the other hand, showed pure panic. He was bug-eyed, ashen-faced, and already struggling to his feet.

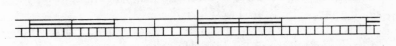

Chapter 14

Taylor caught up to Rodrigue on the other side of the boat ramp. "C'mon, be serious," he said. "Is my boat taking on water?"

Rodrigue looked at him for a moment with what he imagined was Morgan's inscrutable stare, then burst into his own sharklike grin. "Nah. Just jerking your string. I wanted to get you away from that writer so we could talk fishing and not embarrass ourselves. Caught any good snapper lately? My freezer's empty."

Taylor wasn't the most astute character in Galveston, but he might find it odd for Rodrigue to be quizzing him about Vandegriff, and the last thing Rodrigue wanted right now was any further association with the Kindlers, the *Abaris*, or her crew. Being secretive about snapper fishing was second nature to Taylor, however. So now if Rodrigue could artfully let Vandegriff seep into the conversation, all Taylor would remember was that they had talked about fishing. They were strolling slowly across the lot toward A Row.

Taylor said, "Might have a spot or two I could give you . . ." The way the sentence trailed off made it clear it wouldn't be a gift, exactly.

"Don't do me any favors. I have a spot or two of me own. I just want to know if there've been any snapper caught inshore at all. Say inshore of the Two-oh-six?"

"Like that sunken crew boat I been hearing about?" asked Taylor, rubbing his hands together. He collected places to catch red snapper like barflies collect matchbooks.

Inshore of the Two-oh-six, twin offshore platforms, were several wrecks and artificial reefs. They were hit-and-miss during the summer but much better during the winter. While most serious snapper fishermen like Taylor ran right over them on their way out to more productive water, Rodrigue with his big slow boat had thoroughly explored them all. One in particular, the crew boat *San Antonio,* had evaded Taylor. This could be the basis for a long and involved negotiation.

"Hey, you wanna run out and get some snapper?" said Taylor suddenly.

"Nah, my boat's hauled over at Port Bolivar," said Rodrigue.

"Hey, we'll take mine."

Rodrigue frowned. "That little open boat? No thanks, I got a shower at home."

"It's slick calm out there," Taylor said angrily. To him, not wanting to go fishing was idiocy. "That boat'll run forty knots if you're in a hurry."

Well, why the hell not? Rodrigue thought. Nothing he could do here but sit around and twiddle his thumbs until the *Abaris* came in that evening, anyway. Maybe a little fishing trip would do him some good. "I'll get the beer if you get the bait," he said.

"And we split the fuel?" Gas at the dock was almost two dollars a gallon.

The water turned blue within a mile outside the jetties. The seas were gentle two-footers and the Shamrock was steady and comfortable at about twenty-five knots. The Islands Invitational boats were all having an easy time of it as far as the weather was concerned, but the conditions weren't the best for fishing. The participants were prohibited from using natural baits, which meant they had to troll plastic lures. And plastic lures, it was said, worked a lot better in rough water. Kindler had it all going his way.

Rodrigue drank with one hand and shielded his eyes from the blazing sun with the other, steering the boat with his bare foot while Taylor tied new snapper leaders in heavy monofilament.

"Why don't you get a top for this damn thing?"

"It's just a stopgap," said Taylor, not looking up from his task. "I got me a Black Fin on order. Little bigger, little faster. Got a top."

Taylor was an operator at a refinery and unmarried, so he had plenty of disposable income. The way he spent it, though, was like an investment. His tournament winnings were already legendary.

The twin platforms in High Island Block 206 loomed large and distinct. Rodrigue turned his attention to the loran on the console. It was an unfamiliar model. "You gotta show me how to work this thing."

"Sure. What's the numbers?"

"Never mind the numbers, just set it up."

"Aw, Rod. I can't believe you're not gonna let me have the numbers."

"Rodrigue the Pirate don't let *nobody* have something for nothing."

"Oh," said Taylor, grinning with simian wisdom. "A swap, huh?"

"That'll work. Those car bodies east of here." Rodrigue already had the loran time differences—TDs or "numbers"—on the car bodies, but it didn't do to let people think he was easy.

Taylor opened his loran logbook, a ragged spiral notebook with pages of penciled notations and six-digit figures. He pointed and Rodrigue nodded.

"Ain't you gonna write it down?"

"Don't need to." He tapped his temple with a forefinger.

Taylor tuned in the loran as Rodrigue circled. When the lighted display was alternately flashing 11053.4 and 25867.3, he backed down to apply the "brakes" and ran forward to lower the anchor. Taylor logged the numbers into the notebook.

Taylor handed Rodrigue a sturdy Penn four-aught reel on a solid glass rod with the flexibility of a pool cue. Rodrigue watched his friend—who wasn't waiting for anyone—to learn how to put the reel in free-spool. On his own boat, he used a hand line—heavy monofilament wrapped around a spittoon-shaped mahogany spool he had picked up in Veracruz.

They immediately hooked fourteen-inch snapper—two on each line—that could've come from the same mold. Rodrigue had been hoping for a slow day. After they had iced down a dozen or so, he insisted they run over and try the car bodies.

"What the fuck *for?*" demanded Taylor. If the fish had been big sows, he would've backed off immediately, to save them for the next tournament. But a good mess of snapper could also be sold, and Taylor didn't mind if they wiped the wreck clean of these little ones. The idea that, left alone, little snapper would grow into big snapper had never occurred to him.

"You think I'm gonna take your word on those numbers?" said Rodrigue. "I want to try 'em out."

He could make a show of being distrustful and create a little breeze on the way. Hatless as usual, he was starting to feel broiled. And as long as Taylor was winching in red snapper, there was no hope of drawing him into idle conversation.

On Taylor's signal, Rodrigue dropped the anchor and assisted the line in slithering out of the boat. Taylor watched his depth finder with the intensity of a air-traffic controller. When it told him they were over the discarded automobiles—an artificial reef intended for this very purpose—he held up a clinched fist in the manner of a roustabout directing a crane operator. Before Rodrigue finished snubbing off the anchor line, Taylor's baited hooks were on their way to the bottom.

Finally, after a long period with no bites, Taylor uncoiled and the furrows melted from his forehead. The car bodies were picked clean. But this was no tournament and he had what he wanted anyway, so why not relax. Drink a beer—if fuckin' Rod hadn't polished 'em all off.

"Ever do any billfishing?" Rodrigue asked casually, his eye still trained into the blue water, thumb still caressing the taut line as though he might feel a peck at any moment.

"Are you kidding? That's for the big boys."

"I mean as mate or somebody's captain."

"I don't want to be nobody's fuckin' mate." Taylor looked at him with a grin that said Rodrigue should know better. "Besides, that's a full-time deal. You gotta be able to travel all over. I gotta make a living, you know."

"So how do you know Vandegriff?"

"Aw, Bones brought him around the bait camp. Pretty neat ol' guy."

"Maybe you've been around him more than me."

"Yeah, he comes off kinda cobby, I guess. Don't take no shit off nobody, that's for sure. You hear about the big fight with the band?"

"Band? What band?" Leigh had said something about a band the night Vandegriff was attacked, Rodrigue remembered.

"Kindler sent him up to Houston to pick up the band he brought over special from Jamaica, and it's a bunch of these wild-looking, woolly-headed blacks, like something out of Africa or something, and they got into a big pissing match right there in the fuckin' airport."

"Rastafarians?"

"Hell, I don't know what *tribe*. All I know is that Vandegriff left their asses and Kindler wound up having to charter two planes to carry them and their drums down to the island. And you know what they was arguing about? *Religion!*"

Taylor might loosen your teeth over which was better snapper bait, white squid or brown shrimp, but he didn't deem religion worthy of serious discussion.

And that was all he knew about it: Vandegriff had made enemies of a reggae band.

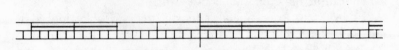

Chapter 15

"Let's don't fillet them," said Rodrigue as Taylor laid the first Mercurochrome-colored fish on his makeshift cleaning board. Taylor would later remember that his fishing buddy had seemed a little preoccupied on the way back to the yacht basin.

"I'll just gut 'n gill 'em," Rodrigue continued. "We can smoke 'em right here. We'll commit a party."

"Why? They'll be partying like crazy over at the hotel."

"Too rich for some of us's blood. Let's offer the proletariat an option, eh?"

"Huh?" Rod was hard to figure. Sometimes he talked like a normal person and sometimes he talked like a college professor. Sometimes he didn't even talk English. 'Course he *had* polished off half a case of Budweisers. . . .

Rodrigue had been looking at the benign, lifeless face of the man in the wet suit, reviewing it over and over in his memory. It was a face sculpted in modeling clay, gray and clammy and not quite finished. With the jowls pared down a little, it would've been . . . well, not exactly handsome, but pleasant. Like a grown-up teddy bear.

Rodrigue looked at the man and saw a neighbor who would

help you fix your car, but not too well. He saw a high school football coach or a small-town TV weatherman. But he could not see a hired killer—especially one hired by a bunch of Rastafarians.

Of course, they probably weren't Rastas at all. A lot of blacks in the ghettos of the Caribbean wore dreadlocks nowadays. It was a style, a statement of discontent. Rodrigue had been reading about the troubles in Jamaica—strikes at the government-run bauxite mines, shots fired at tourists on a golf course—but was Christian Democratic Socialism so virulent that a reggae band would hire someone to bump off a crabby old boat captain just because he was a racist? Or maybe these guys were terrorists and the whole mess was political.

The gunman hadn't had a Caribbean accent. He had sounded more like West Coast to Rodrigue's talented ear. And of course he wasn't black, so the terrorist hypothesis stunk worse than two-day-old bait.

Rodrigue put the cleaned snapper on fresh ice in one of the fish boxes recessed in the Shamrock's deck, and then he went home to change clothes. He showered and shaved and put on a peach-colored guayabera and a pair of khaki shorts identical to the ones he had taken off.

In spindly defense against tropical storms and high tides, the houses in Sea Isle were all built atop tall pilings. The space underneath served Rodrigue as carport and utility room. In the room was a barrel-shaped Old Smokey barbecue grill. He loaded it into the trunk of the Coupe de Ville along with an armload of mesquite, an aromatic hardwood he picked up in south Texas every spring.

On the way back into town, he stopped at the store and bought limes, real butter, salt, coarse-ground black pepper, and a case of Budweiser longnecks, which he iced down in the forty-eight-quarter Igloo cooler he kept on the front seat of the Caddy.

Taylor wasn't around. Rodrigue helped himself to one of the lawn chairs hanging at the back of the storage cabinet and he started the slow process of building a bed of mesquite coals in the Old Smokey. In a short time, the aromatic smoke attracted some of the regulars, who drew up more chairs and either plun-

81

dered Rodrigue's ice chest or brought their own, and the party was on.

The beer finally numbed Rodrigue's sensibilities. He decided to wander around and watch the first day's weigh-in, after all. He had never seen a tournament boat enter a *human* carcass before.

An expectant crowd had gathered at the roped-off perimeter of the weigh-in area, spilling across the dry portion of the double boat ramp. Ahlmark demonstrated that he knew his way around a weigh station, quietly overseeing the positioning of the forklift and cradle that might or might not be necessary. It was conceivable that nothing larger than a forty-pound sailfish would be weighed.

Rodrigue saw Leigh and she looked right through him. She was socializing, and not with her usual cool friendliness. The smile was too ready and too wide, and as fragile as an icy glaze on still water. She was holding a drink, too, which was another departure from the norm. Mrs. Kindler had been taught that a lady always has a place to set her drink. She took a long taste and, for an instant, gave him a hot stare over the rim of the red plastic tumbler.

It was a look of promise, but it left Rodrigue cold. He couldn't think about her right now. He was too . . . *vulnerable*, he decided. He had killed a man he didn't know, and for a reason he didn't understand. He had also become a criminal—not for the first time in his life, certainly, but there was a new, dirty feeling about it. Maybe he was getting old. Or maybe he was just drunk.

The first of the returning boats entered the breakwater and idled to the temporary berths, ignoring the weigh station. Several more joined the sullen parade. Then Rodrigue's old friend Mickey Aimes appeared in *Wahoo Too*. When she forked right at the fuel dock instead of left toward her permanent berth on A Row, the crowd rustled expectantly. Aimes deftly backed her into one of the two slips reserved for boats with fish to weigh. A burlap-covered form became visible in the cockpit.

The weigh-in committee took the lines and Aimes stayed on the flying bridge, hands on the neutraled gear levers—despite the fact that they needed no attending at that point. He was letting the owner descend and claim the spotlight.

The owner was shaped like Humpty-Dumpty, barrel chest and a belly to match, and he was civilly drunk—dead eyes in a glowing face. His thirty-one-pound sail was the first fish on the board.

More tournament boats came and skulked back to their moorings without weighing fish. Then came a big Bertram with Harry Morgan at the helm. They weighed a forty-four-pound sail *and* a one-hundred-fifteen-pound white marlin. Unlike Mickey, Morgan took center stage while his bespectacled owner beamed like a proud owl from the sidelines. Even on the rebound from Kindler, Morgan was something of a catch in his own right.

Morgan was a little flinty, but in that arena it was impossible not to admire him. His face was beginning to show the ravages of almost constant exposure to the sun and wind but it was still handsome and engagingly enigmatic behind the ever-present sunglasses. He wore his faded blond hair shoulder length and slicked back. He was trim with ropelike muscles, and the conspicuous lump in his Speedo bikini tortured all the women on supplemental estrogen. A New Guinea talisman on a leather thong around his neck added just the right savage touch. Men envied his style.

The weigh-in crew took the marlin from the scale, looped a line around its tail, and hoisted it to a high crossbeam where it would hang in the sun, gathering tourists and flies, until the stench became noticeably unpleasant. Then it would be rolled into the water, where it would float like a rotting log, and it would be towed into the Bolivar Roads on an outgoing tide and simply cut loose, to feed multitudes in the sea.

There had been a campaign to have the fish butchered immediately and the meat donated to orphanages the way king mackerel and dorado were utilized in the small-boat tournaments. But because of the difficulty of keeping such large carcasses cool in the cramped cockpit of a sportfisherman, most of the billfish were already too spoiled for human consumption when they were weighed in.

Morgan threw his plastic-tipped cigar down and took the water hose from the helper who had been using it to wash the marlin's blood from the concrete wharf. He hosed himself down, slicking his long hair back and making the definition glisten on his chest and shoulders. Then he stepped between his owner and the angler—the sunburned guest who had merely winched in the fish—to have their photo taken.

Meanwhile, other boats continued to ignore the weigh station.

And then, just before the deadline, just as the crowd was beginning to grow restless, *Abaris* swung around and backed to the bulkhead, with Bones alone on the flying bridge and a huge shapeless pile of damp burlap in the cockpit. When Bones gunned the engines in forward to check the boat's rearward motion, Kindler and Vandegriff stepped out of the saloon—Vandegriff a little gingerly, Rodrigue noticed.

And Kindler was sporting a bandage on his right hand.

"This is the one to beat, gentlemen," he said as he stooped and uncovered the marlin with his left hand. The huge fish was packed with fifty-pound bags of crushed ice. That would help account for its freshness. With the bags removed, the fish still had blue on its back and silver on its flanks—a tribute to Shokaito's skill. Kindler and Vandegriff stepped aside as Bones and the weigh-in committee manhandled the big fish onto the wood cradle and the forklift operator hoisted it to the scales.

"Five hundred and *six* pounds!" Ahlmark announced with a trace of awe in his voice. Excitement swept through the crowd like a fresh breeze.

There was another day of fishing left—day after tomorrow—but the tournament, as Vandegriff had said, was in the bag.

"Hi, Captain Rodrigue," said Susan Foch, unexpectantly at Rodrigue's elbow. "Where'd they get it?" She wore a hard smile.

"How the hell would I know?" His face was burning but his deep tan would hide it.

"You know these waters," she said. "Venture a guess."

"A long damn way from here, that's for sure. You've got to run about a hundred miles due south just to get to the hundred-fathom curve."

"All that running doesn't leave much time for fishing, though, does it?"

"You'd know more about that than me. I get the idea ol' Vandegriff is some kinda wizard at catching marlin."

There was a commotion behind them that caught their attention. Winking red and blue lights reflected off the walls of the fish-cleaning house and the bait camp. At the top of the boat ramp, two uniformed Galveston police officers were trying to wade into the crowd. Two more cops appeared in the weigh-in area, followed by two men in loud sport jackets who had to be detectives.

"Clear this area, now!" one of the cops behind them was saying. "You people are going to have to move on, now! Let's clear this area." The crowd thinned, shrugging shoulders, murmuring among themselves as they fanned out across the parking lot.

Rodrigue could see an ambulance waiting at the top of the ramp. Kindler must've called them through the marine operator, he thought.

The cops reached the weigh station's rope cordon and turned to face the crowd, which had already begun to regroup. With his height, Rodrigue could see the detectives step inside the *Abaris*'s saloon. In a moment, one of them reappeared and barked a command at the uniformed policemen. The farthest of the cops disappeared and returned shortly, followed by the ambulance crew bearing a stretcher. The crowd buzzed loudly.

The men with the stretcher disappeared into the boat. By then, everyone there was expecting human cargo—but supine, like on "Eyewitness News." When the saloon door slid open again and the stretcher bearers emerged carrying a large shapeless lump under the blanket, a common gasp washed back from the cord.

"What the fuck is it?" asked Susan, who was too short to see clearly over the sea of heads. "What's going on?"

"Ah, uh, well . . ." Rodrigue mumbled.

"Looked like there wasn't nothing but body parts piled up under that blanket," said a man, face screwed up in disgust. "Must'a been a shark attack."

"It's all right! It's all right!" Kindler shouted over the clamor. He had climbed halfway up the ladder to the flying bridge and was looking from face to face. When he spotted Rodrigue, he pointed solemnly with his bandaged hand.

"We had a hijack attempt on *Abaris* last night, but we had been forewarned," he announced. "I hired John Rodrigue to protect us and, by God, protect us he did!"

The dark sea of heads turned pale. Everyone turned and stared at Rodrigue. . . .

Everyone, that is, except the weighmaster. Ahlmark was staring at Kindler.

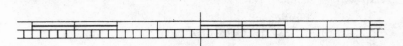

Chapter 16

Two of the uniformed cops had elbowed their way through the crowd to Rodrigue.

"Could you come with us, sir?" one asked, as though there was a choice.

"Not you, miss," the other one said—with diminished kindness—to Susan as she fell in behind them.

Rodrigue turned and looked at her: The expression could've been worry, anger, fear—even hate. He nodded glumly. "I'll see you later, okay?"

Up on the concrete wharf, more uniformed cops were whisking aside Ahlmark, his team, and the handful of newsmen with cameras who were covering the Gulf Coast's first million-dollar tournament.

A lean figure advanced slowly, a man Rodrigue recognized as one of the B-Row regulars, Bruce Phillips. He was a quiet, gray man of about fifty who often showed up on B Row in western dress clothes and then shed jacket and boots to go out fishing alone in his thirty-one-foot Bertram Flybridge Cruiser.

"I've got a boat on the next pier over," Phillips told one of the detectives, "if you want to separate the witnesses."

Detective Sergeant Eckles squinted suspiciously at Phillips. "Can we get inside?" he asked.

"It's got a cabin, yeah."

"Okay, Bruce," said Eckles tiredly. "Lead the way."

"On this next row over. We can just walk around if you want to."

Eckles was a bearish fellow with a thick brown toupee that was an ill match for what was left of his thin, oily hair. He wore a polyester leisure suit and a silken shirt open to expose black chest hairs that looked obscene on his pink puffy flesh. The heavy gold chain around his neck was the perfect accessory for the outfit.

Galveston PD had no homicide division per se. Robbery took it all—rapes, narcotics, and murders. But for a city with a population of only 73,000, give or take a few thousand transient souls, Galveston's detectives were very experienced. Eckles's partner, Detective Sergeant Sulpevida, took Vandegriff into *Abaris*'s saloon while Eckles and Phillips marched Rodrigue around to Pier B. It was an awkward, silent walk.

Rodrigue tried to use the time to organize his thoughts, but the alcohol made his thoughts slippery and he kept having to go back to square one: He was committing a million-dollar fraud. What was that shit Kindler had said about being forewarned? Was he being set up? Well, there was no use in trying to be clever. Best thing to do was to stick pretty close to the truth— and pretend he was born yesterday.

"The gun's in my car if you want to get that now," said Rodrigue as they turned the corner at the end of A Row.

"Might as well," said Eckles. He stood back and appraised the six-year-old Coupe de Ville as Rodrigue fetched the chromed pistol from the glove compartment. The gun looked tiny next to the .45 auto that remained in the compartment.

Phillips took the pistol and squinted at it through a cloud of cigarette smoke for a moment before handing it to Eckles. Rodrigue was beginning to suspect what Phillips did for a living.

"Twenty-five," said Eckles simply. Then they went down B Row. There was no one else on the pier except Taylor, hunched over in a lawn chair, dutifully tending Rodrigue's Old Smokey.

He watched in puzzled silence as they filed aboard Phillips's boat.

"You know the victim?" the detective began as they crowded into the small cabin.

Rodrigue didn't like his choice of words but he attributed it to jargon. "Nope."

"Okay, let's start from the beginning." Eckles sounded as though he was already bored with the story. "What were you doing on the boat?"

Rodrigue wedged himself into the settee. "Watching it. While Vandegriff, Bones, and the Kindlers all went to the Calcutta."

"Watching it for what?" He took the seat at the table opposite Rodrigue. Phillips continued to stand in the doorway.

"A guy in a wet suit, come to find out. I really didn't have a clear idea beforehand."

"You mean to tell me that Mr. Kindler *knew* somebody might try to come on the boat and he didn't tell you that?"

"Well, I suppose he might have—told me, I mean. I'm not a real attentive fellow, Officer. What he said or didn't say, I don't really remember. All I know is what I was expecting, and that was nothing in particular. If that makes any sense." Rodrigue had to watch himself; it wasn't his nature to cooperate with the authorities.

"Hmmm. Okay, what exactly happened?"

Rodrigue sighed deeply and scanned the overhead in the cabin. "I was watching a videotape of a marlin being caught, as I recall, and suddenly this guy slammed the door open and pointed that pistol at me."

"You hadn't heard anything. Total surprise."

"Total surprise. He busted in and told me to start drinking rum."

Eckles stopped writing and squeezed his eyes shut, his shtick for incredible testimony. "He said, 'Start drinking rum.' Like that."

"His exact words, I don't remember. Pointed at the drink I had and told me to get the bottle and start drinking. And it was not a friendly invitation."

"You were drinking before this happened?"

"Yep."

"The Kindlers know that?"

"Mrs. Kindler fixed the drink. In *Mr.* Kindler's presence."

"Kind of unusual, don't you think?"

"Not for me. I drink a lot. Ain't that right, Bruce?"

Phillips said nothing.

Eckles closed his eyes again, trying to visualize it. "You're there to guard against an intruder . . . were you armed? No? Not armed, having a drink, and watching a videotape. Okay, the victim enters, tells you to drink and you drink, right?"

"I gargled a half a bottle of Bacardi Dark, letting most of it run out of my mouth. Then Vandegriff walks in and the guy shoots him."

"Why? Did Vandegriff take him by surprise?"

"Not entirely. I mean we both heard the boat bump alongside and we heard Vandegriff climb into the cockpit. He even mumbled something when he found the victim's—as you call him—mask and fins."

"*Vandegriff* mumbled something."

"That's right. We heard him say 'What the fuck,' or something like that. So he didn't just break in on us."

"And?"

They had come to a crucial point; Eckles had his eyes open, studying Rodrigue's face.

"And as soon as Vandegriff walked in, the 'victim' turned and shot him."

"No words between them?"

"Nope."

"Any hint of recognition in Vandegriff's face?"

This was a subject on which Rodrigue was eminently qualified to expound. He could still see the look on the old skipper's face.

"Total surprise. Like 'What the fuck!' 'Who the fuck!' '*Why* the fuck!' all rolled into one."

"Then what happened?"

"Well, the guy shot Vandegriff and I hit the guy. Then we tried to save him, but—I don't know, I guess I don't know how to do a tracheotomy, after all."

90

"You didn't intend to kill him?"

"No. Just stop him from shooting again, that's all."

"And that's the wound in his throat, you attempting a tracheotomy to save his life?"

"That is correct."

"What do you think he was up to? Your opinion." Eckles's eyes were still open.

Rodrigue shrugged. "Shooting Vandegriff. If he had come to steal the boat, he would've ordered me to get the hook in and got the hell out of Dodge. If he was there to shoot me, he would've shot me."

"What about the information Mr. Kindler had gotten in advance?"

"What information?"

"That's my question."

"I don't know anything about any information."

"Mr. Kindler said he had been forewarned, and that was why he hired you. Forewarned of what?"

"You'll have to ask Mr. Kindler about that."

Eckles jumped to his feet, bumping his thigh on the table, but he ignored it. "I'm asking *you*. What do you know about it?"

Finally, Rodrigue was at a crossroad. He had sobered up enough to recognize it, but not enough to come up with an answer that would satisfy all possibilities. "Like it or not, you're going to have to ask Mr. Kindler," he said coolly. "Because I don't know a fucking thing about it."

Eckles sat down again and massaged his thigh. "Why did you freeze the body?"

"I didn't freeze the body. Kindler froze the body. I just helped him put it in the freezer."

"*Why* is what I want to know."

"Because Kindler wanted to go fishing instead of spending the morning answering questions, that's why. And it looks like he's got the stroke to get away with it." *Watch it!* he told himself. Cool down.

"Is that what Mr. Kindler said, that he didn't want to answer questions?"

"No, he said he didn't want to take a chance on being delayed

91

the next morning. I never got the impression he didn't want to answer any questions. He was pretty nonchalant about it—freezing the body, I mean."

"What was his reaction to the shooting?"

"I think he would've rathered it took place out in the cockpit."

"You know what I mean, Rodrigue. Listen, let's cut the cute act, okay?"

Rodrigue sighed. "Okay. I'm just in a bad position because I don't know half of what you expect me to know. I was in a damn daze by the time Kindler came on board." Kindler might turn out to be his enemy, Rodrigue figured. No point in giving him any help.

"But what was his reaction to the victim?"

"*Vandegriff's* the fucking victim, Officer. He was very sympathetic. Not enough to keep him from going fishing with him, but—"

"Not Vandegriff. The dead man. What was Mr. Kindler's reaction to the dead man? Could he have known him?"

"Well, he asked us who he was, so I guess not."

"Did he seemed surprised?"

"Yep."

"Did he offer any theory as to why the man shot Vandegriff?"

"Said something about someone stealing the boat. Just thinking aloud, it seemed."

"Do *you* know of any reason why anyone would want to shoot Vandegriff?"

"He's pretty crusty, may have made some enemies. I heard he had a run-in with a reggae band day before yesterday."

Eckles closed his eyes again. "A reggae band. What reggae band?"

"Evidently the one that Kindler hired for the tournament. I heard—probably thirdhand, now—that Vandegriff went to pick them up at the airport and got into an argument over religion with them."

"Religion."

"That's all I know."

The two men stared at him for a full second. "Well," Eckles said tiredly, "don't leave the island."

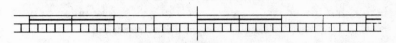

Chapter 17

Taylor had done a good job with the fire. The bed of mesquite coals had crusted over nicely when Rodrigue arrived to take charge again.

"I think that little writer gal wants your bod," Taylor said gleefully. "She was by here a while ago wanting to know where you were. I thought the cops had hauled you off. What the fuck happened, anyway?"

"Aw, some clown crawled on the boat the other night and shot Vandegriff . . . Flesh wound. I popped him a little too hard and he died. Fucking Kindler didn't want to miss a day of fishing so he dumped the body in the freezer. Now they're trying to sort it all out."

"Why in the fuck would anybody want to shoot *Vandegriff?*"

"I wished I knew. Say, what's the deal with Bruce Phillips? He a cop?"

Taylor gave him the incredulous look he used when he discovered he knew something someone else didn't. "Hell, yeah," he said indignantly. "He's a deputy sheriff. Used to be with the feds is what I hear. You know he don't talk much."

Rodrigue nodded. He sure didn't.

93

Rodrigue buttered and seasoned the fish and arranged them closely on the grill. Flames reared angrily at the first spatters of butter, but the lid smothered them. Pungent smoke billowed out around the edges. Rodrigue opened a Budweiser and settled back with a flood of relief. The fresh grilled snapper would be a balm on his troubles.

A few of the regulars gathered, drawn by the smoke. Bruce Phillips was not among them. There were questions, of course, which Rodrigue fended off with protestations of ignorance that few believed. The talk as they ate, even the joking was tentative and intoned. There was none of the good-natured rowdiness of a typical B-Row cookout. Everyone acted as though there were an important stranger in their midst.

He *was* a stranger. It had become as much a part of his act as the piratical swagger and the eye patch he sometimes affected. It was the part that kept the other parts from being too pathetic. He might be a drunken has-been but at least he didn't dwell in the past.

Most of what little the people around the yacht basin knew about him, they had learned from Mickey Aimes, not a man given to hyperbole. But Mickey's reluctant testimony had been tantalizing.

He had first seen Rodrigue in Cozumel and initially assumed he was a local, albeit an unnaturally riotous one. Discovering he was a U.S. citizen, Mickey decided Rodrigue must be one of the scuba divers who filled the downtown hotels. Then he learned that this Ugly American—always drunk, usually in the company of one or more women, and yet somehow beloved by the local populace—was a commercial diver whose long winter vacations overlapped the beginning of the fishing season.

He didn't see Rodrigue again for years, but he kept hearing tales. Some said he had moved permanently to Belize and opened up a dive resort. Others said he had been killed in a diving accident in the North Sea or somewhere. Aimes tended to believe the latter. Live every day as though it's your last and pretty soon one of them will be.

Then one day, Aimes was in a restaurant in Grand Isle, celebrating a big win in an important billfish tournament. The boat's owner and his friends had wandered off to get drunk and chase skirts, leaving him to finish his coffee alone—and who should come through the door but John Rodrigue.

There was something different about him—he was alone, for one thing, and apparently sober. He came over with his usual display of even white teeth, but then after Aimes had asked him to sit down and he accepted, there was a quietness to his demeanor that Aimes had never seen before.

Later Aimes heard that Rodrigue had been involved in some kind of trouble in Africa and now he was suing a diving company. He was still free-lancing for other companies—Aimes was surprised to learn that Rodrigue was considered one of the best deep-water divers in the trade—but he had violated the code of a very strong brotherhood. Two things you didn't do in the oil field were talk union and file suit. Now, Rodrigue, affable and fun-loving, was relegated to the strange role of a grudgingly respected outcast.

As far as most people around the yacht basin were concerned, Rodrigue simply appeared and began hanging out, as though he had sailed out of the morning fog like some Flying Dutchman on parole. A few like Jerry Taylor took him at face value. Most had their private notions about him.

Now, sitting with the others around the smoldering cooker on B Row, the increased burden of his notoriety grew too heavy.

"Arr," Rodrigue said in his pirate voice, looking at Taylor in his one-eyed squint. "Methinks I'll go piss in the sea."

"Here, want my key?" The rest rooms at the foot of the piers were locked and only slip occupants had keys.

"Nah. I hate plumbing."

Rodrigue was halfway across the lot to his car when he heard a happily familiar voice call, "Captain Rodrigue!" He turned; it was the writer, Susan Foch, an almost childlike shadow against the lights of the piers. She hurried to catch him.

"We missed you at the party," she said.

"You missed an excellent grilled snapper. We had a little cookout on B Row."

"I, uh, I just wanted to . . . are you leaving?"

"I thought I'd go to the beach and sulk. I'm having a hard time getting over killing that guy."

"Want some company?"

She was dressed in another T-shirt, still boyish-looking except for the unmistakable flare of her hips and the points of her hard little breasts. Her big eyes were full of intelligence, but warm. Rodrigue decided he liked her. She was probably just chasing a story, but what the hell.

"Why not," he said softly.

They swung around the parking lot so he could relieve his bladder into the plumbing at the bait camp's toilets, then Rodrigue let all the windows down in his car to admit the salty night air, and they cruised slowly past the sportfishing yachts, gleaming in the pier lights, some glowing from within as the festivities splintered into private parities.

When they paused for the light at Strand and Holiday, they could hear the syncopated reggae rhythm echoing from the glass-and-concrete canyon of the hotel—a rhythm as darkly primitive as the drums of Africa.

Chapter 18

"What do you know about Vandegriff?" Rodrigue asked. They were sitting on the seawall with the lights of the city behind them, staring into the whispering black curtain of the Gulf.

"He's kind of a John Wayne figure on the circuit," Susan said. "Irascible. Been around forever. There're a lot of rising young stars who'll tell you in a heartbeat that they learned everything they know from Ed Vandegriff."

"So is working for Kindler a step up for him?"

She shook her head sadly. "Garrett Kindler is not exactly considered a serious contender even though he usually buys talent. I mean the *Abaris* is set up more for dinner parties than billfishing. Doesn't have a tower—doesn't even have a covered *bridge*, for Christ sake. Stubby little outriggers not worth a damn for plastics." She looked out into the darkness with a sigh of disgust. "He's a bait man, anyway. Only reason he limited the Islands to plastics is 'cause the others shamed him into it."

"What others?"

"You know, the other heavy hitters. The others in the tournament."

"So why is Vandegriff working for him?"

"It's a tough circuit. He's getting old. Lotsa young lions around who'd eulogize the shit out of him after they cut his throat—but not literally. I mean nobody would actually kill him."

"Do you know Harry Morgan?"

"Sure. He's about two waves behind Vandegriff. Former young lion fixin' to be a has-been."

"Hell, I thought he was at the top of his craft."

"He knows a lot about *boating* big marlin, no question about that," she said. "But this is the toughest marlin fishing in the world right here. To catch marlin in the northwestern Gulf of Mexico, you gotta know how to find 'em and how to raise 'em. Over in Australia, they're so thick at times, you can't help bumping into one now and then."

He felt a nasty twinge of satisfaction. "So why doesn't he go back to Australia?"

"He's probably already a has-been in Australia."

"I guess you knew that he worked for Kindler for a while."

"Sure. Kindler brought him over here. Listen, I kinda enjoy being the interviewee for a change, but where are you going with this?"

"Would there be any bad feeling between Morgan and Vandegriff for Vandegriff taking his job?"

"Nah. Morgan might be pissed at Kindler, but he wouldn't have any hard feelings toward Vandegriff. Not enough to want to kill him, that's for sure."

"Well, goddamn it, *somebody* did."

She shrugged. "He's kinda short with people sometimes—"

"I'm not talking about reaching down the bar and wringing his neck; I'm talking about setting him up to be killed, hiring a pro."

"Who didn't count on meeting up with another pro." She eyed him evenly. "That's what they're saying you are, you know."

"I'm a professional diver," he said heatedly. "Used to be. Okay, so this guy was a semipro. Question remains, why'd he shoot Vandegriff?"

"Why don't you start at the beginning and maybe I can help you," she said.

"Just between you and me?"

Susan chewed her bottom lip. "Rod, I don't want to have to promise to forget everything. Obviously, it's the major story here, regardless of what happens in the tournament. All I can say is that I don't want to hurt you in any way. That's all I can say."

He stared at the broken trails of phosphorescence left by the tumbling waves. It was a lonely sight. Vandegriff had been right—he was a babe in the woods when it came to these people. Susan at least knew who all the players were. She'd probably get to the bottom of it sooner or later. Better to get her on his side early on. Besides, he instinctively trusted her—to a point.

He rehashed the fiction about being hired to watch out for and protect against generic danger, ending with the truth about the episode with the rum bottle.

"I mean the guy didn't bat an eyelash. As soon as Vandegriff walked inside, he shot him. It seems plain to me."

"And was going to set you up as the killer?"

"I guess. Either that or anesthetize me."

"If you were the prime suspect, it would sound like a pretty fantastic story—this commando comes out of nowhere. . . . You think it could be you he was after? I mean to frame you?"

Rodrigue laughed. "C'mon, Susan. He's mad at me, so he shoots some poor old fart dead just to send me to prison? I'm just glad it was *me* he was mad at."

"Well," she said carefully. "Could it have something to do with the tournament, then?"

He looked at her with a half-squint. She gazed steadily back at him, her big liquid eyes like open doors. He wanted to tell her. But he couldn't. The secret wasn't his alone.

"It might indirectly," he said finally. He chuckled at the absurdity of it. "The only clue I've got is that he had a run-in with the band. Vandegriff did."

"The band? The reggae band? At the hotel?"

"Uh-huh. Vandegriff went to pick them up at the airport and got into an argument over religion. If they're Rastafarians, it's easy to see why. But it's hard to imagine genuine Rastamen hir-

99

ing a gunman to kill him over it—especially a white gunman. 'Course I got all this thirdhand."

"Then let's go find Vandegriff and ask him about it."

"Was he at the party when you left?"

"Naw, come to think of it," she said, rubbing her jaw thoughtfully, "I hadn't seen him all evening."

"They probably took him to the hospital. He's a tough old coot, but he had a hole punched in him. If he's around tomorrow, I'll corner him about it."

"What about what Kindler said—that they were after the boat?"

Rodrigue shook his head. "Why didn't he just *take* the boat? Why try to get me soused, and then shoot the guy who knows best how to run it? I'm telling you, the guy was out to kill Vandegriff. And if I hadn't've killed *him*, we'd know why. I need a drink."

He woke up fully clothed on his own couch, his head throbbing from the rum. Then he remembered Susan. They had gotten drunk together, sitting out on his sun deck in the muggy night. They had become chummy—and maybe she had even come on to him a little, but he had lost faith in his ability to read those kinds of signals. They had separated and gone to bed without so much as a lingering handshake.

He rose quietly and peeked into the bedroom. She was curled on her side, clutching the bunched-up sheet at her chest like a security blanket, and exposing a taut brown back and round white buttocks. Her T-shirt, jeans, panties, and worn Top-Siders were in one pile on the floor beside the bed. He stared for a moment, wondering about his feelings, then he gently pulled the loose bedspread over her and went into the kitchen to start the coffee.

While the pot was dripping, he sneaked back and got a change of clothes, showered, shaved, and dressed—all without waking her. He stirred cream into a cup of the strong Cajun coffee, fetched the morning paper off the drive, and sat out on the sun deck, bathed in the undiluted rays of the new day rising from the Gulf.

Not surprisingly, the shooting incident was a footnote on a back page, while the tournament was getting feature coverage out front. The unofficial Jamaican delegation had been given every opportunity to confess how much they admired Galveston. There were no comments about the upcoming election in Jamaica and how the much-ballyhooed twinning of the islands hinged upon a change in government there. A voracious—if passionless—consumer of news, Rodrigue knew the current government of Jamaica would sooner twin with Cuba than Galveston.

"Well!" said the tough little voice. "Some baby-sitter *I* am." She was standing in the open sliding glass door, wrapped in the bedspread, hair tousled and eyelids puffy.

"Coffee?"

"*Please!*"

"Cream and sugar?"

"Black." She shuffled across the gritty deck and seated herself at the table, the blossoming sunrise capturing her gaze.

"I brought cream just in case," Rodrigue said, returning quickly with her coffee and a small stainless pitcher. "Most people find this dark-roast coffee too strong to take black."

She sipped and comically grabbed her throat and made a face with her tongue out—not the kind of face permitted by the usual female vanity. When she reached for the cream pitcher, Rodrigue got a glimpse of one hard, pale breast in the folds of the bedspread, and he averted his eyes. It was too much like window peeping.

"What is this, shock therapy?" she asked, smiling. "Drinking battery acid by the sea."

"How about some breakfast?"

"I dunno, Rod. My stomach's kinda queasy."

"I make a breakfast specially formulated for hangovers. It's like hyperbaric therapy."

"Say whut?"

"Time may be the only cure for a hangover, but this'll hurry it along. It's like going on oxygen in a recompression chamber. Speeds up nature's curing process."

101

"Sounds great," she said without enthusiasm. "Mind if I use your shower?"

"Help yourself. Towels are in the cabinet."

She took her coffee with her into the bathroom, which was a good sign. Rodrigue fixed a platter of fresh fruit—watermelon, pineapple, banana, even mango. He softened corn tortillas in a lightly buttered skillet and stacked them, steaming, in a tortilla basket. He put a half a stick of butter in a saucer and set it on the counter to soften. From the refrigerator, he took a large can of whole peeled tomatoes, opened it, and separated the contents into two bowls. He spiced each bowl lightly with cayenne, cumin, salt, and pepper. He opened a can of frozen orange juice, added the water, and set it stirring in his blender.

With the fussiness of a waiter at a good restaurant, he hustled the food out to the sun deck and arranged it on the table. For the crowning touch, he took a bottle of cheap champagne from the refrigerator, sneaked it open, and spiked the glasses of orange juice with it. Then he fixed himself another cup of coffee and settled down with the paper to wait.

"Gawd!" she said, toweling her hair and eyeing the table. "I feel like I've died and gone to Puerto Rico."

"Eat, your breakfast is getting warm."

She sipped the spiked orange juice first, sniffed it, and sipped again. "What *is* this, fresh mandarin juice? God, what a layout! *Mangoes?* Look at all this vitamin C! What's this, cold stewed tomatoes?"

"The tomatoes are the active ingredient. The rest is just for show, like parsley on a stuffed flounder."

"You are *not* the kind of guy I expected, Captain Rodrigue," she said, leaning toward him confidentially.

"If I was the kind of guy people expected, I'd be locked up or buried."

"Hey, this ain't *bad!*" she said of the tomatoes. She tossed down the orange juice and Rodrigue winced. "Got any more of this stuff?"

"Oh, you bet."

They finished the orange juice and half of the champagne and everything else except one tortilla that was cold and greasy in the

102

bottom of the basket. Rodrigue surreptitiously poured the rest of the champagne down the drain, trashed the bottle, and began cleaning up the kitchen.

"Can I help?" she asked, coming in with the empty fruit platter.

"Nah. Relax. Just take a second."

"God, I feel *great*! You weren't kidding about a quick cure."

She watched him carefully dry, then oil the cast-iron skillet. "You know, this is the *cleanest* bachelor pad I've ever been in. You are really neat, aren't you?"

"Ten years in the navy. Cleanliness ain't exactly an option aboard ship."

It came out a little brusquely. He had been enjoying himself too much.

Slightly stung, she got back to business. "So, what do we do now?"

He dried his hands and looked at her. "Find Ed Vandegriff, of course. You're with me, aren't you?"

"Like ugly on a toad. Long as you level with me."

"Need to go change clothes?"

"I go days tournament fishing without changing clothes. Why? Do I stink? I used your underarm stuff."

He laughed. "You smell great."

He wished he could have told her the whole story.

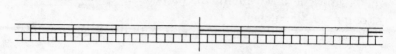

Chapter 19

Bones was poolside at the Holiday Inn, looking drawn and tired. He eyed Susan warily.

"Seen Vandegriff this morning?" Rodrigue asked.

"He's in the hospital. He got infected."

"Bad?"

"I don't know. How bad is an infection?"

"Oh, uh . . ." Rodrigue remembered his manners. "Susan, this is Bones McKenzie, mate on the *Abaris*. Susan Foch."

Bones looked at her with a careful sideways twist of his head, as though it might topple to the table if twisted too fast. "*Marlin* magazine, right? I've seen your stuff. Pretty good."

"Thanks."

"What hospital?" pressed Rodrigue.

"UTMB, right over yonder. That's where they took him to the emergency room after they finished questioning him. You could tell they were kinda pissed at Kindler for not reporting it Thursday night, but they didn't say a whole lot about it."

"You there when they questioned Kindler?"

"I was below, but I heard it all."

"What was that business about him being forewarned?"

104

Bones stretched painfully. "Yeah, they grilled him pretty good about that. Turns out all he meant was that once someone broke into the boat and stole a bunch of trolling rods and reels, and from then on he's kept someone on board whenever he anchors in an unpatrolled anchorage."

"You sure that's all he said?"

"Sure I'm sure," Bones said angrily.

Kindler had apparently just been winging it, Rodrigue decided, maybe trying to convince his rich buddies that the situation was under control; then when the cops called him on it, he had to come up with something plausible. Pretty damn reckless, though, since he couldn't have known what Rodrigue would tell them.

"What the hell happened to you?" he asked Bones.

"Aw, too much fruit juice in them rum drinks, I reckon."

From the emergency entrance off the Strand, they found their way deep into the labyrinthine complex of the University of Texas Medical Branch. There was a uniformed policeman at the door to Vandegriff's room. "You John Rodrigue?" he asked.

Rodrigue nodded.

"Got some ID?"

Rodrigue pulled out his wallet.

"Miss, you're going to have to stay out here with me," the policeman said. "Doctor said one at a time. And I'm afraid I'm going to have to pat-search you," he said to Rodrigue. "Miss, if you want to go in later, we'll have to get a female officer up here."

"Obviously," Susan said dryly. "But I'll just stay out here."

It only took a second to frisk Rodrigue, who was wearing a cotton dashiki and shorts.

It was a semiprivate room. The other bed was empty. Vandegriff was lying on his back, staring up at the ceiling with a look of pained determination.

"What're you in for, matey?" asked Rodrigue in his pirate voice.

"I guess they swallowed that fuckin' theory of yours that someone wants to kill my ass." He grinned.

"How's your bullet hole?"

"Aw, it's all right. They swabbed it out and that hurt like hell. You know, the damn thing punched clean through me. The bullet fell out of my pants when I went to take a crap and there was a hole in the back right underneath my belt. That's what stopped the bullet. But, shit, it passed through fat and didn't hit nothing. They're just keeping me in here 'cause they think somebody wants a piece of my ass."

"I take it you don't think the guy was after you."

"Shit, I don't know! Sure seemed like it, didn't it? But, fuck, I don't know why anyone would want to kill me." He grinned again. "I'm such a fuckin' sweetheart."

"I heard you got into a little scrap with the band Kindler imported."

Vandegriff laughed and the laugh turned into a painful coughing spell. He took a few gulps of air and said, "Them wild, woolly-looking niggers they got in Jamaica, you know? Jumped on me about some fuckin' porno movie or something. *Babylon*—that was it. Kindler didn't say shit to me about it. Motherfucker ain't got the right after what he's put me through. Fuckin' bridge with no top . . . get wet half the time and broiled the other half. Then there's that goddamned propane griddle! Propane's fuckin' dangerous to begin with; shit's heavier than air and if it gets loose on you, you got a floating bomb. Not to mention the grease and smoke everywhere. You ever seen a fishin' boat with *white* fuckin' furniture? Me and Bones spend half our time scrubbing up stains."

"What about the band?"

"Left 'em right there in the airport, ranting and raving. Probably got thrown in jail—or the bayou." He chuckled. "Fuckin' Houston."

"Nah, I heard them playing at the hotel last night. Taylor said Kindler had to have them flown down. No way *they* could be behind it, eh?"

Vandegriff chuckled. "You kidding? Fucker that shot me was whiter than my ass. Until you turned him blue."

Rodrigue gazed out the window over the tarred roof with its galvanized vents shining dully like tombstones in the antiseptic morning sunlight.

"How'd the transfer of the marlin go?" he asked absently.

"Like a Chinese fuckin' fire drill. That one little skinny meskin is dumber than a rock."

Rodrigue laughed. "That's my man Ignacio. Shows a lot of promise, eh?"

"He's a lucky son of a bitch, I'll tell you that. Shokaito had run a cable from the winch to a block overhead, to a block at the end of one of the booms, to another temporary block just over the ice-hold hatch. So when he starts lifting, the marlin comes straight out of the hold. Then someone just cuts that temporary block free and the marlin swings out to the boom block, where it can be lowered straight into the cockpit, you see?"

Rodrigue had no trouble visualizing it. He nodded.

"Well, Shokaito's on the winch, and the other two meskins are manhandling the marlin as it comes out of the hold. Poor dumb Ignacio gets the job of taking a hatchet and chopping the rope that holds the temporary block, and you'd think he'd been made president of General Motors. He eyeballs everything, like he's lining everything up just right, and then—even though Shokaito and the others are yelling at him not to do it— he hauls up a crate to stand on and cuts the rope in two with one whack."

Vandegriff laughed, painfully.

"He cut the wrong rope?"

"Nah. He cut the right rope, all right. Just that he was standing between the marlin and the boom when he did it. Would've been gigged like a skinny frog if the crate hadn't broken right when he swung the hatchet. Now, is that luck or what?"

Rodrigue shook his head with wonder. God dearly loves dumb little shits like Ignacio, although He doesn't always spare them like that.

"So what did Kindler do with his time out there?" he asked,

wondering about the man's odd behavior at the weigh-in. "Did you fish at all?"

"Yeah, we drug baits goin' out. But that was just me and Bones pissin' around. Kindler, he just rode up on the bridge like the king of Mardi Gras—until he busted his hand, that is. Then he kinda sulked below."

Rodrigue remembered the bandaged hand. "How'd he bust his hand?"

"Punched out the goddamned door to the head is what he did. Claimed it slammed shut on him, but shit, it was slicker'n WD-Forty out there."

"Why would he punch out the head door?"

"Fuck 'f I know." He thought about it. "He had gone below for a bit, then he came hustling back up wanting to know what the pistol looked like that the son of a bitch shot me with. Well, fuck, pistol's a pistol, right?"

"Well—"

"But I did have the bullet. When it fell out of my pants, I stuck it in the medicine cabinet. He went down to get it and he never came back up. Then I got to feeling bad and had Bones relieve me, and when I went down, the door was busted and Kindler had his hand all wrapped up. But he didn't say shit."

Rodrigue looked out the window again. What in the hell would Kindler want with the bullet? Did he turn it over to the police? Bones didn't say anything about it. But Bones probably wouldn't. He was like Taylor—if it didn't have to do with fishing, it wasn't worth comment. Plus, people didn't hold Kindler to their own standards of behavior. He did pretty much as he pleased.

He kept gazing through the window for a long time after he quit puzzling over Kindler. He was remembering another hospital, an older building with smaller windows. He remembered staring through the dingy pane at the jumbled rooftops of Marseille, staring long past any purpose of seeing so he wouldn't have to look at Jean-Marc, who was grinning and talking as though nothing was wrong. Finally, he turned and looked at Vandegriff.

108

"Well, you're out of it. But your interests are protected. I'll see to that." He winked.

"Aw, I don't want the money, Rodrigue. I'll *take* it, but money ain't what it's about. It ain't, is it?" The uncertainty made him look younger, somehow.

Rodrigue shrugged. "If it is, you'd think we'd all have more of it."

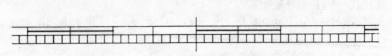

Chapter 20

While Susan waited in the car, Rodrigue knelt in the confessional and recited "Bless me, Father, for I have sinned. . . ."

Confession was like a bracing slap of Mennen first thing in the morning. To his people, religion was manly. His daddy, his uncles, his brothers—all were religious men, at least to the extent that they went to Mass and confession religiously. During his formative years, virtually every male role model he had had crossed himself when he drove by a church, or when an ambulance wailed in the distance, or when seas crashed over the wheelhouse. They might be buck naked, glasses off and teeth out, but they still had a St. Christopher's medal or a Latin cross or a scapular around their necks.

They also drank heavily and fucked anything in skirts except nuns and jailbait. That was the beauty of it: You didn't have to deny your human nature; you just had to be heartily sorry for it.

". . . took the name of the Lord in vain about eighteen times," he was saying. "Masturbated three or four times, seriously coveted another man's wife once but never touched her . . . and I killed someone, too, but only in self-defense."

"Do the police know?" the shadowy form asked in an irritated tone. Priests in Galveston heard unimaginable sins.

"Yes, Father. It was in the paper this morning."

"But do they know you, ah, committed it?"

"Yes, of course. It was self-defense."

The priest thought it over. "What it was in the eyes of the law is not God's concern. What was in your heart is what concerns God. You might have been entirely proper in your actions toward the other man's wife, for instance, and yet in your heart you committed a dangerous sin with her. This lusting, this . . . this self-abuse offends God greatly and you must make an effort to keep your thoughts pure. It is not enough for the one hand not to know what the other is doing . . . ah . . . so to speak. You are responsible for both of your hands. For your penance, I want you to read and meditate on Matthew, Chapter Five, Verse . . . let's see . . . Verse Twenty-one through the end of the chapter. In the name of the Father, and of the Son . . ."

From long habit, Rodrigue paused in the gloomy back pew of the cathedral to pray. He never actually prayed—he didn't really know how—but instead, he let his mind free associate, rise with the dust motes in the shaft of sunlight, flicker with the candles in blood-red glass. As always, his eye was drawn to the frail figure on the cross, and he allowed himself to wonder about the man, Jesus.

The pale visage was as mute as the dead gunman. It was too stylized now, like a poodle after generations of breeding for fluffy hair. Poodles used to be hunting dogs, Rodrigue had read. Now they were just for show.

The Rastas, while rejecting the hate-mongering *Jee*-sus of the white man, acknowledged the spiritual presence of an entity they called "Jess-us." Rodrigue, too, believed the real Jesus was out there somewhere, not out of reach exactly, but certainly out of touch. Out of sight, out of hearing.

Out of *direct* touch, but Rodrigue imagined his thoughts, both noble and ignoble, proceeding either in some real physical sense like electromagnetic waves or in whispers from St. Anthony to

Our Lady to that unfathomable mystery we call God. Now if it would only work the other way.

Faith was what you had to work with, like in diving. You know you've got a tender up there, but he can't help you find your way around in the dark, cold world below. You've just got to act and hope for the best.

Rodrigue knew now he hadn't meant to harm that gunman. He might not have been in a good mood, exactly, but he struck out in reflex—to stop hurt, not cause it. It was nobody's fault but the gunman's.

He couldn't shake the primitive notion that when you caused hurt, you got hurt—and he wasn't exactly innocent himself, helping to steal a million bucks just so he could fuck another man's wife. This wasn't the first time he had followed his dick into a bad situation. But what *was* the situation? Who was trying to kill whom? And the big question: Why?

What was to have been the finished product? A crusty old skipper shot to death, a drunken ex-commercial diver passed out cold, and the contract killer vanishes in the night. Obviously the skipper dies and the diver gets the blame, but what's the value in that? Dead skipper or jailed diver? If either benefited anyone, Rodrigue couldn't see it. The why was more intriguing than the who.

Or maybe it was simply more complex. Sleight of hand—the killing of a boat captain like the topple of the first domino that turns clack-clack-clack into the American flag waving on the floor.

And maybe while everyone is standing around in the parlor watching dominoes fall, the silver is being snatched from the china closet. Or somebody's wife is giving somebody's husband a blowjob in the library. Or poison is being slipped into the brandy. Probably the gunman himself didn't know the reason—beyond his own, which was undoubtedly money. He was the left hand who didn't know what the right one was doing.

"Boy, *now* I need to change clothes!" said Susan. Her sweat-soaked T-shirt was plastered to her hard, conical breasts. She

112

peeled it away to allow airflow inside the shirt. "What kept you so long?"

"I got fifty Hail Marys and forty Our Fathers for killing that guy . . . that and a few other trespasses. Where are you staying, Holiday Inn?"

"No, they put me up at the yacht club. Let's swing by there and then hit the Jamaican buffet at the hotel before we do any more sleuthing, want to? Partying clears the mind."

He patted her on the knee—the first time he had touched her, he reflected immediately. "Just remember that I have just been cleansed of all my sins and I'd like to stay that way for a while." He grinned his evil shark grin.

"Don't fucking worry, Rodrigue. Say, don't you have an air conditioner in this tank?"

"Of course," he said, starting the engine. "But it doesn't work."

It had been broken for two years and hadn't seen much use before that. What was the point in owning a big black Cadillac if you couldn't cruise around with your elbow out the window? Rodrigue didn't mind the heat as long as there was shade.

He bypassed the main entrance to the Bob Smith Yacht Club and parked at the fence that bordered the drive along the yacht basin's A Row. There were locked gates there that any room key would open, and the two-story wing of rooms was just on the other side.

"I'll meet you back here in, what, ten minutes?" he said.

"Fifteen."

He saw her through the gate and then walked back around to B Row. Phillips's El Camino was in the parking lot.

The deputy was sitting in a deck chair in the cockpit of his Bertram cruiser, cigarette drooping from his lips, methodically reassembling an old Penn reel—very methodically.

He was one of the piddlers. Every marina had them—boat owners who spent their weekends polishing chrome or oiling teak or rewiring bridge instruments instead of actually going boating. A few had to constantly work on their boats to keep them from sinking in their slips. Others were uncomfortable on the open sea and perfectly satisfied to lounge around with all the dock lines securely attached. Rodrigue had always put Phillips down as one of the few who genuinely liked to piddle, but now he wasn't sure. Maybe the deputy was there to keep an eye on activities at the yacht basin, the way apartment complexes let cops stay rent-free.

Or maybe *he* was just getting carried away with this sleight-of-hand business.

Phillips had been watching him approach. "Hey, Rod," he said around his cigarette. "Grab that other chair there and sit down here awhile. Drink a beer?"

"Anytime." Rodrigue took the folding deck chair that was leaning against the storage locker and opened it carefully in the cockpit while Phillips raked two dripping cans of Coors from a small ice chest.

"Any word from Eckles on the identity of the guy in the wet suit?"

Phillips choked on a swallow of beer. "No," he gasped. "You boys froze him solid. I mean it. At the morgue, they sat him in a chair and just had a whale of a time with him, dealing him a hand of poker and whatnot. Then they didn't know what to do with him, so they wheeled him across the street in the chair and put him in a walk-in freezer on the docks somewhere and froze him even solider."

The deputy's words had come out increasingly ragged and now both men were blinking tears. It was ghastly, of course, but all the more reason to laugh.

"Finally, someone with some authority came along and had him thawed out enough to get some prints, which weren't on file. Now they're waiting for his head to get soft enough to get his jaw open and do an inventory of his teeth. Goin' to all this trouble to keep from messing him up, and then some pathologist's gonna saw him all to pieces doin' an autopsy."

"Hell of a thing!" Rodrigue wheezed. "No guesses, even? No other clues? I mean this thing is bothering me, Bruce. It really isn't funny."

"Naw, it's not, Rod," Phillips said evenly. "You got any guesses?"

114

"I just had a sudden, sticky feeling that it doesn't have anything to do with Vandegriff. Did you know that Kindler has the bullet Vandegriff was shot with?"

"So what? Eckles has the gun. They know who shot Vandegriff; they just don't know why."

"What about this fellow Ahlmark, the weighmaster . . . you know him?"

Phillips shook his head. "Seen him is all."

"He and I know each other from Vietnam . . . except I can't place him exactly. I was in the brown-water navy and I ran a river patrol boat. I had to carry a lot of passengers—SEALs, CIA goons, and so on—pretty unsavory characters, a lot of them. I'd insert them in the jungle, they'd crawl up to a village and turn some priest's brain to mush with a silenced twenty-two, then be back on the bank waiting for me in a day or two. I'm pretty sure Ahlmark was one of those guys."

"That was a long time ago, Rod."

"I know it, but look . . . Ahlmark knows a lot more about me than I know about him. Better memory? I don't think so. When I first saw him aboard *Abaris*—Mrs. Kindler was hiring me to inspect the wheels—he seemed genuinely surprised. But then later, he came up with a detail about my navy career that came after my service in the PBRs. That tells me he has some way of checking service records, that maybe he's government."

"I still don't see what you're getting at."

Rodrigue started at the worn fiberglass deck between his feet. It wasn't easy for him to discuss his worries with others, and Phillips wasn't making it any easier. "I don't know either, I guess. It's just that this tournament and this whole island-twinning business might be something of an affront to some people back in Jamaica. I don't know if you're aware of it or not, but politics down there are pretty hot these days."

"Well, that figures," Phillips said with a billow of cigarette smoke. "First religion and now politics."

"I'm serious."

"I know you are, but . . . ." He shrugged. "I don't know, we don't get too many professional hits around here. Maybe over in Jamaica a hit might be ordered on account of politics or religion

115

or whatever, but ninety-five percent of the murders we see around here are over money, drugs, nookie, or some combination thereof. Anyway, it ain't none of my business. It belongs to the city."

Susan was standing beside the Coupe de Ville. The heat radiating from the concrete drive made her shimmer like a mirage. And she was different—wearing white shorts and a hot-pink halter with touches of the same color on her lips and earrings. Her hair was pulled back and eyelashes darkened and she looked thoroughly feminine. Rodrigue was flabbergasted.

She regarded him warily. "Wanna walk? It's not that far over to the hotel, is it?"

"Er, no . . . no. We have to jump the fence at the back of the yacht basin, but you can do that, can't you? How many years have you?"

"Twenty-nine. Divorced. No children. No history of PMS-related violence. Anything else you want to know, Rodrigue?"

"Guess that covers it."

"How about you . . . you ever been married?"

"No, never was."

"Ever get close?"

He thought about it as they trudged across the parking lot. The asphalt was already gooey from the heat. "Not in any real sense," he said finally. "There have been women . . ."

"So I hear," she said, filling the abrupt silence.

"Aw, you know what I mean. Listen, don't believe everything you hear about me. A lot of it is due to the overactive imaginations around here."

They came to the chain-link fence and Rodrigue paused. He wasn't sure what was going on between them and it made him uneasy. As an ally, she was a comfort. But *was* she an ally? Did she like him as much as she seemed to, or was she just after a story. "You have a boyfriend back in Florida?" he asked.

Susan bit her bottom lip, a nervous gesture Rodrigue found engaging. "Sort of. I have somebody I've been seeing for a couple of years. We don't seem to be going anywhere. Why are we talking like this, Rodrigue?"

116

He decided he liked her too much not to warn her. "I saw an old friend, an old high school friend, a year or so ago, and there he had this cute, chubby little wife and a houseful of beautiful kids, and you could tell he was on the top of the world."

He gazed across the parking lot, preparing his case. "I come from a big family myself, and I have some idea of what a sacrifice—what a *brave* thing it is to head up a family." Now he looked at her, locking on to her large, intelligent eyes. "See, me, I don't regret not having that. I guess what I regret is not regretting it, if that makes any sense. I feel a little selfish . . . a little inadequate, if you want to know the truth. But I am what I am. So quoth another famous boatman."

She smiled tenderly. "Rodrigue, I look at you and I see you today. I don't see you tomorrow . . . well, maybe tomorrow, but not down the line. Next year, let's say. I see you now and I like what I see."

He tried a kiss and it worked—she kissed him back with a slow grinding of her surprisingly soft lips.

"Are we going to stand here and smooch," she said a little breathlessly, "or are we going to a party?"

He boosted her onto the sagging chain-link fence, savoring her smell. She hopped athletically to the ground on the other side. He backed up a few steps and took the fence at a run, swinging heavily over—and nearly collapsing in pain on the other side.

Susan rushed to support him. "What's the matter?"

"God-*damn!*" he said, hopping on his left leg. He made a mental note of the blasphemy—just counting.

"What happened?"

He knuckled a tear out of his eye. "Whew! When am I gonna learn to quit showing off for a pretty girl?" He took a tentative step and grimaced. "I had a bad case of the bends some while back and it's led to some arthritis in my right knee joint. Thank God it goes away when I drink."

He smiled a different smile than she had seen before—a sort of sad smile, she imagined. Because of the pain, maybe.

"I get better looking, too," he added. "When I drink, I mean."

They walked together so that Rodrigue could lean on her

117

slightly. The pain eased somewhat with each step and he was scarcely limping by the time they reached the breezeway between the buildings. As if on cue, the *shoomp-pomp! shoomp!* drumbeat echoed from the pool area. Susan grinned and snapped her fingers. "We have arrived," she said happily. "Let the circus begin!"

"Aye. *Laissez le bon temps rouler!*"

Let the good times roll. After all, it *had* been his credo.

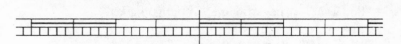

Chapter 21

The band was grinding out a cheerful instrumental. They were "dreads," all right, bearded, with the long hair that naturally wound itself into a mass of quarter-inch rope, like Medusa's headful of snakes. It made them seem untamed—like African warriors who had learned to play electric guitars. They made the rich white folk nervous, which was part of their appeal.

The lead guitar was a young man with a sparse beard and dreadlocks that sprouted in all directions with righteous vigor but hadn't yet begun to droop and take on the appearance of a lion's mane. The oldest, tall and thin and the only somber one in the group, played bass guitar. He played stoically and didn't move to the beat like the other three. The keyboard player, light-skinned with a cruel-looking face, and the drummer, who was approaching fat and wore his locks in a knit cap, were playing off each other, giving each other musical high-fives. They played too well to be terrorists, Rodrigue decided.

It was early yet and there were empty tables. Trying not to limp, Rodrigue led Susan under a naked arbor of two-by-six beams, where the shade fell in parallel bars. A waiter detached himself from the temporary serving station near the Jacuzzi and stood at their table, slightly bowed, eyebrows arched, hands praying. He had a gold stud in his right ear.

"So, what'll it be, madame?" Rodrigue asked.

"Bloody Mary," she said.

"I believe I'll have a beer myself."

"May I suggest the Red Stripe?" said the waiter. "It's an excellent Jamaican beer imported especially for the occasion."

"Good idea. Make it two."

"What a *scoundrel*, you are, Rodrigue." She touched his hand when she said it, and her head dipped playfully. Her eyes were full of amusement—the gritted smile, slurred *s* . . .

Called by the music, the Beautiful People were filling the patio. The pina colada smell of suntan lotion wafted with every bronze, nearly naked body that passed. The swimming pool was a shimmering liquid sapphire set in lush tropical foliage.

"*Yah-maan!*" yelled the lead guitar, and he launched into the lyrics of a happy soca, a fun-in-the-sun tune that played well on the beaches of Jamaica's north coast, hidden from the wretched poverty of the real Trench Town in West Kingston.

Rastafarians thought of their own island as a modern Babylon. Ethiopia was their spiritual home, and had been since the 1930s, when a Jamaican-born American civil rights leader named Marcus Garvey announced that a black Messiah would soon emerge. Right after that, a little guy named Ras Tafari was crowned Haile Selassie I, Lion of Judah and Emperor of Ethiopia. He was an enlightened and progressive ruler who never quite seemed comfortable with the fact with an increasing segment of the Jamaican population considered him to be the living God.

Rodrigue rubbed elbows with Rastamen in Belize. They were serious people despite the fact that they smoked staggering amounts of marijuana, which they considered to be a sacred herb. They were all dedicated to peaceful struggle against the white race and everything it stood for—which to them was corruption, greed, and pollution.

Although Rodrigue's friends were Belizeans, Jamaica's ugly history had formed them, as it had all Rastas everywhere. With the coming of the English in the 1600s, the island became the slave clearinghouse for the whole Western Hemisphere. Even though emancipation came nearly thirty years earlier than in the United States, British ethnocentrism kept the Africans at arm's length. They were left to their own religions, their own languages, their own culture. That was why even today a black Jamaican could consider his native island an alien place.

And yet they could come before a crowd like this and play their music. It wasn't hypocrisy. It was survival. But it had to taste bitter. No wonder they had blown off steam at the airport.

The drinks arrived and Rodrigue used Susan's brief preoccupation with her Bloody Mary to case the crowd. There was one of those gold leaping-marlin pendants on a mat of gray chest hair. Here was a gold Rolex probably worth ten thousand bucks, and there a thin gold chain lodged seductively at the flare of brown young hips. Here was a mass of bracelets on a ravaged ash-blonde who had to be an Owner's wife, there a ropelike neck chain on a red-eyed mate—here rings, there earrings, here medallions, everywhere neck chains.

He felt like a shark swimming in a school of unwary bonito—unwary because the shark wasn't acting hungry. But with gold at nearly three hundred dollars an ounce and climbing, Rodrigue couldn't keep from wondering what the haul would be if he was to go get his gun, stand these people against the wall, and pass a hat. A shark doesn't have to be hungry to smell blood.

"What's the matter, Rod?" Concern was etched between her eyebrows. "Is your knee still hurting?"

"Nah," he lied. He took a long drink of the icy beer.

"What causes the bends, anyway? I mean I know it's from diving and all, but what happens?"

"Air is almost eighty percent nitrogen," he said. "You breathe it in, it gets dissolved in your bloodstream and makes the rounds with the oxygen. But while the oxygen is absorbed by the cells, the nitrogen just goes full circle and dumps back into the lungs as a gas again, and you breathe it back out. Breathing air under pressure means that you've got a lot more nitrogen floating around in your tissues than usual, and the longer you breathe it, and the deeper you go, the more nitrogen you accumulate. So if you don't stop long enough on your way up and give it time to

121

work its way back out through the lungs, it'll turn into a gas prematurely—nasty little bubbles in a joint, maybe, or . . ."

He thought of poor Jean-Marc. Maybe he sort of liked Morgan because Morgan sort of reminded him of the slender Frenchman, with his bikini bathing suits and long mane of hair. Jean-Marc was the total hedonist. He made Rodrigue look like John the Baptist. He was dangerous to be with whether you were in the water or on the beach, but he was fun. It was because he so blatantly enjoyed himself, like a kid.

"It can be a lot worse," he said finally. "It can hit you in the spinal cord, the brain. . . . A really bad hit is in the tissues of the lungs themselves—called the 'chokes.' Really nasty."

"Do you miss it, though?" she asked. "The deep diving?"

Rodrigue sighed. "I do. I do indeed. But . . ." he made a helpless gesture. "A diver is just a peon with an air hose when you get right down to it. It wasn't always that way, but now you're just a piece of meat with a goddamned Oxy-Arc torch in your hand. They say jump, you say how deep."

"It's not any different for Morgan," she said. "Or Vandegriff, or Bones. Look around you." She twisted in her chair. "Look, see that table over there?"

Rodrigue followed her gaze. At a table in the sun, a balding, graying Owner type with an amused look on his face silently read something while a bikinied blonde of about twenty looked over his shoulder. Also looking on, and with the same tempered amusement as the man, was a striking raven-haired woman of about forty. She had an angular face, high cheekbones, and huge breasts for such a lean frame. Also at the table, laughing with the blond girl, were a husky blond teenage boy, and a lean man in his twenties with a girl about the same age sitting close to him. The Owner type put the scrap of paper down and said something, and now everybody was laughing raucously except the raven-haired woman, who continued to smile patiently, as though she was minding playful children.

"One big happy family, huh?" said Susan. "See the young blond? His name is Ricky. He and the other guy are mates on the boat—except Ricky's main job is screwing Paula. She's the

122

Morticia-looking one. No kidding. It's an Islamorada boat—I know 'em."

She took a drink of her Bloody Mary.

"Her husband—he's the bald one there—he not only knows about it, he *arranged* it. He's probably screwing that little blond bimbo hanging all over him. You know, it's like it's his wife's payoff for him having the boat. Look around you, Rod. Boats are just toys to these people. And so are the people who run them."

Rodrigue saw something in her eyes, something that challenged him.

He shrugged. "So what? Ricky probably loves his work."

She laughed. "I like you, Rodrigue. You're a tough nut to crack."

"Do I prey on the rich? Is that what you're trying to find out?"

It was her turn to shrug.

"Well I do . . . at every opportunity," he said. "The wealth these kinda people have is unnatural somehow. I mean, look at the lengths they go to, and they still can't spend it all."

"Have you seen the scale model of Trenchtown inside?"

"Not yet."

"It's something to see." Her voice had a teasing musical lilt. She took another deep drink.

"I think something's troubling you," he said. He reached across the table and touched her fidgeting hand. She smiled nervously and removed her hand to grasp her drink.

"Maybe I've got some pirate blood in me, too," she said, hoisting her severely depleted Bloody Mary in a toast.

Rodrigue snapped his fingers. Their waiter, hustling a tray of rum drinks to another table, lifted an eyebrow in acknowledgment.

"Another round, my good man," he said when the waiter arrived. "And would you be so kind"—he slid a twenty out of his money clip and proffered it between two fingers—"as to ask the band to play 'Guiltiness'? That's for the band, and this is for you." He leafed out another bill, a five.

"My pleasure," said the waiter coolly. He was insulted, but not sufficiently.

"C'mon," she said when the waiter left. "'Guiltiness'?"

"Bob Marley."

"Oh, I know it. How apropos."

The waiter's request produced smiles on the bandstand. The solemn one asked a question, and the waiter pointed toward Rodrigue and Susan. Rodrigue winked and the solemn one nodded back. After some conferring, he switched places with the lead guitar and stood at the microphone. "Guiltiness," he wailed soulfully, like the great Marley himself.

> Rests on their conscience
> Oh yeah, oh yeah
> And they live the lie of false pretense
> Everyday . . .

The switch in tempo went unnoticed. Joining Susan's Islamorada friends were two more Owner types—overstuffed, tanned, balding men dripping with gold. A waiter with a tray of rum drinks followed.

> These are the big fish,
> Who always try to eat down
> The small fish
> Down the small fish . . .

124

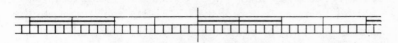

Chapter 22

Trenchtown was a staggering concept, even in miniature. The harbor was entirely artificial, embraced by two elaborate break-waters you could drive along that were lined with shops and restaurants and sailboard liveries. A hotel dominated the small beach, while the steep bluff was lined with condos of Spanish colonial architecture done in earth tones, like cliff dwellings with picture windows. The airport was on the high ground, sur-rounded by several nondescript neighborhoods, presumably where the help would live. A high security fence marched in-land. It reminded Rodrigue of Guantánamo.

The architect's model was in the cavernous restaurant, be-tween the indoor portion of the pool and the elevated lounge area. Here, people were actually whispering, in stark contrast to the welling rowdiness on the patio just beyond the tinted glass wall.

Gray-haired men in linen safari suits and starched yachting khakis paid their respects to Trenchtown as though it were Kind-ler himself, pickled and powdered and laid in his bier. Rodrigue felt uneasy, out of place. He looked around and noticed a beefy man in a cheap suit and sunglasses become patently uninterested in him. Rodrigue moved away from the model and fell into line at the buffet table on the opposite side of the restaurant.

Standing near the end of the line, between the doors to the patio and a burst of potted jungle growth, was another stone-faced man in mismatched polyester. At the hallway to the lobby was another. And across the large room, almost behind the platform that held the lounge area, was Detective Sergeant Eckles. His cold gaze lingered on Rodrigue for several seconds before sweeping on to take in the rest of the buffet line. Rodrigue stacked more salted-fish cakes on their plates and shuffled down to the desserts.

Susan was holding their table against all comers. He set the plates down and looked around for a waiter.

"Yuk. Smells like cat food," she said, wrinkling her nose.

"Cat food'd be fresher. They must've froze this stuff in Port Antonio two months ago and stuck it in a microwave here." He caught the waiter's eye and made a tight circle over the table with his finger, the international signal for another round.

Some of the Beautiful People had gathered around the stage and were bumping their butts together. Another contingent overflowed the Jacuzzi. Gallons of Red Stripe and at least quarts of Jamaican rum had already been pissed away, and the day was young.

Ahlmark suddenly appeared, working his way through the crowded tables toward them. He was wearing his cowboy hat with another bright Hawaiian shirt. "Join you?" he asked.

"By all means," Rodrigue said sadly.

Ahlmark looked back toward the restaurant and waved broadly at the Kindlers, who were standing side by side—yet somehow apart, Rodrigue imagined—searching the crowd. They spotted Ahlmark and walked forward, Kindler with a courtly hand in the small of his wife's back.

At the table, Kindler came to attention, bowed slightly, and clapped noiselessly, like a conductor applauding his orchestra. He clapped gingerly, too, for his right hand was still bandaged. His eyes, Rodrigue noticed, had the detached look of someone who had had a few stiff drinks.

Ahlmark scraped back a chair for Leigh. She looked angry.

"You know Susan Foch?" asked Rodrigue.

"Of course," said Leigh with oleander sweetness. "We met at the party last night. How are you, dear?"

"Fine, Mrs. Kindler, thank you."

Kindler glanced at Ahlmark, then back to Susan. "Would you like to ride with us tomorrow?"

"I'd love it, of course. I was hoping you'd ask. Are you coming, Rod? Repel boarders?"

"Oh no, no, they"—he stroked his jaw and made his one-eyed Long John squint at Kindler—"seem to think the problem's taken care of."

Kindler was dropping the scam. No way he could rendezvous with Shokaito and pick up a second marlin with Susan aboard. But, as Vandegriff had said, maybe it was already in the bag.

"Thieves generally take the path of least resistance," said Ahlmark good-naturedly.

"So you think he was out to steal the *Abaris*?" asked Susan. Ahlmark shrugged. "I don't think anything. I'm just the weighmaster." He grinned to show there were no hard feelings.

"Maybe someone was simply trying to knock Captain Vandegriff out of the competition," offered Susan. "After all, there's a lot of money at stake."

"It might seem like a lot of money," said Leigh with a brittle smile, "but to the type of people in the Islands, it's really not."

The waiter arrived and enthusiastically took a complicated order involving brandies and liqueurs from the Kindlers. "Another beer?" he asked Rodrigue coolly.

"Past noon, ain't it?" Rodrigue glanced at his watch. "Close enough. Make mine a Cuba libre—*Mexican* rum if you have it, and don't forget the twist," he said cheerfully.

He looked at Kindler and surreptitiously arched an eyebrow in Susan's direction. "I guess this means my services are no longer required, eh?" There didn't seem to be any point in staying aboard to listen for Shokaito's transmissions if Kindler didn't intend to make the rendezvous.

Kindler regarded him icily. "Of course they are."

"Uh, Garrett was saying he hoped you'd agree to watch *Abaris* again during the banquet tonight," Ahlmark said quickly.

"Yes," said Kindler. "I'll have Bones run you out a plate. After all"—his smile seemed to crack his face—"one never knows."

"Well, I guess I'd best see to things," said Ahlmark. He stood and gave Kindler a meaningful look. "About eight-thirty?" It wasn't really a question.

"Fine," said Kindler.

Ahlmark said polite goodbyes, then gave Rodrigue a thumbs-up sign and said, "Righteous kill."

"Dewey Rifles," Rodrigue said suddenly, snapping his fingers.

Ahlmark grinned. "Never heard of 'em." He spun on his heel and sauntered off.

"Who or what are the Dewey Rifles?" asked Susan.

"An organization. Where I first met Ahlmark years ago."

He didn't look the same. He had been much thinner then, with darker hair or maybe just more of it. He was an army captain assigned to a group of Dutch and German mercenaries with hearts like industrial diamonds. On several occasions, Rodrigue's group had inserted them into enemy-held territory and picked them up two days later at another location. Ahlmark's job had been to accompany them on their sweeps and take a body count. The Dewey Rifles were paid by the head for officially identified and tallied VC corpses—what the army called "righteous kills."

"Vietnam," said Leigh with a tiny trace of contempt, breaking the silence. She turned to her husband. "Will you be all right?" she asked, moving her fingers toward his bandaged hand without actually touching it.

He nodded sullenly.

"What happened to your hand?" asked Susan.

"Head door caught me," he said angrily. "Wallowing in a side sea."

"Hmmm," said Susan sympathetically.

Rodrigue remembered Vandegriff's assessment—that the sea had been calm and Kindler must've smashed the door on purpose—and he realized that Kindler had solved the puzzle. It was related to that bullet somehow. Kindler had demanded the bullet, smashed his fist through a door, and had acted like some kind of ventriloquist's dummy ever since—with Ahlmark pulling the string.

128

The waiter came with the drinks. Like life itself, the party went on, nasty little secrets in tow. Rodrigue decided he had to piss.

When Rodrigue came back out, Susan and Kindler were gone.

"Where is everybody?" he asked Leigh.

"Garrett has to entertain our guests from Jamaica, and Susan said she needed to get some rest."

Rest? She must've gotten mad at him, he thought glumly. Susan's Bloody Mary was untouched. Leigh must've told her something.

Leigh was studying his face. "So why didn't you tell me about the hired killer when I called you yesterday?"

"Your husband told me not to." Might as well play along, he decided. Find out what she knows. "Didn't want to scare you, I guess."

"He was afraid I would insist he go to the police immediately. But, Rod, I didn't think we had any secrets between us."

"Would you have insisted he go to the police?"

She looked down into her glass. "No. Garrett doesn't give me enough credit for understanding the situation."

"Well, I'm just delighted that *you* do. Perhaps you'll tell me— what *is* the situation?"

"It's political." She glanced furtively around, then leaned forward and spoke in a low voice. "Someone has found out about Trenchtown."

Rodrigue laughed. "I can't imagine how. You've only got an eight-by-twelve model of it in the hotel lobby."

She gave him an angry look. "I *mean* they've found out that the CIA is involved in it. Now keep your voice down."

"And how is the"—he mouthed the initials—"involved?"

"They're providing the start-up money. They want a covert base when the Seaga government takes over—or I guess especially if it doesn't somehow."

"I don't understand, why would your husband need money from the CIA?"

"He doesn't *need* it, of course. But you don't spend your own money when you can use someone else's." She explained it as though it shouldn't have needed explaining.

"So Ahlmark is CIA?" It figured. The Dewey Rifles had been like ghosts. Few men in Nam had heard about them, and fewer still had ever seen them.

She nodded. And took a healthy swallow of booze.

"Does he know about Shokaito?"

"Yes, well, Garrett had to tell him, didn't he? I mean after that attack. Obviously they meant to kill Garrett. Without him, Trenchtown couldn't exist."

"'They' being who?"

"Some Cubans, Garrett thinks. The Cubans are backing Manley. It's complicated."

"But the gunman was an American."

"I'm just telling you what I know." She reached out and grasped his forearm. "I just don't want you to be hurt. Please don't come on the boat tonight. There's no reason—Garrett's not going to pick up any more marlin from Shokaito. Just disappear. Please."

Rodrigue was still trying to sort it out. "So Garrett hasn't told the cops about his suspicions because it would blow the lid off of the CIA deal?"

She nodded.

So that might've been the goal behind the hit—the communists trying to make the capitalist police do their work for them. And they would hire local talent so it couldn't get back to them.

"But the problem is," he said, thinking aloud now, "that it hasn't worked. Your husband is keeping the police at bay. So they might try again—maybe put a bomb on her this time. Does Ahlmark have any help?"

"What do you mean?"

"I mean guys with guns. Agents."

She winced. "Keep your voice down. I don't know. I think he's undercover or something. I've never seen anyone else."

"Well, what do they plan to do? How are they going to protect themselves?"

She bit her lip and shrugged.

"Who's out there now?"

"Bones. But please don't say anything to anyone. Ahlmark's taking care of it, I'm sure. He's very capable. Don't get involved." There was a hint of panic in her voice.

"Look, your husband and Ahlmark are on their own, as far as I'm concerned. I don't play with politics. But we're either going to tell Bones and Susan what's going on and keep them the hell away from the *Abaris,* or I'm going to see to it that nobody can get to her. Which is it?"

The money, he thought bitterly. He didn't want to let go of the money—otherwise, there wouldn't have been a choice.

"What can you do?" she asked.

"I'll top off her tanks and run her up and down the channel all night. That way, nobody can swim up after dark and slap something on the hull."

She thought about it, a tiny smile deepening the creases at the corners of her mouth. "That's a very good plan," she said.

Rodrigue polished off his Cuba libre and declined another. He would slip away and get *Abaris* in line at the fuel dock.

But watching from the edge of the patio, Detective Sergeant Eckles was waiting for him. . . .

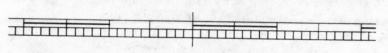

Chapter 23

"But you're not *charged* with anything, right?" The lawyer's voice sounded impatient over the phone.

"No. Just if I refused to go. Then they said they could charge me with being a fucking material witness." Rodrigue looked around in the hallway at the police station. Eckles was standing a discreet distance away from the pay phone, also impatient.

"That may or may not be true, but they can certainly haul you in for questioning. If you're going to retain me, my advice to you is to give them name, rank, and serial number until I can get there."

"Is that free advice?"

The lawyer was a former customer of Rodrigue's, owner of a big bulbous Sea Ray, all cushions and carpeting, who had once run off with a dock line dangling and caught it in his prop. Not realizing the line was still secured to a forward cleat, he burned up his tilt motor trying to raise the outdrive and get a look at the problem. There he was, dead in the water, with an incoming tide sweeping him across the ferry lane and up into the Houston Ship Channel, which is to ships and barges what the Santa Monica Freeway is to cars.

When Rodrigue caught up to him and saw that he and his pals were manicured types out with a load of tail from the office, he might've been a trifle predatory. Now the tables were turned.

"Free advice." the lawyer said. "Here's some more: You'd better get an attorney. If not me, someone else."

Rodrigue didn't like the lawyer. He didn't like *lawyers*, period, but this one he wouldn't have liked if the guy had been a bartender. He had a cold, businesslike attitude that, combined with thinning hair and a puffy face, made him seem older than his thirty-some-odd years. It took an obscene joke just to get a smile out of him.

That was good, though. Rodrigue had recently had a whole team of lawyers, a couple of whom were hip, outgoing fellows who on occasion wound up prowling the French Quarter with him. Somehow that made it worse when they put the screws to him and poor Jean-Marc. Of course, there wasn't any big money involved here. . . . Still, it was better to have one of the son of a bitches that you didn't like right from the start.

"Name, rank, and serial number—gotcha. How soon can you get here?"

"It doesn't matter. They'll wait, once they understand I'm on my way. Let me speak to one of the officers."

Rodrigue didn't realize it, but the lawyer would've left court to come down and bail him out, if necessary. Rodrigue had something he wanted: a profile at the yacht basin. An association with the infamous modern-day pirate couldn't bring anything but good. And as it was, it was only the middle of a boring Saturday afternoon, kids wanting to practice their batting. Of course, he would bill the shit out of him, too. That's how you got the respect of a fellow like Rod.

Rodrigue sat on a bench in the hall at the police station until the lawyer slammed through the door, wearing a new polo shirt with dress pants. He and Rodrigue had a moment together in a large, well-lit room that looked more like a classroom than the sterile, boxlike interrogation rooms in the movies. The lawyer said to answer freely unless he interrupted. Then Eckles and Detective Sergeant Sulpevida filed in.

133

"Ever been to Jamaica, Rodrigue?" Eckles asked, squeezing his eyes shut in anticipation of a trite answer.

"A couple of times, never for more than a few days. Why?"

"We'll ask the questions, Rodrigue," said Sulpevida.

"That right?" Rodrigue asked his lawyer.

"That's the way it works."

"Oh, okay," said Rodrigue, being a smart ass.

"Been there recently?" continued Eckles.

"Where?"

"Jamaica. C'mon, Rodrigue, goddamn it."

"Not in several years."

"Will your passport back that up?"

"You bet." He turned to his attorney: "Can *you* ask 'em what the fuck they're trying to find out?"

"Tell you how it looks . . ." Eckles leaned over and put his face in Rodrigue's, à la the cinema. "It looks like someone from Jamaica wanted Garrett Kindler put out of action. Probably a political motive. We have a witness who says the shooter was hired by someone with a Jamaican accent. And we have this rough character with no visible means of support and known ties in the Caribbean who offs the shooter with his bare hands—"

"Me? Are you talking about *me*? What the fuck do you mean, 'no visible means of support'? I'm a goddamned commercial diver!"

"Who works when he wants to, owns his house outright, owns a big boat, lays around the yacht basin all the time drinking. *And* who dresses like a black—drives a big black Cadillac—kinda dark-complected himself, when you get right down to it. . . . Tell you what it looks like, Rodrigue . . ."

Eckles shut his eyes again, the better to see the big picture, perhaps. "It looks like the shooter was set up. He offs Kindler and you off him—in self-defense, of course. Presto! The deed is done and the motive goes to the grave with the shooter—the motive and the identity or identities of the person or persons who hired him."

"Look, I tried to *save* the motherfucker. Vandegriff will tell you that."

"And so he has. But things are not always what they seem, are they?"

It was plain Eckles was relishing this case. At last, stakes higher than a split beer or a purloined pussy.

"Maybe you were set up, too," the detective said in a kinder tone. "Maybe someone knew you could handle an inexperienced shooter. Maybe you *don't* know what's coming down . . . but you know *something*. You've got the key to this thing, Rodrigue. Give it to us."

"Could I have a moment with my client alone, please, gentlemen?" asked the lawyer.

The detectives left—almost with relief, it seemed. The lawyer hiked up his Sansabelt trousers and put one foot on a chair, assuming the role of inquisitor. "How about this? Is there anything you can give them?"

"Fuck no. Kindler is the one who hired me, and they seem to think he was supposed to be the victim. What are we talking about here, suicide?"

"Let me rephrase it, then." A white strand of spittle, like spider silk, stretched between the lawyer's lips as he spoke. "Is there anything you can *seem* to give them?"

"What do you mean? Just make something up?"

The lawyer leaned close and spoke through tight lips. It was as though the spittle were really Super Glue that suddenly set. "They're desperate . . . lot of pressure. They need to be doing something. So give them something to do. In the meantime, something will either break on their case or something else will take precedence, or the tournament will be over and it'll be just another mystery in the file cabinet. You following me?"

"No."

"Look"—he leaned closer—"you don't have to lie—don't lie—I would never advise a client to lie. . . . Well"—he grinned his dirty-old-man grin—"never say never, right? But tell them *something*—anything, as though you yourself attach some kind of importance to it, you understand? Don't *say* you attach importance to it, but . . . Jesus Christ, Rodrigue, you should be able to figure this out."

135

When Eckles and Sulpevida came back, Rodrigue told them the members of the band Kindler had imported were Rastafarians.

"So what?" said Eckles, grinning at Sulpevida. "I'm a Rotarian myself."

"It's the latest black terrorist group. Like the Mau Maus and the Black Panthers used to be, only worse. Haven't you heard about all the looting and killing in Jamaica? Well, that's who's doing it."

"Yeah?" said Sulpevida suspiciously. "How can you tell? Their hair?"

"They have a kind of code language. Easiest way to spot it is the way they misuse personal pronouns—seriously. You'll hear them say 'I' when they should say 'me,' or they'll say 'I and I' instead of 'we.' Get someone close enough to listen to them and you'll pick it up."

Rodrigue was ashamed of himself. But, hell, the Rastas were the perfect patsies. Wasn't that how it always was?

"And that's all?" asked Eckles.

"It's all I know."

From the way Eckles and Sulpevida looked at each other, Rodrigue figured it was enough.

Rodrigue had the lawyer drop him off at his car. He was fumbling for his keys when Susan poked her head through the gate in the yacht-club fence. "Thank God," she said. "I was afraid you had been picked up in the raid."

"Raid?"

"The cops just picked up the whole fucking band. No kidding. The cops apparently have the idea that they're the ones who tried to kill Vandegriff. Not because they were mad at Vandegriff but because they mistook him for Kindler."

He laughed.

"Ever hear anything so stupid? They snatched them between sets. Ahlmark's out scrambling for replacements for tonight's banquet." She stopped and caught her breath.

"What were you doing over there? Leigh told me you came back here to rest."

136

"Rest?" She gave him a incredulous look. "I'll rest when I'm dead. Mrs. Kindler asked me to go get a coat hanger so we could break into her car. She thought she locked her keys in. Turned out she had them in . . ." The words came out slower as she pieced it together. "Something going on between you and Leigh Kindler?"

He studied the hot, pale sky. "There almost was, but there's not going to be. And that's my choice."

"Hey, I'm not trying to pry into your life, Rodrigue."

"Susan . . . I wish you'd stay ashore tomorrow—"

"No way. I've got work to do." Her voice was suddenly chilly.

"Look, you're on to a hell of a story here, all right, but you don't need any pictures of leaping marlin to go with it." He leaned close and lowered his voice. "Leigh thinks Kindler's a target of some kind of terrorist outfit. Not any Rastas, of course. Probably Cubans. It gets complicated as hell, but the bottom line is that they're going to risk their stupid necks to keep from spoiling this fucking tournament . . . but there's no reason you have to."

"Yeah? Well, maybe the terrorist thing is just a red herring. Maybe the real story *is* the tournament. Don't you think it's time you were honest with me, Rod?"

He felt his face burning. Was she guessing? Probably. No way he could ever put things right now. At least he could try to keep her safe.

He took both of her hands in his. "I'll tell you everything I know right now if you agree to treat me as a confidential source—*and* if you stay off that boat tomorrow."

Tears ran down her cheeks. "I don't know how to treat you, Rod." She stiffened and wiped the tears with her bare arm. "No deal," she said, and she stepped inside the gate and shut it.

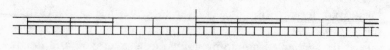

Chapter 24

The last thing Rodrigue wanted was for Kindler to level with him. The less he knew about the CIA in Jamaica—or anywhere else for that matter—the better. But he had to know whether Susan and Bones would be safe. He decided to go ahead and propose his own plan, and if it interfered with anything Ahlmark had cooked up, Kindler would undoubtedly flag him off. They met briefly outside the lounge of the yacht basin, where Kindler was entertaining potential Trenchtown investors.

"I'll just keep her moving," he said. "Up and down the channel. It's well lighted and very public." He didn't speculate on the nature of the threat, nor did he bring up his talk with Leigh, naturally.

Kindler squeezed his eyes shut between his long, bony fingers and said, "Do whatever you think is appropriate."

What would've been appropriate would've been for Rodrigue to kidnap Susan and tie her to his bed with velvet bonds and tickle her until she smiled at him again, but—he told himself—he was not the total rogue people took him for. A deal was a deal was a deal. Without admitting to himself that money might have more to do with his loyalty than any honor among thieves—

selective blind spots were a Rodrigue specialty—he would see it through.

He and Bones fueled up *Abaris*, and then he drove home to shower and change clothes. Back at the yacht basin, he reached into his glove compartment for his navy-issue .45 and tucked it into his pants at the small of his back as an added precaution. Bones was waiting at the end of B Row in the Zodiac.

"So who's taking her out tomorrow?" Rodrigue asked, breaking the silence as they puttered out of the marina.

Bones shrugged. "I haven't heard. Maybe me." His face was solemn.

"What's wrong with that? Go out there and *catch* one of the motherfuckers. This could be your big chance."

Bones cast an angry look. "I know that. That's why I wished we hadn't cheated."

The saloon door slid open and out came Kindler, hair and white dinner jacket glowing a neon pink in the fading sunlight. Rodrigue noticed that the bandage was missing, revealing purple bruises on his knuckles.

"Good," Kindler said simply, which Rodrigue translated as what the fuck took you so long.

"Susan aboard?" Rodrigue asked hopefully.

"No. We'll meet with her at the banquet. She's a little bit of a problem."

"Oh? How so?"

"She knows about Shokaito. That's the reason I invited her, so it doesn't appear as though we have something to hide. We'll just fish normally and stay away from him. And for that reason, it's doubly important that you get his location tonight. Wherever he is, we'll head the opposite way. Wouldn't do to have him hailing us on the VHF."

"She knows about Shokaito? Does that mean she knows we cheated?" Rodrigue felt his face burning again.

"She can't *know* it, of course," said Kindler. "But she suspects it. She lives in Islamorada, as it happens, and must have heard something. Why do you think she's been cozying up to you?"

139

He could have leaned back and kicked Rodrigue in the balls and it would've been kinder.

"How'd you figure all this out?"

"I wondered about some of the questions she was asking around." A storm was brewing behind Kindler's placid expression. "It all comes back to me eventually."

He slid the saloon door open and stepped up. "Al has some contacts in Islamorada. He called them this morning, and sure enough, she had been out to the yard. Asking all the right questions."

"So Ahlmark's in on this now?" Rodrigue said, continuing to act ignorant of the CIA deal.

"He knows. It's not a problem."

Bones waited in the cockpit to take the Kindlers ashore. Inside, Kindler led the way around the bar. Leigh was in the galley.

"Quiche on, Mrs. Kindler?" Rodrigue asked cruelly.

"'Fraid not, Rod." She tried a smile. "Oven's on the blink. I would appreciate it if you would just stay out of the galley. The guys will have to do with sandwiches. In fact, I have the fixings in a cooler on the bridge already. Looks like they're going to be shorthanded tomorrow. There's plenty up there for you tonight, too."

"You're still not fishing?" Rodrigue asked her.

"Somebody has to play hostess. But I understand little Susan is quite an angler."

"So I hear," he said with an empty grin.

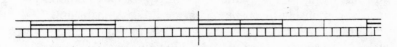

Chapter 25

There was a world of difference between slipping a squat thirty-foot river patrol boat through a canyon of dense jungle in the dark of night and sitting in the command seat of a $600,000 yacht, steering up a well-lighted channel with the noisy activity of cargo docks and grain terminals and shipyards on each side. But the sensation was similar. Rodrigue had that old electric feeling of being in someone's sights. Just as in the unarmored PBR, there was no place to hide.

The banks of the Galveston Channel, on the other hand, had dozens of spots where a man with a scoped rifle could wait unseen.

There wouldn't be a whole lot to gain by knocking off Kindler's hired hand, he tried to tell himself. As slowly as he was going, *Abaris* would wind up nudged against a crew boat or a tug or barge, protected by the rubber-tire fenders. Kindler would probably dump him in the deep freeze and go on about his business as though nothing had happened.

On the other hand, the terrorists had been pretty bush-league so far. Maybe, as Ahlmark had said, they would take the path of least resistance.

141

Thieves, he had said, take the path of least resistance. But he was just trying to muddy the water in typical CIA fashion. The man was probably incapable of saying things straight out.

Rodrigue pivoted *Abaris* by the Pelican Island bridge and started slowly back down the channel, now seeming even narrower, an obstacle course with too many pools of glaring yellow light. Uneasiness was turning into raw nerves and Rodrigue decided there was no way he was going to waddle back and forth like a duck in a shooting gallery all night long. When he reached the point where the channel opened into Bolivar Roads, he threw the throttles forward and climbed on plane, turning northward and aiming for the quick-flashing red light that marked the other side of the Houston Ship Channel.

He followed the channel north for a distance, then turned off into the open bay, the lights of Galveston shrinking behind. Past a few lighted gas wells he found a big patch of blackness. When the radar told him he was a good mile from anything, he went forward and dropped the anchor. Now if they tried to come after him in a boat, he'd be able to hear them.

And if they hired another combat swimmer. . . ? Well, after he had swum a mile in the dark with the tide going out, Rodrigue would be glad to dance with him.

Hell, they couldn't even know where he was, he thought. This was the best kind of plan—impromptu. Nobody knew except him. There was no need to sit up in the dark all evening eating sandwiches. He looked at his watch: seven minutes until Shokaito's report. Then he would go below and make himself comfortable.

The Japanese couldn't conceal his excitement when he radioed to report the capture of a blue marlin that would weigh at least 650 pounds, maybe 700. It made Rodrigue angry, all that fish going to waste. He climbed down to the saloon and poured himself a rum—which he promptly poured back into the bottle. He was too miserable to drink.

What the hell is wrong? he wondered. Was he letting Susan Foch get to him? She was hardly his type—and yet there was something about her that had made him feel good. Or maybe it was the death of the mysterious, neighborly-looking gunman that was troubling him now. But the bastard had asked for it, hadn't he?

Suddenly Rodrigue noticed a fullness in his gut and suspected happily that he was merely constipated. That, at least, he could do something about.

An old fart like Vandegriff was bound to have some kind of laxative on board. Rodrigue went down to the forward spaces, being careful not to trip over the garden hose Leigh had installed to drain the sink.

The top panel in the door to the head was splintered apart. Swinging doors were always a minor hazard aboard a boat. There were latches to hold them open as well as closed, but if a door got away from you when the boat was rocking, it could mash your fingers or bloody your nose. But Vandegriff had said it was calm when it happened. If Kindler hauled off and punched it, as Vandegriff suspected, he must've done it from inside. Maybe the latch jammed on him and he panicked— which might be reason enough to lie about it. Rodrigue shrugged it off. He found a package of Ex-Lax in the medicine cabinet.

He took two fingers of Tia Maria in a glass, thinking his stomach would appreciate something besides Ex-Lax. He found the thermostat—finally—and turned it five degrees warmer, picked up a *Forbes* magazine, and stretched out on the white suede divan.

By nine o'clock, he was getting hungry. He scrounged around in the galley and found a can of tuna, a head of lettuce, celery, banana peppers, and some sharp cheddar and made himself a salad, washed down with a cold Red Stripe from the fridge.

Then he noticed that the water from rinsing the lettuce had not run out of the sink. Leigh's garden hose had stopped up, no doubt. It was hardly his job to fix it, but little things like that nagged him. He stooped and opened the cabinet with the intention of slipping off the hose and huffing and puffing into it like the big bad wolf. If that didn't clear it, he'd haul it out in the cockpit and flush it with the stinging stream from the raw-water wash-down.

The hose wasn't attached beneath the sink anymore, however.

The funnel was stopped with a wad of paper towel that was dripping into a large puddle that had spread around the usual assortment of kitchen cleansers. There was a faint smell like rotten eggs in the cabinet—probably the result of soured food particles in the water. Or maybe it was bilge smells coming up through the hose. Yeah, that was probably it. The end had been fed through the opening for the regular overboard drain line. He tried pulling it back out, but it was snagged on something.

Rodrigue crawled around the cabinet, looking for another way in—and then he remembered Shokaito. It was almost time for Shokaito to report the rendezvous location.

As he was going up the ladder to the flying bridge, Rodrigue felt his insides churning. And then the urge hit him and hit him hard. One of two bad things was about to happen: He was either going to miss the location call or make a hell of a mess of his pants. And cleanliness, he had been taught, was next to godliness.

He sat on the toilet with his head in his hands, studying the carpet. There hadn't been time even to grab a magazine. The carpet was a deep pile, white, of course, and Rodrigue noticed rust-colored flecks at his feet, trailing toward the sink. Vandegriff's wound must've bled a little when he came in to change the bandage.

Then he saw another spot, much larger; and looking closer, he saw it was a small copper-jacketed bullet. He slipped his foot out of his shoe and coaxed the bullet through the pile with his big toe, close enough for him to reach with his hand.

He examined the bullet, turning it over and over. Nothing about this made sense. Vandegriff had said he put the bullet into the medicine cabinet, and here it was on the carpet—after a calm day at sea. . . .

And why would a gunman all dolled up like a navy combat swimmer and supposedly working for some terrorist group have chosen to arm himself with a goddamned .25 automatic—a woman's *handbag* gun, for Christ sake? Unless . . .

Unless the gun belonged to someone he wanted to frame. Leigh, maybe? But hell, Leigh was at the Calcutta, with several hundred very reliable witnesses.

Still, the only logical reason for a contract killer to shoot someone with a .25-caliber weapon was to incriminate someone else—if not the owner of the gun, then someone with access to it. If the gun belonged to Leigh, maybe she kept it on the boat. So anyone who was on the boat with Kindler when he was to have been shot could've found the gun and grabbed it.

Of course, it would help tremendously if that someone had a shady reputation and was drunk out of his mind when the cops arrived. . . .

And who poured him the first drink? Leigh Kindler.

Rodrigue stared at the bullet in his hand. Why hadn't Kindler recognized the gun that night? Of course—he never saw it. Rodrigue had kept it in his pocket. "Hang on to it," Kindler had said. So maybe while they were at sea, he had gone looking for his wife's gun and couldn't find it. Things had begun to click into place for him. And then when he saw the bullet, he knew. Couldn't be that many .25s around: It had to be his wife's. And when the realization hit him, he had thrown the bullet down and, in a rage, smashed his fist through the door.

He hadn't confronted her with it last night, though, and of course he didn't go to the cops. Rodrigue would've liked to think Kindler was going to take it all in stride—no rocking of the boat in these dangerous waters.

Fat chance.

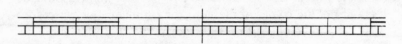

Chapter 26

At the appointed hour, Rodrigue brought the *Abaris* back up the channel to the flat outside the yacht basin. In a few moments, the Zodiac appeared on the light-streaked water, two persons aboard.

"I'm it!" Bones said happily, carelessly bumping the inflatable boat against the yacht. "Kindler's gonna pick up a mate in the morning."

Susan was in the bow, holding on and grinning widely. They both had had plenty to drink, Rodrigue judged.

"Congratulations," Rodrigue said, shaking the mate's hand. He reached over the gunwale to help Susan up.

"Thank you, Captain Rodrigue," she said cheerfully as she scrambled up into the cockpit.

"Don't mention it. Sleeping aboard, are you?"

"Yep. We won't be in billfish water until mid-morning. Might as well sleep in until we get out there. Not going ashore yet, are you?"

It was definitely a conciliatory tone she was using, but that didn't mean anything. Probably she regretted turning down his offer to become her source, and now she was going to be his pal again. Women did what they had to. If he hadn't known that before, he certainly knew it now.

"No, I'm going to squire you and Bones around while you sleep," he said. "That way, if someone wants to swim up and drill holes in our bottom, they'll have to work at it." He laughed in spite of himself.

Rodrigue knew damn well that he had accepted the ridiculous notion of a terrorist attack in the Galveston Channel simply because he had wanted to believe Leigh. Her innocence certainly would've been easier on his ego. But no, he had to face it: He wasn't suave and irresistible, after all. He was being led to slaughter like some prize fucking beef. John D. Rodrigue: big as an ox and twice as smart. It might've made another man bitter, but Rodrigue already had come to terms with most of his weaknesses, and certainly his weakness for women. And, what the hell, it *was* comical—him puttering down the channel into an imaginary ambush, hair crawling on the back of his neck. So he laughed.

Susan was glad to see Rodrigue lighten up. She could deal with him lying about terrorists and whatnot, but it had begun to look as if he actually believed it. "Oo, I don't know if I can sleep now," she said jokingly.

She was dressed in her working clothes—Islands Invitational T-shirt, khaki shorts, and Top-Siders, carrying a camera bag and a small duffel. She looked like a cute little urchin someone had turned out of the orphanage for reaching puberty. Just standing there smiling at him, she put a stitch in Rodrigue's wounded heart.

"Well, since you're going to sleep all morning," he said, "why don't you join me on the bridge for a nightcap?"

"Don't mind if I do."

"I noticed nobody invited me," said Bones, straightening from the task of looping the Zodiac's painter around a stern cleat. "But I don't mind. Nossir, I don't mind a bit. I'm goin' to get me some rest. Tomorrow's a big day." He winked broadly at Susan and stumbled into the saloon.

"Make mine a Cuba libre," Rodrigue told Susan. "I'm going to head us back toward the bay." He put a foot on the ladder to the flying bridge, then leaned over and called after her. "Don't forget the twist."

It was a beautiful night. The sky was fuzzy with the lights of Galveston, Texas City, Port Bolivar. The air had cooled well below the water temperature of eighty-three degrees and produced a silky sheen on the surface of the bay. Riding on the open flying bridge was a majestic feeling—which was made all the better by the company Rodrigue was keeping.

Hell, he couldn't blame Susan for sticking to him like last year's wet suit. She was just doing her job. And, he was just doing *his* job. Just because they worked on opposing teams didn't mean they couldn't get along.

She had been studying the water, a languid hand on her forehead, the breeze pushing her hair back and revealing a slender, attractive neck. Now she looked at him with sleepy eyes.

"You're not really worried about commandos storming the boat, are you, Rod?"

"No. Not now." The question had been unexpected—his mind had taken leave of the Kindlers and their problems—and the answer came out sharply.

"Aw, don't tense up on me," she said. "I'm not pumping you for information. I was at first, I admit. I'm not even sure when I stopped. I just want to know—are you in trouble?"

Rodrigue looked back at the lights of the channel. He decided they had come far enough, so he pulled back the throttles and put the engines in neutral.

"I may be," he said slowly, measuring his words. "A little innocent fraud. The murder attempt, I believe, is completely unrelated to the tournament. But it'll all come out sooner or later. Bound to."

She slid out of her chair and went to him, putting a cool hand on his face. "I was all through with you this afternoon, but I changed my mind. Well, that's not exactly right. I haven't changed my mind at all; I just don't seem to be able to help myself. I've known about the long-lining from the beginning and yet I was hoping you would come to bed with me the other night."

148

She surrendered herself to be held. "I was afraid you didn't like me, but you do, don't you? You were just too bummed out." She looked up again, eyes questioning.

"I like you very much . . . have from the first moment I saw you," he said.

"And Mrs. Kindler?" She laid her head against his chest to await the answer.

Rodrigue thought carefully; he wasn't sure himself. "Lust. Unrequited, thank God."

"Aw, come on, Rod. Don't you wish you had the memory, at least?"

"A memory is all I ever thought it would be. Listen, I might be something of a tomcat, but I can't chase two women at the same time. You showed up and she turned into just another rich man's wife."

The transition hadn't been quite that neat, but why confuse the girl?

"You're a scoundrel, Rodrigue . . . too lovable a scoundrel to kiss off over matters as paltry as lying and cheating and stealing."

"You know what stings the worst? The lying part."

"Aw, I could tell you wanted to tell me about the long-lining the other night when we were sitting on the seawall. You *are* an honorable man, Rodrigue. It's not conventional honor, is all. Anyway, I'm not going to do anything to hurt you, I promise. May not be able to *help* you, but I'm not going to hurt you. There—that's my speech. You're free to do with me what you will."

He kissed her, gently, and brushed back her hair. "I'm sorry I got in the way," he said.

"I probably will be too, pretty soon. But right now, my hormones are raging. Do you affect all your women this way, Rodrigue?"

He laughed. "Not many who would say it out loud, anyway."

"Lust," she said softly, her eyes focusing on his mouth.

"It's not good for you to fight it. It's like a snee—" She shut him up with a tender kiss that grew heated, with a tentative flicking of tongues.

149

"Got to anchor," he said hoarsely. *This*, by God, was the way to be used.

"Hurry. If I sober up, I'll lose my nerve."

This is a mistake, he thought miserably, lumbering about on the foredeck. He ought to tuck her in bed and leave her alone. Even if she wasn't jerking him around—and what could she possibly get out of screwing him except screwed?—it seemed there was a delicate balance here that could easily be upset. She wasn't just a woman, she was a friend, and Rodrigue needed all the friends he could get. Yet she was undeniably a woman. As he climbed back up the ladder, he found he had a jutting erection. There was no turning back now.

Bones was up a little after midnight, barfing over the gunwale. He slapped a towel into the bay and rinsed his face with it. "Whew!" he said. "Why do I do that to myself?"

"For the fun of it," said Rodrigue from the darkness of the flying bridge. He was glad for the company—being alone had gotten too confusing. Susan's smell still clung to him. He was giddy and scared at the same time.

It had taken a long time for the euphoria of their lovemaking to subside, Susan cuddled in his arms like a sleepy little girl. When they talked again, it was the same candid banter they had enjoyed from the beginning—but more intimate somehow. Rodrigue was overjoyed. They had gotten over a big hurdle intact. He had tucked her into her berth with a gentle kiss that lingered just enough to prove they weren't through with each other.

He had decided not to tell her his suspicions about Leigh. The less she knew, the better at this point. What Rodrigue needed was professional help.

"How do you feel?" Rodrigue asked as the lanky mate—now captain—climbed to the flying bridge. The question wasn't about his hangover—mates on tournament boats were used to hangovers.

"Pumped," said Bones. "I can't sleep. Where the hell are we?"

150

"Port Bolivar," said Rodrigue, pointing to a mass of lights. It was all the orientation Bones would require.

"Fuckin' stinks below," said Bones, twisting his rubbery face into a grimace. He belched loudly and then smacked his mouth with disgust. "I need some coffee. Want some?"

"Yeah. Tell you what, I'll go down and make it. You bring us back to the anchorage at the yacht basin. You guys are safe now, and I've got things to do."

Bones slid into the helm chair. He had felt safe enough all along.

While the coffee was dripping, Rodrigue found a note pad and wrote down a set of loran numbers. They were the numbers to nowhere in particular.

He turned around to search for the cups and stepped on the garden hose. He recoiled as though it were a snake. His nerves were not in terrific shape, he decided.

Bones came to the ladder and reached down for the two cups of coffee.

"You need to get that fucking hose off the cabin sole," Rodrigue said grumpily. "I stepped on it and nearly did a back flip. Felt like a goddamn water moccasin."

Bones laughed. "I searched every yacht supply store from here to Clear Lake and I can't find a damn sink trap anywhere. And now the fuckin' hose is stopped up."

"It's not the hose that's stopped up, it's the sink. Mrs. Kindler plugged it and just poked the end of the hose behind the damn cabinet. You must have a sour bilge and the stink was coming up through the sink."

Even a billionaire's fine fucking yacht could be nasty and smelly on the inside, he thought with satisfaction.

"So that's where it's coming from. I was afraid the carpet below was mildewed. I'll tell you one thing, though; she tries to be helpful, which is more than you can say for Kindler."

Rodrigue pulled the paper with the loran numbers from his pocket and handed it to Bones. This was what he could say for Kindler.

"That's where *Colinda* is swinging on the hook—with a hell of a big marlin. Shokaito says maybe seven hundred."

Bones threw his head back and looked up at the charcoal sky. "Holy shit," he said miserably.

"Seven hundred fucking pounds of marlin that's going to be shark shit this time tomorrow."

It served no purpose to alienate Bones. Rodrigue was just indulging himself. But it felt good.

"Aw, that fuckin' gook'll sell it," said Bones.

"He better not. Whomever he sold it to would make a dandy witness for the prosecution. Does Kindler keep any guns on board?"

"Yeah, there's a stainless Mini-14 underneath the sofa." Bones grinned after he said it. He wasn't sure he should have.

"No pistols?"

"Not that I know of. Why?"

"Aw, nothing. I was just wondering if Kindler had armed himself," Rodrigue lied.

It didn't mean anything. Bones was not the kind to prowl through the owner's belongings. Odds were that the gun Rodrigue had taken from the man in the wet suit belonged to one of the Kindlers.

The cops would figure that out sooner or later. Best thing he could do was help them figure it out sooner. Ever since he had found the bullet, he had known what he would have to do. Only now was he prepared to do it: Fuck the money and fuck honor among thieves; it was every man for himself.

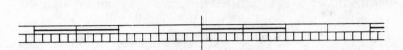

Chapter 27

Rodrigue left the inflatable boat at the end of B Row and went straight to the pay phone at the foot of the pier. He called the sheriff's office and convinced the dispatcher his message was important enough to call Phillips at home. He gave the number of the pay phone and then hung up to wait.

Phillips called in less than five minutes.

"What is it, Rod?" he said. He sounded the same as always, neither sleepy nor even faintly irritated at being called in the middle of the night.

"I've got a better guess and I thought it was important for you to hear it now. Also I have a little confession to make."

Phillips sucked at a tooth with a noise like a maiden aunt's kiss. "I told you, it's the city's case."

"Yeah, but I want you to hear it. I trust you, for some reason. Then you can call Eckles. He'll take it better coming from you, anyway."

"Naw, he won't, either. But go ahead."

"First, did they find out who owns the gun?"

"Don't think so. Heard the NCIC query drew a blank. Only thing to do is start at the manufacturer—the importer, in this

153

case—and trace the serial number down through the system—what wholesaler got it, then what retailer, and finally who the retailer sold it to. But that's next to impossible to do on a weekend. I doubt they've got anything yet."

"I'll bet you it turns out to be Kindler's gun."

"Oh?" said the deputy flatly, without a hint of surprise. "And what makes you say that?"

"Why would some fucking commando be carrying a chrome-plated twenty-five automatic? Unless it was supposed to look like I got drunk and got into an argument with Kindler and shot him with a gun I found on board. Vandegriff blundered onto the scene and the gunman thought he was Kindler."

Phillips had apparently already given the theory some thought. "The only thing that bothers me about that idea is him leaving his mask and fins out in the cockpit. If he's setting up an ambush, why would he leave his calling card out like that?"

"Well, he wasn't very good at it, was he? Maybe he was so worried about getting the jump on me that he didn't think about it."

"That's possible, I guess. How'd all this come to you?"

"I went to see Vandegriff in the hospital, and he told me he had found the bullet in his pants when they were out at sea Friday, and that he had put it in the medicine cabinet. He said that Kindler later came up to the bridge in a kind of a huff, wanting to know about the gun—I think because he had been looking for *his* gun and couldn't find it, and had begun to put two and two together. The telling thing is that he went down to the head and busted the door with his fist. It looks to me like he saw the bullet was a twenty-five—which aren't that common anymore, right?—and then blew into a rage. I found the bullet in the carpet."

"So Kindler figures he was the target, and maybe even has an idea who set him up."

"Leigh Kindler, who else?"

"She's got a hell of a motive, I suspect, money-wise . . . which makes more sense to me than religion or politics."

"She'd been coming on to me for a couple of months, Bruce. I gave her the chance to do something about it the other day and

154

she backed down. She was always flirting in public, though—I think so people would be quick to believe that Kindler and I were fighting over her."

He remembered also how Leigh had insisted he stay in the saloon to watch the quiche the night of the shooting—so he wouldn't be up on the flying bridge when the gunman climbed aboard?

"This the confession you mentioned?"

"It gets a little stickier."

"Well, does it ever get around to explaining why Kindler hasn't gone to the police?" the deputy asked.

"You're not going to like this, but I think that part of it *is* political. Leigh told me Kindler was involved with the CIA in that marina project in Jamaica and doesn't want to jeopardize it with bad publicity."

"And you believe her?"

"It'd be easy to. I remember Ahlmark from Vietnam now. He was regular army, but his job was to count the corpses produced by a kind of shadowy mercenary outfit—the Dewey Rifles, they were called. Doesn't seem like a big jump from there into the CIA."

Rodrigue paused for a moment, gathering his nerve.

"Bruce, even if she's lying about the CIA, Kindler's still got a pretty good reason to keep it quiet; try a million bucks."

"How's that?"

Rodrigue told Phillips all about rigging the tournament. The phone was silent for a long time. A mosquito buzzed around Rodrigue's ear and then bit him on the neck. The warm breeze off the Gulf smelled faintly of sulfur.

"Well," drawled Phillips at last. "Is this the last of the surprises, I hope?"

"You now know everything I know. You and Eckles can take it from here. I'm going home and get drunk."

"Naw you ain't, either. You're gonna meet me at the courthouse annex in about—make it fifteen minutes. If Kindler wasn't worried about it, I wasn't gonna worry about it. But this throws a whole different light on the subject."

"I thought you said this was the city's business."

"It is, but unfortunately Eckles likes the Jamaican angle too much. If I take this to him, all that's gonna come of it is me gettin' a memo from the sheriff telling me to keep my nose out of city business. Detectives don't generally like ideas that other detectives thought of. I'm just as guilty of that as anyone."

"What the hell do you want me to do at this hour?"

"Help me stick my neck out. I suspect you'll be good at it."

Rodrigue stuffed his .45 back into his glove compartment and locked his car in front of the sheriff's office. Inside, the dispatcher directed him into a large room full of small cubicles formed by gray metal partitions. In one of them, Phillips waited, propped back in a chair with his feet on his desk. The atmosphere smelled of stale cigarette smoke and Old Spice.

Phillips rose and poured them both a cup of coffee from the community pot outside his cubicle.

"Ever wear a body mike, Rod?" the deputy asked, taking his seat again. He hooked his thumb at a box with a long wire running from it that was lying on the desk.

"Never had the occasion. I usually run with a better crowd."

"Well, stay away from AM radio, that's the main thing to remember. And don't let her give you a hug. Slip your shirt off." Phillips took a roll of bandage tape from his desk drawer.

"What the hell do you want me to do?"

"Feel her out about the gun. If you can get her to draw you into the murder conspiracy somehow, that'd be fine. Raise your arm. You might casually bring Morgan up, too."

"Harry Morgan? He doesn't work for them anymore." The microphone was cold against his skin.

"They got an ID on your boy yesterday," said Phillips as he spread the tape across Rodrigue's broad flank. "A pharmacist from Modesto, California. Just divorced. Two young kids."

"Aw, that makes me feel great, Bruce. What the fuck was he doing climbing on boats and shooting people?"

"Second childhood, I guess. Decided he wanted to be a soldier of fortune all of a sudden. At least he had the sense to start small. Advertised his services on supermarket bulletin boards."

"You're kidding."

"Nope. Now drop your arm. Naw, the ol' boy made up some details from a military career he never had and hand-lettered an ad on index cards—'Situation wanted: high-risk assignments'— and thumbtacked 'em up in grocery stores all around the Clear Lake area. Swing it a little."

"It pinches."

"Well, no one said police work was comfortable."

Phillips smoothed on another strip of tape. "Eckles said Seabrook PD believes they can tie him to a killing there last month. Man was taken out with a deer rifle as he drove over the Kemah-Seabrook bridge. They had written it off as either an accident or a random killing until a rifle of the same caliber turned up on a boat your boy was living on there in Kemah. Still waiting on ballistics, but the bridge-killing widow is acting awful nervous. That ought to make you feel a little better."

"Some."

"He was living on the boat with a little gal right out of high school. She reported him missing when he didn't show up Friday. Identified the body—now that they got it thawed out."

He finished his taping and sat back to admire his handiwork. "Just let your arms hang naturally. That's better, ain't it?"

"Yeah, great."

Phillips stood up and tossed the roll of tape onto his desk. "The girlfriend is the one who gave Eckles the idea it was a Jamaican who hired her boyfriend. Took some strong deductin' on his part, though. I went over last night and sneaked a peek at her statement. Call it professional curiosity. You wanna know what it was she actually said? Said her boyfriend told her it was a man and he had a kind of an English accent."

"Morgan."

"Could be. English-sounding accent could be Australia, Rhodesia, lots of places. And Jamaica, of course. 'Course it ain't exactly evidence, but it sure fits with what I had always kinda figured about Morgan and Mrs. Kindler."

Rodrigue sat down and finished his coffee in a gulp. It was lukewarm and too weak for his taste. When you got right down to it, he didn't give a shit about Leigh and Morgan. But he sure hadn't suspected anything, either.

"What about them?" he asked tiredly.

"They were careful—real careful—but a feller like me, sittin' around the yacht basin kinda quiet . . . he sees things. It seemed to me she had a little trouble keeping her hands offa him. When Kindler fired him, I figured it was because he'd caught them at something, or at least suspected it."

Rodrigue shook his head and chuckled bitterly. "I think I'm gonna enjoy this."

"Well don't enjoy it too much. Even if she confesses, it won't be worth a hoot in court. Just get enough to convince Eckles— without spookin' her, preferably."

Phillips took his summer-weight double-X Resistol from the old-fashioned hat rack.

Rodrigue rose and put his shirt on. "What about the god-damned tournament?"

"We'll worry about the tournament later. First thing we gotta do is get this here attempted murder solved."

The deputy lit a cigarette and inhaled deeply.

"Otherwise," he said through the yellow smoke, "she's liable to get it done one of these days."

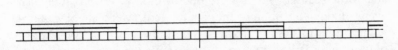

Chapter 28

The Kindlers' condo was adjacent to the yacht basin. Leigh came to the door in a white cotton robe. She was meticulously made-up, hair a vision of obedience, and smelling faintly of scotch.

"What happened?" she asked. Her eyes were wide, flitting back and forth from his good eye to his bad.

"Nothing," said Rodrigue. "Sorry about coming by so late. Didn't wake you, I take it?"

"What are you doing here?" Her voice lowered a sliver of an octave and she clutched the robe between her breasts.

"It's about the shooting. Purely business, I assure you. May I come in?"

"I'm sorry," she said, standing aside. "Of course, come in. Can I fix you a drink?"

"Sure."

"Rum and Coke?"

"With a twist."

"Make yourself comfortable." Her hips undulated tantalizingly in the thin robe as she walked to the bar.

Too bad, Rodrigue thought.

The living room decor was glass and chrome, black lacquer and white leather. There were photos of anglers with their fish everywhere. The photos, though modern, were all black-and-white prints in chrome frames. The only splash of color was a blue-purple marlin hung against the white brick of the fireplace.

She brought the drink and a fresh one for herself. "Thank God it's over. I've been worried out of my mind."

"What makes you think it's over?"

"Well . . ." Her eyes widened again, questioning. "They *did* arrest those men. . . ?"

"Yeah, they did. But I think they're barking up the wrong tree. I think Vandegriff was the one who was supposed to be shot all along."

"Ed?" she said with a trace of a smile.

"Yes, and I think Bones is behind it."

"Bones?" This time she laughed. "*Why*, for God's sake?"

"For the win. He wanted on the bridge real bad. Now he's there. And if Vandegriff would've died, his share would've been one-fourth instead of one-fifth."

Leigh thoughtfully stirred her drink with a long, blood-red fingernail.

"And Vandegriff probably would've died if the gunman had used something bigger than a twenty-five-caliber automatic," said Rodrigue. "But I think there must've been a reason for that, too. I think it was supposed to look like I killed him, with a gun that I found on board somewhere. Do you or your husband own a twenty-five automatic?"

A look of panic came into her face and her hands went to her mouth. "My God! Was it . . . silvery? With black handles?"

"That's the one." He *was* enjoying himself.

"My God!" She looked wildly around the room. "My God, it has to be Al!"

"Ahlmark?"

"He knew about the gun. Garrett showed it to him down in Jamaica when he quizzed us about protection. That and the rifle under the divan. He laughed about the pistol. Said it was too . . . puny."

"Who else knew about it? Bones?"

"I'm sure Bones wouldn't know, unless he went through our things in the master stateroom. We kept it in a drawer. I just can't imagine Bones doing anything like that. But Al . . ."

"Why would Ahlmark want Vandegriff dead?"

"Not Vandegriff. Garrett."

"But why?"

"Al was suspicious of Susan for some reason or another, and he checked up on her. Of course, she turned out to be exactly who and what she said she was. It was her questioning that made him suspicious. He thought she knew something about Trenchtown, but of course it was Garrett's plan to finesse the tournament that she was trying to uncover. Al found out about that in the process, and he was livid."

"Yeah, but enough to kill him over it?"

"I don't know. No, I don't think so. Maybe . . . to keep anyone from finding out about the CIA and Trenchtown?"

"Sit down, Mrs. Kindler." She looked on the verge of buckling at the knees. Rodrigue guided her to a sofa and sat beside her.

"I just don't know how anyone else would've known about the gun," she said, almost angrily.

Rodrigue squeezed his eyes shut in an impish imitation of Detective Sergeant Eckles. "Let's see now, Ahlmark is afraid your husband would reveal the CIA's involvement in Trenchtown if we got caught cheating on the tournament. But why would he do that?"

She sighed. "Leverage. The CIA would have to quash the investigation. But that would be terribly embarrassing for Al, wouldn't it?"

"So let's say the gunman had been successful in killing your husband and pinning it on me. How would that have kept the CIA's role in Trenchtown a secret? After all, you knew."

"Yes, but Al wasn't aware I knew. All I know is what Garrett told me in private. Garrett admonished me in the strictest of terms not to let it slip. I was made to feel—without actually being told, you understand—that the knowledge could be dangerous to me."

"Why did he tell you, then, was he asking your advice?"

161

A sad smile. "Oh, no, of course not. It's just that Garrett and I . . . talk. But as far as Al was concerned, all we knew was that he was an old friend who was familiar with the fishing out of Port Antonio—a sort of consultant, I guess."

"Who's we?"

"Why, Ed and Bones and myself."

"What about Harry Morgan?" he asked evenly.

"Harry wasn't with us in Jamaica."

"Did Harry's firing have anything to do with the CIA thing?"

"I told you—"

"Yeah, you told me. He played too much with the girls. Were you one of those girls, Mrs. Kindler?"

Her blue eyes darted to her hands for a moment, then calmly rose and looked unwaveringly into his face. "I owe you an apology, Rod. And an explanation."

"If it's for why you've been coming on to me, please."

"To win Garrett back." She moved an inch closer. "I love him. I love him, and I used you to make him include me in his—" She jumped up suddenly and walked toward the fireplace. "In his agenda."

"Making him *jealous*?" Rodrigue almost laughed.

She nodded, her back to him. "At first, I thought it would be enough if another man was interested in me, so I flirted with Harry . . . but very discreetly." She turned and smiled. "Harry's not the gentleman you are, Rod. He tried to press it further than I wanted, and I had to ask Garrett to dismiss him. And he did it with about as much passion as if Harry had missed one too many oil changes with the engines."

She sat beside him again. "I wanted him to think I was attracted to you. I'm sorry if that sounds cruel; it *is* cruel, but—" She sobbed and covered her face with her hands.

"C'mon, Leigh," he said coldly.

Unexpectedly, she lunged at him, burying her face in his neck. He held her awkwardly, his right arm clasped against his side to keep her from feeling the body mike. She was softer than he thought she would be.

"I just wanted him back," she croaked. "I'm so sorry, but I just wanted him back."

"Back from what, Leigh?" he asked gently.

"From his . . . almighty *plans!*"

She drew away, tentatively, and found her drink. "I was so afraid something would happen," she said. "And now it has."

"But Ahlmark botched it."

"He'll try again . . . I'm sure of it." Her face seemed bloodless. "It's not just Trenchtown at stake. If all this got out, imagine how damaging it would be to Edward Seaga. They'd risk anything to prevent losing that election down there."

Detective Sergeant Eckles listened to the entire tape with his eyes closed. Then he opened them and looked at Rodrigue.

"You seemed to have left out a few details the other day. What's this about 'finessing' the tournament?"

"We cheated. Caught that marlin on a longline beforehand."

"You know about this?" he asked Phillips incredulously.

"Not till tonight. Tell you the truth, I didn't figure the tournament had anything to do with it. I figured she and this Morgan fellow had cooked it up between themselves to do the ol' boy in."

"What about now? Think she's just protecting Morgan?" Eckles asked.

Phillips shrugged. Eckles looked at Rodrigue.

"I don't know what to think," said Rodrigue. "She changes like the wind. One minute it's the Cubans trying to kill Kindler, and the next it's Ahlmark. First Morgan is fired for chasing skirts, then it's because he was chasing *her*. Hell, maybe she's telling the truth now. I don't know how she sounds, but she sure as hell *looked* scared."

"If he's CIA, he might be talented enough to mimic a Jamaican accent and smart enough to cover his ass that way," mused Phillips.

"Give me a break!" said Eckles. "What's the CIA doing hiring some goon who advertises in supermarkets?"

"Ahlmark may be a rogue, hiring the best talent he could find on short notice."

"A rogue secret agent with enough money to build a small city?" said Eckles. "What does the CIA pay?"

Phillips rubbed the cigarette smoke out of his eye. He was beginning to look tired. "Let's suppose it's a CIA project and Ahlmark is in charge. Let's say maybe he picks Kindler and has a little something invested in him—like maybe a kickback from the start-up money, or for whatever reason, he's had to put up some pretty heavy sponsorship with the brass. Kindler is his man, in other words. Then Kindler screws up, and Ahlmark is in no position to go running back to Langley with it. He has to deal with it himself."

"Still, somehow I'd expect more from a CIA agent," said Eckles, shaking his head.

"They've got professors and clerks and airplane pilots in the CIA, too, you know. They can't all be professional thugs."

"Okay, so we've got two different suspects." Eckles looked at his watch. "What time do the tournament people start fishing?"

"They can't break the jetties until five," said Rodrigue. He glanced at his own watch. It was 4:40. "They're all out in the Roads by now."

"We can't do anything with Morgan until he gets back from fishing. I'll drop in on this Ahlmark right now and have a little chat with him. Any idea where he's staying?"

"I don't know, they've got people everywhere—the yacht club, the Holiday Inn," said Rodrigue. "No telling."

Phillip's cigarette ash was half an inch long. He cupped his hand under it until he got it safely to the ashtray.

"I'd put her under surveillance if I was you," he said to Eckles. "Just to be safe."

Eckles nodded glumly. "At least her old man is in the safest place he could be, under the circumstances. Safe at sea." He stood up, opened the interrogation room door, and waited for them to file out.

"What about the reggae band?" asked Rodrigue. "You going to release them?"

"We already have," Eckles said dryly. "Despite the fact that, just prior to being arrested, they all ate their cigarettes."

It was nearly dawn by the time Rodrigue got home. He stood in the doorway to his bedroom, looking at the bed. It was still rumpled where Susan had slept in it. Maybe it even smelled of her. But it was too late to go to bed.

He went to the liquor cabinet and stood there, looking at the bottles with the same vacant stare he had cast upon the bed. About four fingers of straight Pusser's would feel good. But it wasn't a good idea.

He slammed the cabinet door impatiently. He didn't like waiting.

The open refrigerator was no more comforting than the liquor cabinet had been. There were three six-packs of Budweiser longnecks in there, but he needed something more substantial. Maybe he ought to cook some breakfast. But he wasn't hungry.

He went downstairs and found his rusting chaise lounge in the storeroom, and carried it to the water's edge. The Gulf of Mexico was like an inheritance to Rodrigue. Its expanse made him lonely, but it was a connected, good kind of lonely, like gazing at an old photograph or standing at a grave site. It connected him to his past, and even beyond. The breakers murmured softly and the warm, salty breeze caressed his hair. He stretched back to await the new day.

Why couldn't he have met Susan while he was just minding his own business at the yacht basin? Why did he have to be tangled up in killing and stealing?

Fatigue was clouding his thinking. The real question, he realized, was why in the hell he was involved in killing and stealing to begin with.

The light came in a breathtaking starburst, rays of gold and pink and turquoise shooting from the low clouds. The sea was brassy and the sky was lemon yellow. In about two seconds, it was over, and the sun was just a weak orb low in the gray morning haze.

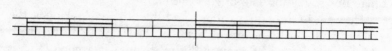

Chapter 29

Breakfast smells woke Clayton Guidry, and for a moment he wasn't sure whether he was at home or at work. He was twenty-seven years old and still lived with his momma and daddy in a sprawling, much-added-on farmhouse near Pecan Island, Louisiana. There were two other brothers and two sisters there, plus the husband of one of the sisters, who was like a brother, anyway.

Daddy farmed rice, and Clayton and his brother Loveless, who also worked offshore, helped out on their seven days off. His other brother, Melvin, was still in high school, and he worked at the gas station in town part-time. George, their brother-in-law, also worked on the farm, especially in the summers. He was a teacher at the high school.

They had a big old kitchen, and every morning Momma got up before daylight and cooked sausage and biscuits and eggs and French toast, and of course lots of good coonass coffee. The bodies moved slowly through the darkened rooms, pulled into the light by the smells—it was just like mornings in the living quarters offshore.

Lying still for a minute, just half-awake, Clayton could tell he

166

was still on his seven-on. Eighty feet above the surging Gulf on hollow steel legs, there was always a trembling, a constant vibration that Clayton liked.

The twin platforms stood in 151 feet of water, give or take 10 feet for changes in bottom contour. The living-quarters platform had about a fourth of an acre of deck space. The adjacent production platform, which had once supported the drilling rig, was a little larger. Now it served to link a dozen natural gas wells to a shoreward-bound transmission line, producing nearly 100 million cubic feet per day, all told. The two platforms were linked by a two-hundred-foot catwalk suspended between their decks—the production deck where the wellheads were, and the deck of the quarters platform that housed their washers and driers, air-conditioning units, electric generators, and hot-water heater.

Clayton enjoyed being out in the Gulf. He appreciated all the sea's moods, from iron gray with towering whitecapped peaks, to deep, endless blue, to glassy and shining with coppery morning light.

The beauty of it was that he could enjoy being at sea without the discomfort and downright danger that the men on the boats had to put up with. The platform trembled constantly but it never rolled or bucked. The men had rib eyes and fried shrimp and ice cream, and could watch TV or even shoot pool when the weather was bad and the boat crews had to eat cold sandwiches—if they could keep them down—and couldn't even make coffee.

The rest of the platforms in the field were smaller satellites, manned only during daytime shifts. A four-passenger helicopter—the ubiquitous Bell 206-B Jet Ranger—distributed workers from the twenty-man crew around the field in good weather. And when conditions were too bad for flying, there was an eighty-foot standby boat hanging off a mooring buoy a half a mile northeast of the production platform. The platform would radio the captain, who would dog-ear a page of his paperback, wake up the deckhand/engineer, and they would go run the crew around the field.

Bodies were stirring in the darkness of the bunk room. The hands who would be making the rounds this morning were

167

quietly pulling on their coveralls and boots in the semidarkness. As they dressed, other men continued to snooze.

Clayton, whose job kept him on the main platform, could've slept another hour. In the winter, he would've. But summers in the Gulf were so glorious that he usually rose early and drank a couple of cups of coffee outside, watching the big fish chasing the little fish in fluttering sheets, like gusts of rain blowing up from the bottom.

Sometimes he just watched the sun come up, or just smelled the warm salt air and daydreamed.

He pulled on his boots and slapped on his hard hat—company policy—and slipped into a shirt—which was Raymond's policy—and wandered into the galley in his boxer shorts.

Raymond was the cook. He was a grouchy son of a bitch with red eyes and dandruff like rice who claimed he used to work at the big hotels in New Orleans and Biloxi before his back got too bad to be manhandling those big pots. He had the temperament of a chef, at least. He was busy turning out biscuits by the square yard and bacon by the pound when Clayton came in.

Les Bruning was there, too, drinking coffee and trying to get Raymond's goat, which was child's play for a guy like Les. He was the helicopter pilot, and a real maverick—wore muscle shirts and jogging shorts to work usually and got away with it. They said he had been through hell in Vietnam, got wounded several times, won a bunch of medals, a real hero. But he never talked about it himself—never talked about anything serious. He just liked to cut up.

"Yo, my man Clay!" Les greeted him. He stroked his sandy handlebar mustache evilly, as though he were about to tie Clayton to a railroad track.

"Fuck you, Les." Clayton always liked to make a show of being grumpy before he had his coffee.

"Give'm coffee, Ray," said Les.

"Coffee," said Raymond, pouring it himself. The pilot's hale friendliness made him nervous and he was grateful for someone to share it with.

"Well, your ol' *cousin*'s not doing so damn good this year,"

Les said, snapping the wrinkles of the early edition of the Baton Rouge *Morning Advocate*.

Yankee pitcher Ron Guidry was not Clayton's cousin and Les knew it. It was just some more of his shit.

"Lemme see that," said Clayton, commandeering the sports section. "Hey, they're playing today. Wanna make a little wager?"

"Well, mebbe," said Les, stroking his mustache. "I'll put ten bucks against the Yankees but you gotta pay up in some more of your daddy's good boudin."

The first of the crew came in, teeth brushed and hair combed, and before long, the galley table was full of laughing and arguing men, being orchestrated by Les with one foot on a chair and a half-eaten sausage biscuit for a baton. Clayton refilled his cup and went out into the dim, still morning.

He walked around to the southeast rail and looked seaward. The horizon was a glowing ribbon, visibly widening. Clayton leaned on the rail and prepared himself for a treat.

On the pad above, Les warmed up in the helicopter in the semidarkness. Clayton felt the first rotations of the rotor at the base of his skull. *Whup-whup-whup* . . . Then there was a buffeting down draft as the Jet Ranger roared off with the first four men—Les undoubtedly still yacking away at the controls.

The coming sun did not disappoint him. Low clouds quickly took shape, outlined in gold, with rose-colored bottoms. . . .

Clayton's daydreams were pretty ordinary. Mostly he wondered about how things worked and why things happened—ordinary things, like waterspouts and microwave ovens. Loveless, who was four years younger, said he wasn't ambitious enough. Clayton didn't even have a girlfriend now that Lydia had broken off with him and married the druggist she worked for in Gueydan. But he figured, What the hell—he was making a good salary, had great benefits, retirement, the whole bit. He liked working seven-and-seven—and he liked living at home, too, which Loveless thought was an insult to be tolerated only until he could save up for the new Z-car he wanted.

The Gulf was pink now. Clayton looked over the rail to see

whether any fish were feeding. A big black-and-white yacht was backing up to the east corner.

Clayton casually propped his elbows on the rail. Sometimes the girls on those yachts went topless. You really couldn't tell much from way up here, but it gave a nice little kick to the old imagination.

There was a guy on the back deck, line coiled in his hand. They were going to tie up and fish. It happened all the time in the summer.

Officially, company policy didn't allow it, but nobody enforced the policy. Fishing boats didn't bother anything and it was kind of entertaining to watch them catch fish—especially when the fisherman was a topless girl.

The guy in the boat lassoed a landing bitt and another guy appeared, climbing down from the control station—dragging a damn raincoat for some reason. Must've come through a thunderstorm on the way out, Clayton thought. He looked back to the north. The sky was pale blue and clear. Maybe they caught a lot of spray on that open bridge.

Clayton looked back down again in time to see the man with the raincoat jump onto the platform. *That* was definitely against policy. Maybe they were in trouble. Maybe they needed a pump on the boat, or somebody was hurt. He flipped the rest of his coffee overboard, set the empty cup on the grate at his feet, and ran to the stairway.

He was halfway down the long stairs to the cellar deck when the man with the raincoat roughly shoved the other man forward. That was when Clayton knew something was really wrong. Then the raincoat slipped aside and he saw the rifle. Then the man with the rifle saw him. . . .

Clayton wheeled and started to climb, but the stairs flew up and hit him on the bridge of the nose. That was the only pain he felt. A numbing warmth spread from his back into his arms and legs. He remembered hearing the shots just as the sunlight faded.

Harold Broussard heard the shots and instinctively recognized them for what they were. His mind said no, it had to be a com-

170

pressor acting up over on the quarters platform, but he jumped for the emergency shutdown station, anyway.

He was in an office on the main deck of the production platform, overseeing the morning's production report to the field office in Lafayette. He was the only one there; the other men were having breakfast on the other platform.

The head office in Houston once had sent out a confidential memo initiating what was to be the formulation of a contingency plan in case anyone ever tried to overtake an offshore platform. It never went past that. Nobody wanted to talk about it—almost as though it might give the wrong person an idea.

Probably they had realized for the first time just exactly how vulnerable they were out there: no arms on board—ages of policy against that; sitting on a dozen columns of explosive gas; Probably a hundred miles from the nearest coast guard cutter.

At least they had instantaneous communication. Broussard flipped open the fax machine's clear plastic lid and scribbled MAYDAY SHOTS FIRED on the production record. Then he slowly turned and went to the door like a dead man reanimated, like a zombie.

He had been teaching high school physics, helping to coach football, and working on his master's at SLI in Lafayette when their third daughter came along and he could no longer afford a career in education. The money was too good in the oil field. Now at forty-five, hair falling out and needing to have his teeth pulled—and not a goddamned thing to show for it except twenty years of bills paid on time—he was about to go out and get killed.

The hell of it was, he had been expecting it all along. Everyone knew it was dangerous offshore.

Maybe it *was* just a compressor. Broussard had experienced these feelings of dread before—and, just as now, he had simply gone ahead and done what was expected of him. A couple of months ago when that front whistled through and they had to change crew by boat instead of helicopter, he had a strong premonition that the boat would founder and sink in the cold, angry Gulf. Still, he'd climbed woodenly onto the Billy Pugh net and let them lower him to the heaving vessel below. And while it was a booger of a ride in, they had made it.

So, what to do? . . . He had to assess the situation, that was first. Then call Lafayette—microwave communications made that a matter of picking up a phone. But what if the men were in danger. . . ? Of course they were in danger, but what if he could do something—take some kind of action. . . ? What? He had to go see . . .

Broussard got to the rail in time to see a man with a gun herding his men back into the quarters. The man looked toward the production platform. Then he disappeared into the building. Broussard walked back to his office and stared at the phone.

It rang in seconds.

"Broussard," he answered matter-of-factly.

"Bruce, this is Raym—" The cook's voice broke. "Guidry's dead," he said, sobbing.

"What's the problem?"

"What's the *problem*? There's a guy over here with a fucking gun and he's going to kill every one of us unless you do what he says—*that's* the fucking problem!"

Situation. That's what he had meant to say, not problem. Well, so that was the situation.

"All right. What does he want?"

"He does not want you to call out; if he finds out that you called out, he'll kill us all. He means it, Harold. He wants you to come over here. Come right over here to the quarters and come inside."

Broussard heard other talking but he couldn't make it out.

"With your hands up," Raymond added.

"Tell him I'm on my way."

After the receiver had rested in the cradle a full second, Broussard carefully picked it up—hollow silence. It was still off the hook over in the living quarters. Again he raised the lid of the fax machine and scribbled ARMED MAN ONE DEAD.

Then he walked slowly, almost casually, along the long catwalk to the other platform.

172

Les Bruning knew something was wrong when he approached the living quarters and nobody was waiting for him. The next group out should've been waiting to run over and jump in. Instead of setting down, he circled for a look at the other side of the elevated landing pad.

Someone appeared on deck, coming from below: Broussard. He was waving him off; pointing out toward another platform. Les keyed his mike, but there was no use in that. If Broussard was over here at the living quarters, there probably wasn't anyone back in the office to answer the radio. He shrugged and banked around toward the nearest satellite.

Probably nothing, but he had a bad feeling about it.

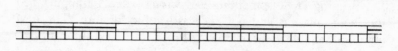

Chapter 30

Rodrigue went straight to Hell, there to be literally barbecued on a grill, his own juices teasing him with a cruel imitation of coolness as they trickled down his thighs. The Devil came, the hot coals crunching under his sharp hooves. He stopped and leaned over Rodrigue's body. His breath smelled of sulfur and cyanide when he spoke.

C'mon, Rod, get up. Something's goin' on.

Rodrigue opened his eye into dazzling brightness and quickly shielded it with his hand. Bruce Phillips was bending over him, cigarette drooping from his lip.

"You just about got time for a shower. I'll make us some coffee while you're at it." From the redness of his eyes, it was apparent the deputy hadn't slept at all.

"Then we've got to get our asses down to the coast guard station," he said.

"Coast guard? What happened?" Rodrigue thought of Susan and panic grabbed him by the throat.

Phillips was already headed for the house, his low-heeled ropers crunching in the sand and shell. He turned and waited at the crest of a low dune.

174

"From what it looks like, Ahlmark has taken over the *Abaris* and hijacked an oil rig." He resumed walking as soon as Rodrigue caught up to him. "Got Kindler, and his captain and mate, and whoever else was on the boat with him. We've got to fill the coast guard in on the background."

"Hijacked an offshore platform?" Rodrigue said incredulously. "What the fuck for?"

Phillips shook his head. They had reached the stairs to Rodrigue's sun deck.

"What about Susan?" It was the only thing that really mattered.

"Far as we know, everybody who was on the boat is all right. But she's being held hostage by an ol' boy who's already killed at least one hostage on the platform, so we can't take nothing for granted."

Rodrigue nodded grimly and headed up the stairs. This was not a time to go rushing around wildly. When moments mattered, what worked best was economy of motion. He would clean up, maybe force down a bite. It was contrary to Rodrigue's natural impatience, but years of training and experience had molded him: Take care of the little things and the big things will take care of themselves.

He hoped. He fervently hoped.

The invasion of Sunday visitors hadn't begun yet and traffic was sparse on Seawall Boulevard. Phillips threaded the El Camino through the slow-moving cars and pickups effortlessly, almost distractedly. The speedometer was slapping eighty, but there was little sensation of speed. Outside, the hot, moist breath of the Gulf weighed like an invisible blanket, causing even the spiny palm fronds to droop. A sheet of discarded newspaper barely had the energy to raise one corner as they shot by, then it settled back on the concrete like butter melting in a pan. Cars floated by like cardboard cutouts. "Look, if there's anything you haven't told me, now's the time to do it." Phillips chanced a sideways glance. "Don't make me wade into a mess of feds half-cocked."

"You know as much as me," said Rodrigue. "*More* than me. How do you know it's Ahlmark on the boat?"

"He wasn't in his room last night—hadn't slept in the bed—yet all his stuff is still there, toothbrush and socks and the whole bit. Eckles said they did manage to get good prints off the glass tabletop, but they bounced right back. Not on file."

"Hah!" said Rodrigue.

"Yeah, exactly."

"But why in the hell would a government agent hijack an offshore platform?"

Without as much as a touch of brake, Phillips wheeled onto Ferry Road. The El Camino's tires shrieked and one hubcap went clanging off on a diverging course.

"He's a rogue. No tellin' what he'll do or why."

"What about Leigh, she all right?"

"She's right where you left her. Eckles set up a surveillance. Her light stayed on until just before daylight."

Minutes later, they whisked through the open gate of the federal government's compound on Fort Point, the northwestern corner of Galveston Island. Marine reserve armored vehicles were parked in scattered confusion like kids' bikes. On the softball field, a civilian helicopter, a Bell Jet Ranger with MACDONALD OFFSHORE painted on the streamlined tail, squatted in a bowl of swirling dust.

Phillips squealed to a stop at a tall Caribbean-style building on the Galveston Channel. The ground floor was open except for a closed space that served as a garage, and a veranda surrounded the second story. The steep hip roof was punctuated with dormers.

At the top of a flight of stairs, they found a solid-looking door with a closed-circuit TV camera, a box of push buttons that operated a crypto lock, and a single door buzzer. Phillips rang the buzzer.

"Come in," said a speaker hidden in the acoustic-paneled ceiling. At the same instant, the latch began to hum loudly. Phillips pushed and the door opened with a click.

They had reached a small rectangular room in the attic. The ceiling sloped in steep contour with the roof. The room was divided lengthwise by an elbow-high counter composed of electronics bays, like squat metal lockers.

On the far side of the counter—seated, so they could see him only from the nose up—a young man acknowledged them with his eyes, all the while speaking earnestly into the phone cradled on his shoulder. Behind him, a dormer window overlooked the glittering channel.

The instant the door clicked shut behind them, an officer leaned from another doorway at the far end of the room. He wore the three bars of a full commander on his shoulders.

"Be right with you, gentlemen," he called. "The circle marks the spot." He pointed at a Plexiglas covered chart on the wall, then he disappeared back into the adjacent room.

Rodrigue recognized it as a block chart—a standard NOAA navigation chart overlaid with a grid of red lines showing how the government had parceled out the Gulf of Mexico to the oil companies. In an area designated "East Addition High Island," around a small square marked "A-237," a circle had been drawn with a grease pencil. With thumb and little finger serving as navigator's dividers, Rodrigue walked off the distance from the Galveston jetties. About seventy miles out, he figured.

The officer reappeared.

"Hello, Commander," said Phillips, stepping forward and offering his hand. "I'm the guy at the sheriff's office spoke to you awhile ago. Phillips. Bruce Phillips."

The officer took the deputy's hand. "I'm Fred Kopek. I'm group commander for this area."

He turned to Rodrigue. "Fred Kopek," he repeated.

Kopek had reddish-brown hair that grew tight to the scalp, and he was groomed almost to the point of skin irritation. Rodrigue shook his dry, talc-scented hand.

"John Rodrigue."

Kopek's eyes flickered with recognition. He had heard stories about the retired diver now running a private rescue service. They weren't all nice stories.

"He's the man I was telling you about," Phillips said quickly. "He knows the crew."

"Glad to meet you," said Kopek without conviction.

He led them to the counter and introduced them to Petty Officer First Class Peter Millet, who looked up and stretched his

177

small red mouth into a tight smile. He had a round, razor-burned face, and a short fifties haircut plastered with hair tonic and combed to the side. He turned his attention back to the phone, red lips pursing thoughtfully as he punched the numbers.

Rodrigue had known dozens like Millet. You wouldn't want him in a deck or engineering rating where too often you had to improvise. And God help those under him when he made chief. But as a middle-rated yeoman or radioman, he couldn't be beat. Routine was joy to him. Red tape was like ice cream.

Kopek reached over the counter and picked up a clipboard. He smoothed his left eyebrow and studied Millet's notes. He was from Oregon and an offshore platform seemed to him well visited by disaster, but he had his duty.

"A production report was being faxed from a platform owned by MacDonald Offshore, Incorporated, to the company's office in Lafayette, Louisiana, this morning. It came over with a message scrawled on top of the normal data: 'Mayday. Shots fired. Armed man. One dead.' The installation's standby vessel, the"—he consulted the clipboard again—"*Mermentau*, radioed the field's production office upon hearing the shots. When the office, which is on the platform, failed to respond, they radioed the information to the Lafayette office. They also reported a distinctive black-hulled sportfishing vessel tied up at the living quarters. The information was relayed to the company's headquarters in Houston, and someone in authority is on the way here now."

"Must've been them we saw as we drove up," said Phillips. "Chopper sittin' down out on the ball field out there."

"Well, gentlemen," said Kopek. "Who are we dealing with?"

"You tell him, Rod," said Phillips. "And don't leave nothing out."

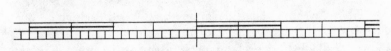

Chapter 31

L. J. MacDonald fanned at the sandy grit clinging to his tropical wool suit. The dirt wouldn't budge, so he simply stood beside the company's Jet Ranger, waiting. He was small and fragile-looking, with a full head of fluffy white hair that had been blown into a youthful-looking mop during his hasty exit from the helicopter. His unlined pink face added to the illusion of youth, but the elegant three-piece suit, the big gold cufflinks, and the impatient scowl didn't let him get away with it.

"We might as well walk, L.J.," said the beefy man who climbed out of the Bell Ranger behind him. Ralph Smith was fifty-four, dressed in a plain brown suit and sturdy oxfords, which were buffed to a high shine but showed the bulge of steel toes. He looked at MacDonald like a horse eyeing a wagonload of bricks. "I believe it's that building right over there."

"I need to stretch my legs," said MacDonald when it was evident nobody was coming. He strode across the softball field a pace ahead of Smith.

Inside the coast guard operations building, Kopek was trying to digest what Rodrigue had told him. "And you're absolutely *sure* this man is a government agent?" he said, looking at Phillips for reassurance.

"We're not absolutely sure of anything," said Rodrigue. "But this is how it looks, yeah."

Kopek diddled his eyebrow nervously. "All I can do is go by the book, and there's nothing in the book about dealing with renegade secret agents. I'm afraid he's going to get SOP treatment."

Phillips nodded. "That'd be the way to do it."

The buzzer rang. Millet consulted the closed-circuit TV. "Civilians," he said. Kopek nodded and the petty officer spoke into the intercom. The electric lock clicked and admitted the two men. MacDonald introduced himself stiffly as production vice president of MacDonald Offshore. "And this is my operations manager, Ralph Smith."

Kopek stepped forward and introduced himself in hushed tones, like a funeral director.

MacDonald waved aside any further introductions. "Let's get Ralph to the radio and see if we can't establish contact with our platform."

"We've been trying to phone them but there's been no answer," said Kopek. "Are you talking about trying to use sideband?"

MacDonald looked at Smith.

"There's one on there, yes, sir," said Smith.

"Very good, then. Let me show you to it," said Kopek. He ushered the doleful Smith into the adjacent room, where the station's radiomen worked.

A phone rang. Across the counter, Millet snatched it up. "Yes, sir," he said. "Yes, sir. Yes, sir." Growing excited. "No, sir, we'll take care of that. Hold on, sir."

Kopek reappeared at the radio room door, eyebrows arched.

"This is the MacDonald office in Lafayette," Millet said, holding his palm over the mouthpiece. "The platform just called *them*. Affirmative on the armed intruder. He wants fuel, food, and a guarantee of safe passage across the Gulf and through the Yucatán Channel into the Caribbean. They're standing by."

180

Kopek leapt to the wall chart and freehanded a grease-pencil line from Galveston through the marked circle and on across the Gulf: a southeast course bound for the channel between Mexico and Cuba.

"They still have the platform on the line?"

"Affirmative, sir."

"Find out if there's another phone line we can call in on without them having to disconnect. We sure in the hell don't want to lose them."

Millet spoke into the phone again.

"No, sir. They have to hang up on the platform first."

"Okay, tell them to hang on; query them about injuries. Oh, and see if you can get a confirmation of the vessel's name and the identity of the intruder."

Kopek remembered that Smith was in the adjacent room trying to contact the platform via single sideband. A second channel of communications could prove advantageous—but it could be disruptive, too, a show of bad faith just when the situation was stabilizing. Better play it straight, he decided. He headed for the radio room to stop Smith.

"And, Millet," he called over his shoulder. "When you get a second, brief Control." He disappeared through the door.

"Who is Control?" demanded MacDonald.

"Coast guard New Orleans," said Millet. "Regional headquarters." He reached for a red phone on the desk.

"Shouldn't the FBI be involved in this?" MacDonald asked.

"They will be," said Deputy Phillips ruefully.

Millet, with phones at both ears now, spoke briefly into the red one. He hung it up just as Kopek was reemerging from the radio room. "Control says to go ahead and contact the platform and set up a com sked."

"Ident on the intruder?"

"Negative, sir. They report one fatality by gunshot and no other injuries. Operations have been shut off."

"Tell Lafayette to advise the platform that we will be calling them at"—he glanced up at the wall clock—"ten hundred hours. Tell them to say that we have the head of MacDonald operations on hand and that we will be processing all of

181

the hijacker's demands from here. Then tell them to disconnect."

"Aye-aye, sir."

They waited in silence, studying the unyielding chart while Millet spoke into the phone. Phillips lit one cigarette with another.

"Make some more coffee, please, Millet?" Kopek said absently. He was beginning to understand the political implications of the situation. Coffee would make it seem less apocalyptic.

When the coffee stopped dripping, Millet poured everyone a cup. They all continued to wait, eyes on the big twenty-four-hour clock, until it said 10:00. Then they heard Millet's finger falling precisely on the buttons of the phone.

"Could you identify yourself, please?" he asked matter-of-factly. "Spell it, please. . . . Bravo, romeo, oscar, uniform, sierra, sierra, alfa, romeo, delta—is that correct? Are you a MacDonald employee?"

Leaning in the doorway to the radio room, Smith nodded his head glumly. "Field foreman."

Millet suddenly tensed at whatever was being said to him on the phone. "Yes, sir. But we have to know who we are dealing with. Will he identify himself?"

Kopek moved quickly to the counter and leaned over it, forcing MacDonald to stand back. MacDonald smoothed his suit coat and became intensely interested in the wall chart.

"I understand, but we'd like to know who we're dealing with," Millet continued. "No, I understand. First I need to know his demands, and then I'll relay them to the proper authority . . . yes, I understand. Hold on."

Keeping the receiver to his ear, Millet cupped his hand over the mouthpiece and spoke urgently to Kopek: "Lot of background noise. Sounds like the guy is going berserk in there."

"Tell him we'll at least need to know the name of the vessel in order to grant safe passage," said Kopek. "And advise Control . . . belay that; I'll do it myself." He rounded the counter and picked up the red phone.

182

A radioman poked his head in the room. "We got a distress working west of the Buccaneers, Milly!"

Millet gave the radioman a helpless shrug.

"Relay it to Freeport," Kopek, hand cupping the red phone, told the radioman. "You guys work all your SARs and overdues through Freeport, Sabine, and Port O'Connor while we deal with this crisis."

"It's the *Abaris*, all right," said Millet.

Kopek spoke briefly and then hung up the red phone. "Call the FBI, Millet. Houston office. They're supposed to have a SWAT team." He stiffened his back and looked around the room. "Control says to keep them advised," he said to no one in particular. "But it's our baby."

Still standing at the chart, MacDonald pulled granny-style reading glasses from his vest pocket. He stretched and peered up at the grease-pencil circle, then he shrank back down, chewing absently on an earpiece and viewing the chart as though it was in extremely bad taste.

His pale blue gaze probed the room and settled on the big, rough-looking seaman standing next to him. He was deeply tanned and had an anchor tattoo on one arm. He wore one of those white Mexican shirts and khaki shorts, and was sockless in a pair of shoes MacDonald wouldn't have let his dog chew, if he'd had a dog.

"What is your role in this?" he demanded.

"I'm a Chinese fire marshal," Rodrigue growled. Standard operating procedure was making him want to reach out and strangle somebody.

MacDonald accepted it without comment. His eyes shifted to Phillips: Lanky frame hanging by the elbows on the counter, Lyndon Johnson hat cocked back on his head, dangling cigarette, he looked like an Ace Reid cowpoke. "And you?"

"Yeah, me, too," said the deputy wearily.

"The agent-in-charge is on the way, sir," said Millet, hanging up a phone.

Wonderful, thought Rodrigue bitterly. More procedure. Meanwhile, Ahlmark's getting dangerously desperate. Or with

183

his twisted Howdy Doody grin and cryptic remarks, maybe he was a touch more than desperate—a little unstable maybe. For a man like that, there had to be other, saner options than stealing a distinctive boat like *Abaris* and then hijacking an offshore platform. It was just not rational behavior, even for a rogue CIA agent.

Rodrigue thought of Susan and his heart began to race.

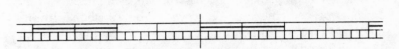

Chapter 32

Joseph Saccone entered the operations center with a keenly developed sense of having arrived. His career as special-agent-in-charge of the Houston FBI office had been a long series of pivotal arrivals.

He was a short, heavy-set man with a pockmarked face and bristly gray crew cut. His eyebrows were dark and thick and he had bluish bags under his eyes, so that he had the look of a huge, ill-tempered raccoon. He immediately took a commanding position at the right of the wall chart.

"Now, can we clear the room of anyone not directly involved in this operation?" He looked at Rodrigue and Phillips.

"We don't have an operation, yet," Kopek protested.

The coast guard officer introduced the two oil men. Saccone responded with a respectful nod.

"Deputy Phillips, there, is acting as liaison with the local authorities, who are very much involved in this."

Phillips sneaked a wink at Rodrigue, which probably meant his "liaison" role wasn't exactly official.

"And Captain Rodrigue has special knowledge of the vessel and its crew," Kopek continued.

Saccone ignored Rodrigue. "I don't have to be invited to take jurisdiction, Commander!" he barked. His eyes glittered in the darkness beneath the massive brows. "This situation carries a precedent that is clearly a threat to national security."

"Fine," Kopek said heatedly. "You want to start from scratch? We'll just clear the room and you can deal with the hijacker all by yourself."

Saccone glared at him. "I want these men cleared if they're going to be involved. How secure are these phones?"

"Against interception, you mean?" asked Kopek. "I don't know. It hasn't been a consideration."

"I'll have to risk it. I need a private office."

"This way." Kopek looked at Millet, the electric lock hummed, and the coast guard commander led the FBI man out of the operations spaces.

"Yes, sir," Millet suddenly said into the phone. "Tell him the demands are positively being processed." His tone was calm now, almost bored. As their link to Ahlmark, he served as an excellent filter for the egos and anxieties that were on the verge of creating chaos at this end.

Not for the first time in his life, Rodrigue was glad God had made people like Petty Officer Peter Millet.

Saccone blustered back through the door and offered his hand to Phillips. "OSI, huh?" he said. "That was my outfit. See Nam?"

"Some of it," answered the deputy flatly.

Saccone acknowledged with a single brisk nod, then he turned to Rodrigue. "Second time this month somebody pulled *your* record. The first time might've been the man you call Ahlmark. Why would he be checking up on you?"

"I was doing a job for Garrett Kindler," Rodrigue said.

"Garrett Kindler? Of the oil Kindlers? How is he involved?"

"It's his boat Ahlmark has commandeered," said Kopek with a trace of impatience. "Let's back up and assess the whole situation, shall we? Okay now, MacDonald personnel on the platform possibly number as many as twenty—that right, Mr. Smith?"

186

"Twenty minus four our pilot reports having carried to other platforms in the field early this morning, that's right."

"And minus one killed. So fifteen MacDonald personnel and an unverified number from the boat, possibly as many as four or five, right, Captain?"

"Five if they picked up the extra man this morning," said Rodrigue. "That'll be Kindler, his captain, Bones McKenzie, and Susan Foch, a fishing-magazine writer, and then whoever they picked up as mate—I don't know who it is. And Ahlmark, of course, who you apparently know more about than we do."

"We're operating under the assumption that he's a government agent, possibly CIA," said Kopek, giving it the inflection of a question.

"Okay, we're under a strict national-security imperative here, remember that," said Saccone. "This Ahlmark—and even the Bureau doesn't know his real name—came to our attention when Galveston PD tried to run his prints this morning. So you don't need to be making any suppositions in that regard. He is government and he is dangerous. Now, what specifically is it he's asking?"

"Fuel, food, and safe passage through the Gulf to the Caribbean. We have granted him the request for fuel and food, which they are loading onto the boat right—"

"And which you took it upon yourself to grant," MacDonald interjected.

"To keep the hijacker occupied," said Kopek defensively. "We're stalling him with the guarantee for safe passage."

Saccone waved the comment aside. "He's not just stealing a boat. They're up to something."

"He might be acting on his own," offered Phillips. He paused to light a cigarette. "Apparently the Agency was fronting a marina in Jamaica. The developer, our own Mr. Kindler, suddenly decided to cheat on a high-dollar fishing tournament here. Then somebody made an attempt on Kindler's life. And we found out that the magazine writer was fixing to expose Kindler. Could be that Ahlmark intends to cut his losses by taking Kindler and the writer out to sea and disappearing them."

The words sent an icy shock through Rodrigue.

"Who the hell tried to kill Kindler in the first place is anybody's guess," Phillips continued. "Same goes for what the hell Ahlmark's doing on an oil rig."

"Could be a double agent," said Saccone, staring at the vacant space a foot in front of his eyes. "His real agenda might be something else altogether. . . ." He looked at Kopek. "My SWAT team is mustering at this moment. If we can get everybody rounded up—not easy on a Sunday—I can have fifteen men down here in three hours. Regardless of his motivation, we can't afford to let him succeed."

"I agree," said MacDonald.

"There are fifteen lives at stake," said Smith.

"Twenty, unconfirmed," said Kopek.

MacDonald spoke directly at Saccone. "We can't let him get away with this, you know that, don't you? If we do, there won't be another safe day of oil and gas production in the Gulf of Mexico."

This was MacDonald's shining hour. He hadn't been a wildcatter like his grandfather, nor worked his way up from a derrick floor like his father. All his adult life he had been little more than a caretaker of the family company—and sometimes, in dark moments, he wondered who was caring for whom. Now, at least, he could stand up and save what he hadn't built.

"Affirmative," said Saccone quietly. "The only solution is to stall him until we can get into position, then tell him he has his safe passage, and take him as soon as he clears the platform."

"Wait a minute!" said Rodrigue. "What about the hostages?"

"Yes, what about them?" Kopek asked Saccone. "My job is to guard life, not endanger it."

"If I get on the phone to Washington and explain what's at stake, what do you want to bet your role will be? This is not a hostage situation, you understand? We can't afford to be held hostage over our domestic energy supplies. You think I'm acting on my own authority on this? Guess again."

"Wait just a goddamned minute here!" Rodrigue yelled. "You mean you're going to just fucking *sacrifice* the hostages?"

188

"We're wasting time," said Saccone to Kopek. "How soon can you roll a cutter?"

Kopek wheeled and studied a white plastic status board on the wall. "Millet, advise the *Point Baker* to prepare for sea immediately. Then brief Control." There was one benefit to being outranked at least. You didn't have to make these ugly decisions.

"*Baker*'s at Freeport," he said to Saccone. "Your men will load on there."

"How long from there to the rig?"

"Figure six hours once they clear the jetties."

"*Point Baker* advises they're taking on fuel and can cast off in an hour and a half, sir," said Millet, again with phone at each ear.

"Very well."

Saccone looked at his watch. His brow furrowed. "Be approaching dark when we get there. That might work out to our advantage."

The prospects dizzied Rodrigue. Either the coast guard would lay a cutter alongside and blast the *Abaris*, or Ahlmark would get away—disappear with Susan, Bones, and Kindler, never to be seen again.

"Hey," he said, the words coming hot on the heels of the thoughts. "I've got an idea! Fly me out to the standby boat in a helicopter. I can get aboard the *Abaris* without Ahlmark knowing it. Then you let him go like fucking J. Edgar Hoover, here, said and I can take him down without hurting the hostages. It might take a while for him to drop his guard, but it's a whole lot better than raking the fucking boat with machine-gun fire, eh?"

"How can you get over to the platform without being seen?" asked Kopek hopefully.

"Swim underwater. I'm a diver." He grinned.

"Look," said Saccone acidly, "I've got a world of respect for any man who has won the Congressional Medal of Honor, regardless of what he's done with his life since. But this is no time for any John Wayne heroics. Let the pros handle it, okay?"

"If the current and visibility are right, I can do it," Rodrigue said heatedly. "It's worth a try."

A phone rang. Millet answered it quietly. "It's for you, Agent Saccone," he said, offering the receiver.

Saccone listened briefly. "That is outstanding," he said. "Rendezvous with the coast guard cutter in Freeport, ASAP. Full tactical gear."

He hung up and glared at Kopek. "Thank you, Commander. I'll take it from here."

"Jesus Christ!" Rodrigue muttered in disbelief.

More careless blasphemy.

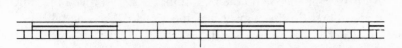

Chapter 33

Years earlier, in block no. 7 on NAVPERS Form 792, "Evaluation of Performance," a U.S. Navy lieutenant commander stationed in Panama had written of Rodrigue: "Extremely cool under fire." What he meant by "under fire" was not being shot at but the more mundane emergencies—pinched hoses, stalled compressors, and the like—faced by his diving teams in their routine work with the fleet. If there was a man to be sent into the engine room of a sunken vessel with a complicated set of instructions on which valves to close and which to open to facilitate pumping her out, Petty Officer Rodrigue was the man. What he didn't say in the semiannual evaluation was that Rodrigue was *not* the man to assign as backup diver. Idle time ate at him like saltwater on carbon steel.

Rodrigue's brain was burning for something to do as he and Phillips stumbled glumly down the stairs. They heard heavy footsteps clattering behind them.

It was the MacDonald operations chief, Ralph Smith.

"Wait up," he said. "Do you think the FBI really intends to just blast away at those people?"

"Naw," said Phillips, shaking out a fresh cigarette. "I think what he intends to do is yell at them over a loudspeaker, give ol' Ahlmark a chance to do the right thing. But if Ahlmark for some reason don't do the right thing, then, yeah, Saccone will blast them out of the water. You bet."

Smith's big sad eyes focused inward. "Why?"

"*Energy*, motherfucker," spat Rodrigue.

Smith pulled himself up and stared at Rodrigue. "I don't know what your problem is, fella, but let me tell you something about MacDonald Offshore. Old Man MacDonald—that little fart in there is not *the* MacDonald—the Old Man, he ran it like a big family. And it's still like that today. We've got a lot of people who have been with us from the beginning. And, believe me, it's our *people* that make MacDonald Offshore. We can build new platforms. But I'm not taking a chance of letting some of our people get shot up in the name of energy or anything else. I'm with you."

"Yeah?" said Rodrigue, feeling hope.

"I've got a Bell Ranger sitting right out there that'll fly a hundred and twenty miles an hour. Hell, I've got helicopters all over the Gulf. I can get you out there, if you really want to go."

Phillips glanced up the stairs. "Let's get away from here, then. We'll go someplace and plot this thing out."

"Why not?" said Smith. "Let's take the pilot with us, too. That way L.J. can't run off with the helicopter."

The MacDonald pilot was a friendly, freckled sort who smacked his chewing gum. He was wearing a western suit with a necktie and new lizard boots—had evidently been yanked out of church.

Sunday best notwithstanding, the pilot rode with Rodrigue in the back of the deputy's El Camino as far as the Kettle Restaurant, where the pilot was told to eat everything on the menu if he had to, but to stay put. Then Smith slid into the middle and the three of them squeezed into the cab.

"Now what?" asked Phillips.

"We need to get Mr. Smith to a phone," said Rodrigue. "I need to know what the current's doing in that part of the Gulf. And the visibility. If I'm going to make an open-water swim, I'll

192

need to round up some extra gear. And we need a chart to plan this all out on."

"My office lacks a little in privacy," said Phillips. "Let's just get a room at the hotel here, if there's any left."

"Good idea," said Rodrigue, happy to be doing something.

The Holiday Inn was just across the lot. Phillips sat out in the car with the engine running while Rodrigue and Smith checked in.

Far to the back, someone opened the door in the huge smoked-glass wall between the restaurant and the pool area, and the sounds of reggae music came echoing down the hall. They were doing Marley's "Guiltiness" again—a little gleefully this time, Rodrigue thought.

> Woe,
> Woe to the down-presser,
> They eat the bread of sorrow
> Woe to the down-presser,
> They eat the bread of
> Sad tomorrow . . .

Rodrigue smiled. He reminded himself to apologize properly to Smith when the time was right.

Rodrigue's cash beat Smith's credit card for the desk clerk's favor. Standing behind the clerk, arms folded, was a tall, thin man in a gray pinstriped suit—a manager, Rodrigue supposed. He was watching the transaction with misgivings, and why not? A couple of rough-looking characters checking in without luggage . . . There already had been enough excitement around there to last the rest of the summer.

Smith took his key and went to the room to make his calls. Rodrigue and Phillips drove around to the yacht basin to borrow a chart.

There was a small gathering at the folding cafeteria tables beneath the tournament-headquarters tent. Rodrigue had a thought. "Let's go see if anyone knows whether the new mate

193

actually got on the *Abaris* this morning—just so we know how many people to account for out there."

"Let's do it," said the deputy.

Phillips parked by the bait camp and they approached the tournament tent, an oasis of shade on the blistering parking lot.

"Hey, anyone here see the *Abaris* leave?" Rodrigue called.

"Uh-uh, they must've left early," said a woman seated at one of the tables. She was in her fifties or looked it, wearing too much makeup to hide the erosion caused by too much sun, and her voice was a husky whiskey rasp.

"There was a young man over here this morning who was left behind," she said. "He was telling us that they were supposed to pick him up off the end of B Row at four-thirty and they never showed up. Pretty sure it was the *Abaris* he was talking about."

"You know this young man's name?"

"I'm afraid not."

Her gaze suddenly shifted past Rodrigue, and his followed it. A fortyish man with horn-rimmed glasses and clean, starched sportfishing togs was wading angrily into the crowd. Rodrigue had seen him before but couldn't place him.

"Here's someone else who got left behind," the woman said in a sympathetic whisper.

"Oh?" said Phillips, addressing the man. "Engine trouble?"

The man's face became red. "No. *Asshole* trouble. I just can't believe it." He shook his head and walked away a few steps.

"What the hell's he talking about?" Rodrigue asked the woman at the table.

"His captain didn't show up this morning. And he's got points on the board, too. White marlin and sail." She pointed to the white plastic tote board propped up against the tent's center post.

Rodrigue remembered the scene with the white marlin at the weigh station, how the captain had rinsed himself off before posing with the fish.

"That's Morgan he's talking about," he told Phillips quickly.

"Where is Morgan now?" Phillips asked the man. His tone did not invite further indulgence in self-pity.

"I haven't the foggiest," the man said bitterly.

Rodrigue and Phillips looked at each other.

194

"You go ahead and get the chart, I'll go lookin' for him," said the deputy.

Jack Bizzell had a Mississippi River-to-Galveston chart over at the bait camp. He grudgingly pulled it out from behind a cabinet in the tiny foyer office.

"You been over to see ol' Vandegriff yet?" he asked. "He was askin' for you."

"Yeah, I saw him yesterday morning, why?"

"That was before they operated on him. They don't give him much of a chance."

"What? He looked okay to me."

"You a doctor?" Bizzell said gruffly. Then his face softened. "Naw, he wasn't healing right, way I hear it, so they cut him open and found him all eaten up with cancer. Nothing to do but sew him back up."

Rodrigue's stomach turned sour. "Jesus fucking Christ!" he said, blaspheming from the heart.

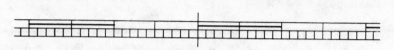

Chapter 34

Vandegriff was in ICU, lying pale and gaunt amidst a mass of tubes and wires. Rodrigue grasped his hand gently. It was cold. He just held it, saying nothing.

Finally, the old man opened his eyes. He chuckled silently. "Son of a bitch," he said in a halting whisper.

Rodrigue shook his head. "What the fuck."

"What's going on?" Vandegriff asked, wincing with pain.

"God, everything. I don't know where to begin. The god-damned weighmaster's hijacked the *Abaris*. Ahlmark. Turns out he's a CIA agent."

"Knew . . . he was something."

"He's holding an offshore platform hostage, trying to get safe passage out of the Gulf and into the Caribbean. Might be intending to go to Cuba. I'm sure they'd welcome him with open arms. But the FBI's hot on his ass."

"Guess it's out about the tournament."

"Not yet. Not entirely. But it will be, I'm afraid."

"Good. Listen—" He grappled silently with the pain. "I'm counting on you to let people know . . . to let people know I didn't like it." He sucked in a ragged breath. "I did it and that

196

can't be changed, but you know I didn't like it, don't you?" He squeezed Rodrigue's hand.

"Yeah. I know."

"Don't know how much time I have. I might not even get out of here." He smiled weakly.

"Aw, shit, Ed. You can't believe these fucking doctors. It's between you and God."

Vandegriff shut his eyes. He drew a long breath. "I'm sixty-seven years old. Shoulda been dead of old age by now."

He shook his head.

"Don't mind dyin'. Pissed at myself on accounta . . . what I was doing at the end. But I'm glad about the tournament getting found out." He paused to breathe. "Been broke all my life—sure in the fuck don't want to die rich."

Rodrigue made it across the Strand before he started sobbing. He hardly knew the old son of a bitch and here he was blubbering in broad daylight on a public street—he for whom the bell would also toll, and soon enough. He straightened up and took two deep breaths of the hot, muggy air.

He cut through the hotel lobby and went into the men's room, dampening a paper towel and wiping his face. Someone slammed through the door, pushed him aside, and vomited in the sink—couldn't even make it to the toilets. It was the thin man in the gray suit—the hotel manager who had watched so skeptically as he and Ralph checked in. He tried to wash the vomit down the drain, a disgusted look on his face.

"It's just horrible," he said, self-consciously swishing the beige water in the sink.

Rodrigue ran out through the restaurant to the pool area. The band had quit playing and everybody was standing and looking up at the second-floor breezeway. A crowd clogged the open stairway. Rodrigue shouldered his way up.

Phillips stepped out of an open room.

"Morgan didn't answer his phone, so I decided to take a look. See if maybe he hadn't skipped out."

His tone was strangely conversational. He put a cigarette between his lips and pointed down toward the lobby with it.

197

"Manager insisted on coming up with me. I sent him down to call Eckles. Another second in here and he woulda been puking all over the evidence."

Rodrigue looked inside the room and his knees nearly buckled. Both Kindler and Ahlmark were there, on the floor, covered with blood.

Blood was everywhere—the rug, the bedspread, even smeared on the TV screen. Ahlmark was facedown, right hand clutched behind him like a man trying to keep the covers from sliding off. But Kindler was unmerciful in his final pose. He sat leaning against the dresser with his legs splayed, the pant cuffs hiked to show shiny white shins. His crimson hands held his bowels, which were spilling from a ragged, bloody rip in his ruffled white shirt. He stared blindly at Rodrigue. His expression was placid.

"Jesus!" said Rodrigue, gagging.

"Looky here," said Phillips. The toe of his boot nudged a bloody, thin-bladed butcher knife, the kind used for filleting big fish.

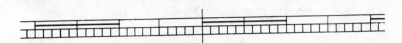

Chapter 35

Detective Sergeant Eckles came out of the room with a plastic bag containing a stubby blued pistol.

"Ahlmark had this on him. Mauser HSc three eighty automatic. In his waistband under his shirt. Didn't even have a chance to get it out." He pinched his eyes closed. "Jesus, I'm sick of the way this thing keeps jumping around."

"Well, we figured all along that it was Morgan who hired the gunman," said Phillips. "But this sure ain't no way to kill someone when you're planning to marry his wife and inherit his fortune. Might've even been self-defense."

"Yeah, let's say all that crap Leigh Kindler fed us about the CIA in Jamaica is really true," Eckles mused. "So what does a man like Kindler do when he finds out his wife and her squeeze are plotting to kill him? We have to assume that Morgan knew about both the CIA and the cheating, right? Mrs. Kindler did and she would've told him. So Kindler can't come to us for protection because if we arrest Morgan, we might find out all his dirty little secrets. So he has to take care of the problem himself—him and his secret agent buddy."

"There is a possibility," Rodrigue said numbly, "that Leigh

199

didn't know anything about it. Remember, she said that she had been using Morgan to make her husband jealous; maybe Morgan just figured she'd tumble once Kindler was out of the way."

Phillips and Eckles stared at him.

"Why didn't Kindler confront her with it, then? He acted like nothing had happened."

"He probably would've confronted her about a hundred miles out in the Gulf," said Phillips. "Him and Ahlmark. You'd be amazed how many wives get lost at sea."

Smith had his coat off and tie loosened and was talking on the phone when Rodrigue and Phillips let themselves into the room. He looked up at them and flashed a palm. He had been taking notes on the hotel stationery.

"All right," he said into the phone. "I'll see you get something out of this. I know, Les. I know, but still . . . Just stand by. I'll coordinate it from here."

He hung up and got to his feet. "Here, let's spread that chart out on the bed. Lafayette says there's a fairly strong sub-surface current out of the northwest, estimated at nearly a full knot." He found block 237 and drew a felt-tip diagram:

"Just how sub are we talking?" asked Rodrigue.

"Dead calm above forty feet," said Smith.

Rodrigue winced.

"Trouble?" asked Phillips.

"Well, yeah. If I would've had a good surface current, I could've stayed above thirty feet for most of the swim and not

200

charged it to my bottom time. Now I'll have to figure in the whole duration. I still ought to be able to make it inside the no-decompression limit, though."

"This is a dual platform," Smith said, referring to his drawing. "The north one is the production platform, south one the living quarters. That's where the boat is tied up. Personnel on one of our other platforms in the area reported that they can see beyond the second cross-members underwater. That probably means at least ninety feet of visibility—real clear, in any case."

He looked at the grim faces. "Something wrong?"

"Well, we just found our prime suspect with his throat cut," said Phillips. "Now we're back with our original prime suspect. Doesn't change anything, I don't suppose."

"Oh yeah it does, too." Rodrigue sat heavily in one of the chairs. "I think the FBI would've made some effort, at least, to get Ahlmark alive—to find out what he was up to if nothing else. Morgan, though, they'll swat like a mosquito. The problem is how to make sure I've got enough time to jump him after we leave the platform." He was just realizing how tired he was.

"You still want to try it?" asked Phillips.

"God, I've *got* to now. After what a mess he left in his room, can you imagine him just pulling over for the coast guard? Susan and Bones'll be right in the middle. What you guys'll have to do is call the coast guard after the *Abaris* leaves and tell them I'm aboard. The cutter has both speed and range on them—they can follow all the way to the Caribbean if need be—so giving me a crack at it will be a reasonable option at that point."

"We'll fly you to a field about halfway out." Smith placed a thick forefinger on a cluster of small black squares on the chart. "We're not really rigged for lowering people out of helicopters, so we'll have to land you on a platform, put you on a supply boat, and run you over to the next field. You'll catch another chopper there that'll run you all the way out."

"Yeah, but then what?" asked Phillips.

"How do you feel about jumping out of the helicopter?" asked Smith.

Rodrigue rubbed his jaw. "Shit, I don't know. How high?"

"Very low—twenty or thirty feet. *But* . . . moving. A hovering helicopter would look suspicious. I just talked to a chopper pilot in the field east of there." He smiled. "Vietnam vet. Loony as hell. He's willing to create a diversion. He'll come in and hover near the platform on the"—he consulted his diagram—"southeast side. He'll be out of rifle range, hopefully, but still close enough to draw your man's attention. Your chopper will be skimming the surface on the opposite side, up current, about a mile away. We'll plot the current and get a loran fix on a spot exactly up current. And when the man says jump, you'd better be ready. Okay?"

"Okay," said Rodrigue with more enthusiasm than he felt. He'd never liked sitting in one of the damn things—never even thought of jumping out of one.

"Goddamn it, though, can you really swim a *mile* underwater?" asked Phillips.

"If I remember the *Navy Diving Manual* right, a man can swim a half a knot just plodding along. That's better than half a mile an hour. But with a good one-knot current carrying me, I ought to be able to do a mile inside an hour without getting too far behind on my breathing."

"That water's clear," said Smith. "Won't he be able to see you?"

"Hope not. I'll have to drop down about sixty feet as I near the platform, and you'd have to be looking pretty close to see a man in a black wet suit swimming that deep. If I go any deeper, I'd probably be out of that mid-level current. Anyway, the good visibility will make it easier for me to spot the platform in case I get off course." He grinned. "I told you guys this was doable."

Phillips sucked thoughtfully at a tooth.

"However—" Rodrigue looked at Smith. "We do need a contingency to get me to a chamber after this is all over. If things go wrong, I could wind up stretching the no-decompression limit a little."

The limit didn't have much give where he was concerned. His age, accumulating bulk, and the fact that he had suffered the bends previously were all high-risk factors.

"I'll see to it," said Smith.

"And I can't be flying at any altitude if I'm bent, Ralph. If they take me in in a helicopter, it'll have to be flying low."

"I'll see to it," Smith repeated, and Rodrigue had no doubt that he would.

"Still seems awful damn iffy to me," said Phillips. "Look, even if you make it to the platform without getting lost—or, hell, *eaten*—how in the Sam Hill will you crawl up on that boat without getting caught?"

Rodrigue stood up and put his hand on the deputy's bony shoulder. "That's what luck's for. Let's go get my stuff."

Phillips parked beneath Rodrigue's house, next to the black Cadillac. He left the engine running.

"Be right back," said Rodrigue. He ran upstairs and came down with a new bottle of rum. From the glove compartment of the Caddy, he pulled out the navy-issue .45.

Phillips ignored the bottle and squinted through a wreath of smoke at the big automatic.

"You know how to use that thing?" he asked.

"I can make it go off, if that's what you mean. I can't hit Ping-Pong balls in the air."

Rodrigue pointed to the gray utility trailer sitting in the sandy yard. "Back around."

Over the years, he had accumulated some scuba gear, including double tanks on a common yoke. He didn't particularly like scuba, preferring the comfort and security of the surface-supplied full-face mask, but he had assiduously maintained all of the contents of the trailer, so everything was ready to go.

What he didn't have—had not had a use for—were a compass, depth gauge, and diver's watch. A commercial oil-field diver didn't generally do much lateral traveling underwater, let alone navigating. His depth was sensed by a pneumofathometer hose that was part of his lifeline and monitored on the surface by his tender. The tender also kept his time, using any kind of timepiece he happened to have.

There were several deputies who were sport divers. Phillips contacted one by radio and they met him at his home in Hitchcock, a mainland village a short drive up the freeway from the causeway. The deputy went into the garage and dug through his diving gear for the compass and depth gauge.

The watch was his personal wristwatch, which he peeled off with a display of misgiving. It didn't help to see that Rodrigue could only fasten the watch to his wrist by the last eyelet, with not enough of the watchband left over to tuck under the buckle.

"You *will* take good care of that, won't you?" he said.

"I certainly hope so," Rodrigue said sincerely.

They rode in silence to Scholes Field, the municipal airport, where Smith had said to meet the helicopter. Finally, Rodrigue reached for the rum. He held it up and, with arched eyebrows, wordlessly asked Phillips whether he wanted a drink.

Phillips took the bottle and held it at arm's length, examining the label. "What, just straight out of the bottle?" he asked.

"Hey, I'd offer you hors d'oeuvres if I had any."

The deputy chuckled sadly. "Why not," he said. Steering with his forearms, he unscrewed the lid and took a moderate pull from the bottle.

Rodrigue took the bottle back and examined the contents in the harsh midday light. He shouldn't drink, he knew. It would make him all the more susceptible to the dreaded decompression sickness—the bends—the literal boiling of nitrogen in his body like bubbles in a Coke when the top is popped.

It had been painful, decompression sickness when he got it off Porto Alexandre. It seized him in the right knee with a dull ache that became worse and worse until it demanded all of his attention.

Poor Jean-Marc had felt little pain. On the contrary, he felt less and less of anything until only his head was left alive, and the rest of his body just numb meat.

It was the result of one tiny little nitrogen bubble that, instead of attacking a joint, or causing an itchy rash, or making him tired and irritable, chose to explode in his spinal cord. It could as easily have lodged in the lungs or heart. It could have killed him. And if it had, Rodrigue probably wouldn't have the fear of the bends he had today. Some things were worse than death.

204

What made the bends especially dreadful was its unpredictability, not only in the range of symptoms from merely inconvenient to fatal but more especially in the mysterious criteria the malady had for picking a victim. Some things, like age and fitness, could be labled plus or minus. But there were so many hidden factors—or maybe it was pure chance—that you found one young, healthy diver stretching the navy tables for years with no ill effects, and another just like him getting the bends after one or two dives crowding the limits.

Cold increased your chances of getting the bends. Exertion increased your chances. Excess body fat increased your chances. Being over forty increased your chances. Having had the bends before dramatically increased your chances.

And alcohol consumption increased your chances, too. It dehydrated you and made your tissues absorb more nitrogen. Ergo, he shouldn't drink. But the alcohol he was consuming was more likely to rot his liver than give him the bends, so what the hell. He raised the bottle.

"*El hígado no existe,*" he said softly. The liver does not exist.

Phillips accepted the unintelligible toast with a nod.

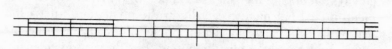

Chapter 36

Flying a helicopter took four arms and three legs, it seemed to Rodrigue, and total concentration. He left the gum-smacking pilot to his work. Rodrigue had flown in helicopters to oil fields all over the world, yet every safe landing was a miracle.

He watched the baked land and the olive-colored shallows and the cluttered offshore anchorage slip by below. There was a glinting blue-black panorama as they flew over deep water. A tiny speck of white at the apex of diverging scratches on the surface was a sportfishing boat, and the little squares of light gray were oil- and gas-production platforms—a vast archipelago of steel islands with Coke machines and subscriptions to *Playboy*.

They flew on and on. He was lulled by the sensation of floating effortlessly over the occasional platform or vessel. But then the pilot made some quick moves, the engine changed pitch, and Rodrigue's heart tried to leap out of his thorax.

They were descending, aiming for a tiny yellow-and-gray square on an equally tiny structure below.

"This is the part I hate," said Rodrigue—the first words he had spoken since they left the ground.

The pilot laughed. "Me, too," he said.

The platform loomed larger, and then the fear of missing altogether became fear that they would wind up against the crane or tangled in a radio mast. One freak gust of wind was all it would take. . . .

The pilot put the machine down smoothly, however. Rodrigue looked at his watch; the flight had taken less than thirty minutes. Three men in blue MacDonald coveralls ran to greet them, ducking under the invisible rotor.

"Boat's waiting!" yelled one of the men. "Let's get your gear and get you down there!"

A Billy Pugh net was sitting on the main deck, dangling from the crane like a lank, skeletal tepee. Named for the man who invented it, it was the standard personnel net of the offshore world—a big, hard-foam doughnut with a canvas center and a cone of large-mesh cargo netting attached to the crane's cable. The men loaded Rodrigue's tanks and dive bag in the center, and Rodrigue, from long practice, stood on the edge of the doughnut, outside the net, with one arm looped through it, and waggled his index finger in the standard signal for "take 'er up."

The crane operator jerkily picked the net off the deck and swung it over the side, still ninety feet from the surface of the Gulf. The two-hundred-foot supply boat looked like a toy below. Slowly—except for the occasional two-foot plunge when the cable unwound into a valley on the winch spool—the net was lowered to the boat's back deck.

Deckhands helped him unload the net, which was alternately stretching and collapsing with the long, low swells. Rodrigue walked over to the bulwark and breathed in the sweet salt air. This was home. The empty net rose, and the boat, belching clouds of black diesel smoke from her aft stacks, pulled away from the looming platform.

"How long's it gonna take us to get to the other field, Cap?" Rodrigue asked a boatman.

"—'Bout an hour."

"Someplace I can lie down? I need a nap."

"Well, you can stretch out right there in the galley if you don't mind the light."

"Nah, that'll be fine."

After he showed Rodrigue to the cabin door, the boatman turned and walked back toward his companion, cupping his hand beneath his crotch as though he were lugging a pair of cannonballs. The crew of the supply boat knew a little something of Rodrigue's mission.

"Time, Cap," said the boatman. The diesels rumbled loudly as the captain lined the stern up with the platform. Rodrigue sat up and rubbed his eyes. The padded galley bench was the most comfortable bed he had ever slept on. He hated to leave it.

Coffee smell hit him like a warm shower. A little wiry man with a gap-toothed smile offered a cup.

"Das frash, *neg*," said the little Cajun.

"*Bien merci*," said Rodrigue. It was dark roast, with sweet condensed milk, just the way he liked it.

The galley was like a comfortable cave, the paneled walls were darkened by years of greasy smoke, and the air conditioner was working overtime. Walking directly onto the shimmering steel deck was like stepping into hell. The sky was blindingly white and the heat felt like a slap. . . .

Rodrigue loved it. It was like old times. His heart raced a little and he felt energized. He wore that old sassy grin that was far too rare these days.

They had already loaded his gear into the personnel net. Rodrigue hopped on and gave the go-ahead signal. The crane operator hoisted him slowly alongside a platform with a derrick towering overhead—a working rig. As he rose and the main deck fell away below, a jutting helipad came into view. And sitting on it was another Bell Ranger.

It looked incomplete, gaping. . . . One door was missing.

He wouldn't think about it. There was too much to be done.

But he'd *have* to think about it, eventually. There were always those ugly little pockets of time when there was nothing to do but think.

Well, goddamn it, he'd think about it *then*. . . .

"Want to dress inside?" asked a khaki-clad man with a blue MacDonald ball cap.

"You the pilot?"

208

"Yeah."

"John Rodrigue." Rodrigue extended his hand. He liked to be on a first-name basis with these fellows.

"Sam Soileau," said the pilot with a puzzled smile. "You wanna dress inside?"

"Sure, lead the way."

It was a dormitory, dimly lit. Sleeping sounds came from the night shift, blanket-covered forms scattered around the bunks. Rodrigue gave his wallet and folded bills in a clip to the cook, a big black man with a ready grin. He neatly folded his clothes and stacked them on an unclaimed top bunk.

He pulled on the black neoprene pants with so much difficulty, he had second thoughts about being able to make the swim. A wet suit had to fit snugly to be effective, but this was ridiculous. Retirement was turning him into a balloon. And it wasn't so much that he had to struggle to get into the suit but that the struggle left him panting—which didn't bode well for someone about to swim a mile sucking air through a little rubber hose. But it was too late to worry about that now.

He put on his weight belt and tucked his cotton work gloves under it, strapped the compass and depth gauge to his arm, and hung his old brass-sheathed navy diver's knife around his neck. When he came to the .45 auto, he realized he had forgotten something. He padded into the gleaming galley.

"Cookie, you got a big Ziploc bag I can have?"

The cook eyed the oily pistol and raised his hands. "Man, you can have anything I got."

"Okay, I'll take a mess of snapper fried light as soon as I get back, but right now, all I want's a Ziploc bag."

Rodrigue put the .45 into the bag and sucked the air out. He slid the sealed package inside his already-crowded wet suit jacket and zipped it up. He was ready to go.

"Fasten this seat belt until it's time for you to get your tanks on!" the pilot yelled over the rotor noise. He grinned nastily. "That way, you don't get out too soon!" He lifted the craft up, then peeled dizzily away from the platform, circling and climbing.

"Not gonna get on the deck until we're close!" he yelled. "Be a little while!"

Terrific, thought Rodrigue. His eye drifted toward the gaping hole at his side. The helicopter seemed to roll that way with the weight of his gaze, and Rodrigue felt gravity tugging him toward the door. How in the world would he get his gear on without falling out?

The pilot pulled out a chart and unfolded it in quick, jerky movements, hand never leaving the joystick.

Need some help? Rodrigue thought frantically.

"I'm gonna take 'er down now!" yelled the pilot. "Better get ready!"

Surprisingly, it was no problem to shoulder the tanks and gather his fins and mask. He hadn't done this sort of thing before, but he knew how to do it. The mask strap was looped around his left upper arm and the mask hugged against his side—lose that and the job was finished before it was begun. Fins were held the same way by the right arm. His left hand would hold the regulator to his mouth. His right hand, grasping the tank harness, would tug the double tanks downward, keeping the valve from slamming into the back of his head as he crashed into the water.

He looked out the open door; the glinting surface was streaking by below—*way* below, it seemed. Rodrigue made a palm-down signal to go lower.

The pilot shook his head. "I don't want to go in there with you! I'll slow down a little and kick the tail to the side so you don't get a haircut on the way down!" He grinned devilishly.

Son of a bitch, thought Rodrigue. Did everyone think he did this for a living?

"Get ready!" said the pilot, eyeing the twinkling loran readout.

Rodrigue pulled on his gloves. Through the pilot's window, far off, twin platforms stood darkly against the silvery sea. He could barely see the white of *Abaris*'s cabin poking out from behind one of the platforms.

"Get ready! *Go!*"

Whatever his misgivings, a commercial diver did not hesitate to get in the water—that was unthinkable. Rodrigue set the bezel

210

on the borrowed wristwatch and threw himself into space. He had a moment to realize that it was actually a relief to be out of the helicopter, and then he was tumbling violently, nostrils stinging.

He quickly pulled the mask on and snorted to clear the water out of it. The agitated surface was fifteen, twenty feet above. He exhaled in order to sink slowly while he pulled on the fins, then he crooked his arm to display the compass and depth gauge, and began a slow, hip-rolling kick—the better to favor his delicate knee—on the heading he hoped would take him right into the mossy, encrusted ribs of the platform.

It was good to be in the familiar thick, cool environment again.

But he was heartily sorry he'd cussed God and skipped Mass that morning.

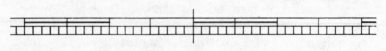

Chapter 37

The afternoon sun gave the pastel world its only texture, a faint radiant twinkle. It was like swimming in Paul Newman's eye.

There was nothing ahead; nothing below but darkening blue mystery. Rodrigue knew that if he rolled over and looked up, the surface would be a liquid mirror, but he didn't have the luxury of sight-seeing; he had to concentrate on the two dial faces on his right forearm.

The compass particularly needed his attention. If it wasn't held at just the right angle, the needle would lock up and lie to him. Only a constantly swinging needle was to be believed.

Maintaining depth was no problem—not yet. Later, when he would go deeper, the closed-cell foam of his suit would compress and lose some buoyancy. But then his tanks would be lighter from the loss of pressure, so maybe the two would even themselves out.

One of the arts in the science of scuba diving, Rodrigue knew, was being able to achieve neutral buoyancy at any given depth. It wasn't something commercial divers had to worry about, generally. More often than not, he had wanted to be heavy, the better to manhandle a high-pressure jetting hose ditching under a pipeline, or to keep a cutting torch gouging away at an abandoned wellhead.

The sensation, in the brief flickers of inattention he permitted himself, was different from the familiar one of hanging alongside a towering subsea platform. That was flying; this was loneliness. It was as though the entire miracle of creation had been erased except for him and the color blue. It could've been disheartening, even frightening, but for the fact that concentrating on a swinging needle to the exclusion of everything else was the sort of thing Rodrigue did best.

That was how he got into these messes, by concentrating on whatever it was that was being dangled in front of him—in this case an untouchable blonde. It made him more susceptible than most to sleight of hand.

It was the reason he hadn't questioned the decision to do stage decompression in the water instead of using the chamber on that job in Africa when he and poor Jean-Marc got bent. He should've, but he hadn't. He was too much like a cobra watching a mongoose.

They were working in an field off the lower coast of Angola. The divers lived in huts on the beach and furloughed in South Africa when the weather was too rough to work, which it often was. The job was taking a long time.

And the ongoing bush war made it a tense situation when they were working. It reminded Rodrigue of Vietnam because you couldn't tell who the enemy was.

One night as he had lain sweating on his cot, an unseen hand had reached up and removed an empty beer bottle from the row of bottles on the window ledge. Many long minutes later, another bottle disappeared. His burglar alarm was being painstakingly deactivated. Rodrigue watched the process with fascination and growing respect, but when the last bottle had been removed and the dark silhouette filled the window, he calmly raised his .45 and shot. The body vanished before the soldiers came with the lantern.

The job had been hanging sacrificial anodes in a large, widespread field of deep-water oil-producing platforms, nailing them into place with a tool that used .38-caliber blanks to fire high-tensile steel fasteners. The divers worked in pairs, one manhandling the barrel-shaped anode into place, relaying instructions to the crane operator on the platform to align the curved steel plates with the leg, and the other diver wielding the potentially lethal Ramset Tool. They were operating from a barge and doing their stages in the water—hanging off a line at twenty and ten feet—while the chamber stayed on one of the platforms for emergencies.

After a decade in the oil fields, Rodrigue was used to cutting corners with his safety. In the navy, where he had learned to dive, these kinds of operations always were done with utmost caution. But then, the navy didn't have to show a profit—nor did it pay nearly as well. So, again, he accepted the risk—but this time not knowing the full extent of it.

The chamber was broken. And the nondiving diving supervisor—a new management position created by the corporation to break up the hegemony of the divers—hadn't told anyone. He didn't want to halt the work until new relief valves and backup gag valves could be shipped all the way up from Capetown.

Then came the storm. Rodrigue and poor Jean-Marc were in the water. The crazy, grinning Frenchman had demonstrated blood-chilling disregard for safety in using the Ramset Tool, so he was manhandling the anodes despite Rodrigue's superior size and strength. The fact that poor Jean-Marc had been exerting himself was why he took the harder hit, everyone figured.

The perfidy of the bends was an ugly fact of life in the oil fields. Nearly all commercial divers had been bent at one time or another, usually exhibiting joint soreness, an itchy rash, or some other mild symptom. But the occasional serious hit like poor Jean-Marc's was enough to keep them from taking the malady lightly. In the old days, when the companies were small and the divers took turns ramrodding the jobs themselves, no one would've dreamed of purposely putting a diver in jeopardy of getting the bends.

The Thompson supervisor hadn't had any reason to do it. It wasn't as if they had to shut down a platform and cost the oil company millions. They were only doing preventive maintenance and the flow of oil would've continued unabated. Sure,

214

the divers and tenders would've continued to be paid while they were sitting around waiting for the parts for the chamber, just as they were when they had to wait out the frequent storms. But standby pay was at a reduced scale, a drop in the bucket compared to the staggering cost of offshore oil production.

Maybe the oil company would've bounced them off the job rather than pay standby, but so what? Jobs went begging in those days.

The diving supervisor had done it, according to his own deposition, for the simpleminded reason that he didn't think anything would go wrong—total ignorance of the second law of thermodynamics, not to mention Murphy's Law. It baffled Rodrigue. He finally decided that that was what you got when you let a nondiver run a job.

The supervisor was fired, of course, but he went right to work for a British company in the North Sea.

For *his* arrogance, Kindler hadn't gotten off so easily. And now Morgan . . .

There it was again—*why*? He could certainly understand the downtrodden rising up and bashing heads now and then—and he supposed he even could understand the wild excesses of the very rich, operating as they did without the constraints of normal people. But the Morgans and Rodrigues of the world got along just fine doing the things they had taught themselves to do.

Morgan could've had any woman on the beach, including Leigh Kindler, so why didn't he just take her? Why did he think he had to have Kindler's money, too? After all, a man could eat only so many seafood platters in his life, could drink only so many bottles of rum, wear so many shirts. What in the hell was he going to do with all the rest of it?

And for Christ's sake, why does a pharmacist with a wife and two young kids climb aboard a boat to kill someone for money?

There was a silvery flicker of movement ahead. Rodrigue shifted his clasped hands to look at the borrowed diver's watch on his left wrist. The minute hand was almost to the forty-five-minute mark on the bezel; it was time for him to sound.

He had long been vaguely aware of a humming, the underwater sound of a platform with diesel engines sending their vibrations down through a hollow steel skeleton. It had come on so gradually that it was impossible to say when it began. Now faint groans and clanks were added, but sounds carry far underwater. The movement he had seen might have been a predatory fish milling around just outside the sheltering legs of the structure. But he couldn't see anything now except unending blue.

Rodrigue's knee ached and he was sucking hard on the regulator. He leveled off at sixty feet. The world was a shade darker, noticeably colder, and he found he had a tendency to keep sinking. He had to divide his concentration between the compass and the depth gauge, and he had to work harder to keep the needle on sixty. His knee was really starting to nag him. His gaze flicked unnecessarily back to the watch.

Time dragged on. He was coming up on his no-decompression limit, and still no platform. The sounds were much louder, seemingly overhead, but underwater you could never tell. Could he be swimming past it? No way he could surface now without jeopardizing the plan. His knee felt as if it were packed with ground glass, but he ignored it—something he knew he could not do for long.

How much air did he have left? Ordinarily, he would have plenty with the twin tanks, but he had been breathing heavily since he'd reached sixty feet, fighting the tendency to sink. He wasn't used to swimming underwater marathons.

He wished now he would have borrowed some more modern equipment—a regulator with an underwater pressure gauge, for example—and, God, an inflatable flotation vest! If he had a vest, he could blow a few puffs into it and not have to struggle so to stay at this depth. If he tired and started sinking, he'd have to try to work one of the four-pound weights off his belt. He'd try it now except he would surely go off course.

It was coming to that, though. His knee was killing him. And here was a shark cruising by, a big hammerhead, aloof, uninterested. It circled widely to the left and was a tiny smudge on the radiant blue curtain long before it disappeared.

The depth gauge showed seventy-two feet; the deputy's watch showed fifty-nine minutes had elapsed. That was it—he was al-

216

ready technically into decompression time, eight minutes at ten feet. Nobody memorized the decompression tables on purpose—it was too dangerous to trust to memory what you ought to be looking up—but Rodrigue couldn't help himself. He struggled to get back up to sixty. He was winded now and the scuba regulator was starving him for air. He yearned for a nostril-flaring blast from his Kirby-Morgan's free-flow.

The dive tables weren't designed for multilevel swims like this, so he had some grace. How much, he didn't know. And where was the platform?

To hell with it! He unfastened the weight belt and pulled it around into his field of view. The cotton gloves made it difficult to work the stiff web belt through the slots in the first weight; he should've taken them off before unslinging the belt. He should've rigged some sort of quick-release for each of the weights before he started the swim. *Shoulda. . . ?* Ever try to eat a bagful of shouldas? old Peg used to say. Hada-oughtas and ifs? Not very nourishing.

His thoughts had big pieces missing from them. His mind was becoming as blank and white as a sheet on a clothesline in the hot, hot sun. Almost blindingly white.

He was getting dyspneic and he felt the panicky twinge that never helped any situation, let alone a problem with breathing.

And to make matters worse, here came the shark again.

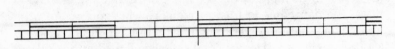

Chapter 38

As he homed in on the distant structures, Les Bruning felt once again the peculiar coldness of combat. It must've had something to do with the heart, because it always radiated from the muscles of his upper back down into his upper arms, and from his rib cage—past his stomach, which was doing its own thing—down into the large muscles of his thighs.

Men didn't usually talk about it, but when they did, they sometimes described it as an "adrenaline rush." That didn't seem right to Bruning. While the feeling radiated, it didn't really seem to be any kind of an outpouring. Actually it was more like a deprivation, as if part of his nervous system was being temporarily shut down so that the resources could be utilized elsewhere.

He liked it. It made him feel focused, calm, deadly.

Vietnam was like some kind of cruel narcotic. It had been hell on earth when he was there, but it had expanded him in ways that left him empty afterward. The hell of war was that nothing else could ever seem so vital.

He wondered who was dead. He knew them all—liked them all. Even Raymond. And he felt a peculiar, cold kind of rage against whoever it was on that platform. He supposed if he had been a grunt, he would be wanting to chew the guy up with an M16. Instead, he concentrated on flying a Bell Jet Ranger straight into danger.

Broussard heard the helicopter approaching but he didn't say anything. He would wait until the man with the gun heard it too, so he wouldn't think it was some kind of a trick.

There were two of them, but the other one was a hostage from the boat. Another hostage, a woman, was tied up on board, he had said.

He was a foreigner—a Britisher, Broussard figured. He went from calm and almost relaxed to a screaming fit in the bat of an eyelash, so sudden moves and even attempts at conversation were not a good idea.

They were in the galley, the man with the gun at the door, where he could look out from time to time. Broussard was nearby, holding the phone. Everybody else, including the man from the boat, was crammed back against the freezer and the refrigerator at the other end of the room.

Finally he heard it. He head jerked back and forth slightly. "Hear that? What's that?"

Broussard pretended to be listening. "Helicopter. Probably one of ours didn't get the word."

"That's a pile of crap! You tell them to get that fuckin' bird outta here!"

"Broussard here," Broussard said into the phone.

"Tell him we're still waiting on word from Washington," replied the coast guardsman.

"There's a helicopter coming. He wants it turned back."

"Helicopter? It's not one of ours. Tell him it's not one of ours."

Broussard set the phone down. "It's not one of theirs. Probably one of ours."

The man motioned with the muzzle of the gun for Broussard to step back toward the rest of the men. Then he opened the door and looked out for an instant.

"One of yours, all right. Where's the radio?"

"On the other platform."

"All right, mate. Here's what we're going to do: You're going to go over there and get on the horn and tell him to get lost. You"—he indicated the others—"are going to file outside behind me. Every one of you. I can count. Let's go."

Broussard started out the door first but the man grabbed him by the shirt sleeve.

"Wait a minute!" he said. "Wait for me."

He backed out the door, gun leveled. Broussard followed into the blinding afternoon light.

It was Les Bruning, Broussard knew instinctively. He was approaching very slowly from the east, still several hundred yards away—hovering now, it seemed.

"You men line up there—quick!" yelled the man with the gun. He spoke to Broussard: "I'll give you two minutes to get him away from here, and then I'm going to start shooting these men, one a minute. Wait—"

Broussard halted.

"After he's gone, you have two minutes to get back here or the same thing happens. Go!"

The foreman's chest was burning and his breath felt as if it were drawn through smoking coals by the time he reached the office. He fumbled with the mike, noticed with surprise that his hand was trembling wildly.

"Les! Les! Go back! This is Broussard. You copy? You copy?"

"What's he doin' out there, Bruce?" asked Les.

"He's gonna starting shooting them if you don't leave. Get outta here!"

"He means it?"

"Yes! Get outta here!"

"I'm gone."

But the helicopter was still hovering off the platform when Broussard ran out of the office. He was running down the stairs to the production deck, where the catwalk led to the living quarters, when he felt the horrible squeezing in his chest. He stumbled down to the deck and sank to his knees.

He couldn't die now. If he did, the whole crew would die with him. He pulled himself up and staggered past the mute Christ-

220

mas trees—the clusters of valves and gauges that had been his life's work.

The helicopter was just sitting out there. Morgan decided to take the one on the right, the last one to come out the door. He must be the cook; he had an apron on which he kept wiping his hands.

Bastard was looking right at him. Everybody else was looking up at the helicopter, but this bastard was looking right at him. He had a pleading look, like a dog. It made Morgan sick. *It's you or me, you bastard!* he thought, as he raised the rifle. . . .

Suddenly the helicopter spun around and took off, and the men cheered softly. Damn lucky for you, cook.

"All right, now," he called. "Everybody settle down. As soon as your mate gets back here, we'll all go inside again and get comfortable."

The foreman didn't return, though. Morgan looked at his watch. He hadn't been keeping time—just going by gut feeling. Now he started. . . .

"Where is he?" he asked no one in particular. Two minutes had elapsed since he started watching the time. "Where the hell is he?"

"It's a long way over there," said one of the men. "You gotta go down to the—"

"Shut up!" Morgan barked, raising the rifle threateningly. He was feeling the panic of uncertainty, like when a radar blip suddenly appears off your bow. He stripped the wrapper off one of his plastic-tipped cigars and stuffed the cigar into his mouth, wagging it up and down as his jaw flexed nervously.

What could he be doing? Do they keep any arms on here? Maybe there were others over there all along. . . .

But it *was* a long way over there. . . .

"What's his name?" Morgan demanded, looking at the man who had spoken.

"Harold Broussard."

"*Harold!*" The shout echoed against the steel water tank.

"Harold, you better get over here! The cook dies first!"

Morgan thought that was kind of amusing. He was glad he

221

still had a sense of humor. He glanced at his watch again: five minutes. . . .

He fished out his butane lighter and thumbed it. His thumb was sweaty and the lighter didn't light. Six minutes now . . .

The lighter refused to light and Morgan threw it at the cook, who dodged it as though it were a hand grenade. Seven minutes . . .

He had about made up his mind to go ahead and shoot the cook when the foreman came up the stairs. He was white and making an expression like a man tasting quinine.

Then he fell flat on his face.

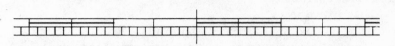

Chapter 39

The platform was faintly visible beyond the lazily approaching hammerhead. Rodrigue could see one thick vertical leg stabbing into the blue darkness below. It bristled with horizontal and diagonal cross-members whose far ends faded and were absorbed in the distant blueness.

He finally got the lead weight off the belt and it dropped like a leaf, its flats reflecting the dimming sunlight as it flipped over and over. The shark exhibited immediate curiosity, arching from side to side in a display of body language that, to a free-swimming diver, is not a good sign.

Grasping the belt in both hands, Rodrigue swam toward the hulking gray-blue tower.

The shark cruised below him—or was *he* going up? He glanced at the depth gauge: right on sixty. It was about time for things to go right. He concentrated on making smooth, powerful kicks. Sharks liked their food weak and erratic. Fifty feet to go until he reached the comparative safety of the underwater structure.

Forty-five feet . . .

Forty . . .

223

Something brushed by him. Or was it his imagination? He decided to ignore it.

Thirty-five feet . . .

The hammerhead appeared again, filling Rodrigue's faceplate with ugly iron gray for an instant. It moved ahead effortlessly, angling off toward the right to avoid the platform and then abruptly circling back like a puppy who wants to play. This time, it came directly at him, veering off at the last second and leaving him with an impression of a mile of crosscut saw.

But it was just a few more kicks, just a few more . . . strong, smooth kicks and never mind the pain. Then he was at the platform leg, mottled with moss and barnacles. Then he was inside the structure, in the dark skeletal shadow, with angular patches of rich blue light. Fuck you, shark.

Looking up, Rodrigue could see the bottom of the *Abaris* bulging the shimmering surface of the water like a dark welt. Luckily enough, he had found the south corner of the living quarters. He wouldn't have enjoyed swimming that open two hundred yards between the platforms with a fractious shark shadowing him. Luckier still was the fact that he found the platforms at all—another couple of yards off course and he would have been drifting past into open water. He shuddered at the thought.

He swam just inside the platform, being careful to stay at depth. With his lighter weight belt and tanks, he might tend to ascend too rapidly now. Better to do it coming straight up a leg, where he could control it.

He had been an hour and twelve minutes in the water, with a maximum depth of seventy-two feet; he needed to linger at the ten-foot depth for—his prodigious memory clicked—twenty-three minutes to adhere to the letter of decompression law. But there was no way. He probably didn't have the air, and he certainly didn't have the time. The coast guard and the FBI had to be closing in on them. He would just have to hope the tables were conservative enough that he wouldn't take a hit—or that he could overpower Morgan quickly and get to a chamber if he did.

Twenty feet under the surface, Rodrigue straddled a crossmember and draped his weight belt in front of him. He unfastened the harness and pulled the twin tanks over his head, rebuckling the waist strap around the cross-member. He took one last breath from the regulator, then rose cautiously to the surface, dampening his ascent with a bear hug on the barnacle-encrusted leg of the platform. Rapid ascents inside the maze of a platform were dangerous enough, even if your body wasn't charged with nitrogen.

He broke the surface and gulped air silently, suddenly aware that the barnacles had shredded the arms and legs of his wet suit and sliced into his flesh. Great, something else to worry about—blood.

Barnacles were terrific at producing spectacularly nasty infections, too . . . but why was he cluttering his mind with these paltry threats? It wasn't like him.

There was nobody in view on the boat. Nobody in view through the open-grate landing above. He pulled off his diving mask and searched the network of stairs and catwalks leading up to the first deck—nobody.

Rodrigue had taken his share of desperate gambles and he knew there was one rule for success: Do the hard thing and do it quickly. He dropped his mask and fins and pulled the plastic-covered automatic from his wet suit. He ripped the Ziploc bag open and clasped his gloved hand around the checkered plastic grips. It felt good. He jacked a round into the chamber and put the pistol on safety.

The *Abaris* rose and fell almost imperceptibly on the low swells. The steady rhythm was magnified by the nylon dock line that connected the boat by one stern cleat to the low platform landing. It slackened and bowed toward the surface, then slowly tautened and stretched, shedding water in a fine mist. When it bowed again, Rodrigue caught the line with his left hand. He put his left foot in the blubbering exhaust port and let the taut-ening line pull him up. And when the boat reached the end of its leash with a small jerk, he lunged, slinging his aching right leg over the wide transom.

He smashed into a steel drum slippery with diesel fuel. There was another drum on the other side of the fighting chair. Rodrigue ducked behind them for an instant, peeking up at the looming platform—no sign of life. Painfully, he gathered his legs beneath him and lunged at the door, jerking it open and stumbling into the cold, dark saloon. He moved quickly past the bar and galley and found Susan sitting on the divan, bound hand and foot, looking more like a little girl than ever. One big tear ran slowly down her cheek.

"My God!" she said, eyes widening. "It's the U.S. Cavalry!"

Rodrigue stepped quickly into the galley, where the cabinets would hide him from anyone entering from the cockpit. He looked regretfully at the wet footprints he had left on the white carpet. But they wouldn't matter. His plan was simple: If Morgan headed for the saloon, he would shoot him as soon as he appeared in the door; if he went to the bridge, he would sneak up behind him and try to take him alive.

"Where's Bones?" he asked. His eye, too, was watering—whether because of the weblike pains now affecting his whole right leg or because he was so glad to see her, he couldn't have said.

"On the rig—" She choked down a sob. "It's Harry Morgan, Rod. He took the boat in the night."

"Bones okay?"

"Yeah, he's okay. Gonna leave him. Morgan. Just have me to watch, he said."

"What kind of gun does he have? A rifle?"

"I don't know. Yeah, a rifle. He got it out from under here and wrapped it up in a windbreaker. He—"

Rodrigue had motioned for silence. He had thought he heard feet scraping on the platform's landing grate. But it was just his imagination. The platform made so much noise, he would be unlikely to hear Morgan until he thumped down on the cockpit sole. Then it would be a matter of staying cool and letting Morgan fill the saloon door. . . . And hoping he didn't notice the wet footprints before Rodrigue could shoot. . . .

"What the shit is all this about, Rod?" Susan asked, suddenly angry. "Morgan hasn't said more'n a dozen words."

"Morgan and Leigh were plotting to kill Kindler and make it look like I did it. Kindler found out." That was enough for now.

"What are you going to do?" She looked scared.

"I'm going to shoot him. I'm not going to hesitate." He was lecturing himself.

"You mean it's just *you*?" She looked even more scared.

"No, the rest of the cavalry is on their way. I'm an advance scout. Helicopter dumped me off about a mile away."

"How'n the hell'd you get over here—*swim*?"

He grinned. "Quite a feat, eh?"

She sighed and shook her head. "I ain't believin' this! This is *crazy*!"

"We might not be out of it yet, but believe me, things are looking up. You just sit there quietly and act like nothing's happened."

"Jesus!" She rolled her eyes.

He didn't realize how tough it would be to take his own advice once he noticed the sensation of tightness, like leather straps shrinking around his chest. He seemed short of breath, but who wouldn't be? That tightness, though—could it be a damn heart attack?

Or nitrogen bubbles erupting in his lungs. . . ?

Rodrigue looked down at his chest. Rips in the wet suit revealed glistening blood. It they had been coral instead of barnacle cuts, he could suspect a reaction to some kind of toxin. No, it had to be a nitrogen hit in the lungs—the "chokes"—the manifestation of the bends most feared by divers because of the horrible helpless feeling of being strangled from within.

And *Abaris* tugged gently at her leash—now sinking slowly between the long, flat swells, now rising again, now coming to a soft halt when the line stretched taut. Behind him, Susan sobbed once.

He still had time, he told himself. He could still draw a breath. And they had to have given Morgan the go-ahead by now. It was just a matter of moments; he would kill the son of a bitch the instant he entered the saloon, and then they would scoot him off to a chamber and everything would be all right.

Everything would be all right. . . .

It rang hollow. *Every*thing was *never* all right. Why was his hand trembling?

227

The .45, an old friend, seemed both too heavy and too small, ungainly. He knew better than to thumb down the safety. He was nervous and excited and far too likely to pull the trigger accidentally.

He was falling to pieces. It wasn't three years ago—or maybe it was, but just barely—that he had lain perfectly still and watched a lifelong warrior creep up on him, intent on killing him brutally, and he had been as calm as though it were a mosquito looking for a place to bite. Now he was shaking. Had he changed that much?

No, he wasn't shaking; he was shivering. It was the cold. They had turned the air conditioner on high again, and it was like a walk-in freezer in here. His wet suit ought to have been more than enough insulation. Instead, it felt stiff and icy. Maybe it wasn't the cold.

Rodrigue desperately searched his mind for alternatives, options. He and Susan could run out and jump in the water right now—hide behind the leg of the platform. But then what would Morgan do when he found her missing? Search and maybe find them? Take Bones or another hostage off the platform? Scratch that idea. . . .

Suddenly something was different. . . . No jerks—that's what it was. No jerks and now a faint sensation of lateral movement. Then the scuffing of feet on the ladder—footfalls overhead—

The idling engines suddenly roared and *Abaris* rose by the bow. Morgan was up on the flying bridge at the controls. Rodrigue looked back and grinned at Susan. Things were working out.

If the coast guard had told Morgan he had safe passage, it meant the cutter was lurking just over the horizon. It would be a race, but the cutter had superior speed. Rodrigue knew he had to act fast.

His breathing was growing more painful. Susan looked at him with wide, fearful eyes. He'd better free her first, he thought. Give her a knife. If Morgan got the best of him, maybe she could save herself.

His hand was too unsteady and the double-edged blade of his navy knife was broad for him to be thrusting it between her slim wrists. He looked through the galley drawers and found a small paring knife. There was the stopped-up sink again, bits of lettuce from his salad plastered to the stainless steel where the water, slowly dripping out, had stranded them. It was a bad omen—bad things happened when you neglected things on a boat.

"Stay down here and stay quiet." He knelt, cutting Susan's bonds with the paring knife.

She nodded, rubbing her wrists.

He noticed then the rotten-egg smell wafting from the stained carpet, a familiar, disgusting odor. "Smell that?" he asked.

Susan sniffed. "Yeah, what is it?"

"I don't know. Listen—if for . . . some reason Morgan comes down here, act like you're still tied up. First chance, go for his chest with this." He handed her the heavy navy diver's knife, unsheathed. "Hide it under your leg."

"Oh, Rod, look—" Her fingers touched his ripped wet suit.

"Nothing." He looked into her big, frightened eyes and he had to kiss her. It wasn't the time for it—and yet she kissed him back urgently. For about a second and a half, nothing else mattered.

Then Morgan's voice boomed at them: "Mother*fucking* Rodrigue!"

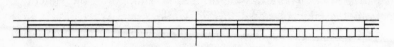

Chapter 40

Morgan was standing beside the galley cabinets, pointing Kindler's Mini-14 at Rodrigue. An unlit cigar protruded jauntily from his mouth.

He had put the boat on automatic pilot and—alerted by the wet footprints on the carpet, Rodrigue figured—come silently through the open saloon door.

But although he had expected someone, he apparently hadn't expected that someone to be John Rodrigue. He had hesitated, and Rodrigue had whirled and now he had the .45 trained on the Australian's belly.

"Hi, Harry. We . . . just talking about you." He had tried to be cool and cheerful, but he had almost gagged on his words.

"How in the hell did you get aboard?"

"Swam. Underwater."

"Yeah? An' where from?"

"I fell out of the sky." Rodrigue coughed fitfully.

Morgan shook his head. "You should've kept right on flying." He removed his sunglasses in the growing gloom of the saloon. His eyes were small and squinty, as though he was constantly flinching, and his face lost its handsomeness.

The *Abaris* sped on.

"I'm here to stop you, Harry." Despite his pain, Rodrigue had become deathly calm, and his voice reflected it. "You've got but two ways to . . . you can live or you can die. Pull that trigger . . . you die."

"Yeah? An' so do you."

"Think of number one, Harry."

Morgan's face was wooden. "Rod, believe me, dying is not that dismal a prospect right now." His eyes flickered to the galley counter, then to the coffee table, but only for an instant.

Rodrigue said nothing. He felt sweat running down his neck like a bead of dry ice.

"I guess we're gonna have to kill each other, now."

Rodrigue gagged, then caught his breath. "I wouldn't be trusting my own judgment . . . too much if I were you. Kinda clumsy . . . kill Kindler and Ahlmark in your own room. . . ."

"It was clumsy, all right—but not of me. I didn't have any choice. That clod was CIA. They said they came to run me out of town—except that Ahlmark was going to drive me himself. Right. Drive me right to a swamp someplace and put a bullet in my head. It was fucking self-defense, nothing less."

"Hire . . . good lawyer."

"Nah. Maybe if I hadn't killed Kindler, too—but I went a little nuts. Smell of blood, y'know? Just like a shark." He smiled again for an instant. "The only thing I could think to do was run. And then I wound up shooting a bloke on the rig back there in the bargain, so think of something else."

Rodrigue knew there wasn't a way out now—for either of them. The maddening thing was, there was no good reason for it.

"Why didn't you just . . . take Leigh away from him? Why did you need his money?"

"It was a package deal, mate. I needed her to get the money. The money was what it was all about."

"For her, too?" Rodrigue asked.

"Her? Nah, the stupid little cunt is in love with me. She woulda chucked it all." He stepped into the galley, and without taking his eyes off Rodrigue, opened a drawer and felt inside.

Rodrigue's chest burned all the way to his back and his breathing was getting ragged. He coughed up phlegm and spat it on the carpet beside the green garden hose.

Suddenly he recognized the rotten-egg smell—propane! Leigh had moved the hose to the griddle and the goddamned boat was filling with propane!

He gasped with raw fear, but he fought it back. "She didn't know . . . you taking the boat, did she?"

"No, an' how'n the hell could she? We hadn't had a chance to talk since Thursday night before that dingo blew the job. What're you driving at, mate?" With increased irritation, Morgan slammed the galley drawer shut and jerked open another.

"We don't have . . . kill each other, Harry," Rodrigue said quickly. "Susan and I . . . we'll jump."

"What?" said Susan quickly.

Morgan laughed. "You'll be killing yourselves. Ain't nobody gonna find you out here."

"Far as they . . . know . . . you've still got . . . hostage."

Morgan thought it over.

The *Abaris* raced blindly on.

"Fuckin' Atlantic's fished out," Morgan said suddenly. "When you made your reputation off the Great Barrier Reef, it's hard to live up to here. I couldn't have stomached a whole season of it."

"Go back . . . Australia." Small talk was the last thing Rodrigue wanted right now.

"You don't go back, mate. You of all people should know that." He smiled—sadly, now, Rodrigue thought. "All there is for me is tellin' stories at the bar. But the money would've made it better, wouldn't it?"

Rodrigue saw then where he had gone wrong. It wasn't lying and stealing or even chasing another man's wife. It was trying to set up everything just right in the face of inevitable ruin, like building a sand castle at low tide.

He thought of Garrett Kindler, sitting back there with his guts in his hands watching the motel room fade. . . . Wouldn't he have traded lives with poor, dumb—and lucky—Ignacio about then? Wealth couldn't buy security; security was an illusion. And nothing stops the clock. Not even a cypress-hulled shrimp boat.

The one who had the answer all along was Jean-Marc. No wonder he could lie there grinning. The son of a bitch had never let a minute get away from him.

Morgan thought it over, absently wagging the unlit cigar up and down in his mouth. . . .

"Okay, mates," he said abruptly. "Over you go."

"Life . . . jackets?"

"Why prolong it?"

"Harry?" Rodrigue raised the pistol. He almost blacked out with the effort.

"In that side cabinet."

Rodrigue pulled out an orange vest and dropped it weakly in Susan's lap. "Here," he croaked.

Out of Morgan's view, Susan shifted her weight onto one hip, revealing the heavy double-edged knife Rodrigue had given her. She looked at Rodrigue with raised eyebrows. A desperate fight was better than a slow death from exposure—or maybe a quicker but infinitely more horrible one as the object of a feeding frenzy.

Rodrigue nearly panicked. He had forgotten about the knife. If Morgan saw it, there would be shooting for sure—shooting that maybe no one would survive. "Put . . . this on and . . . let's get out of here," he said through gritted teeth.

She closed her eyes, heaved a sigh, and slid the knife beneath the divan cushion. With a glazed look in her eyes, she led the way out the door. Rodrigue followed, walking backward, then Morgan, their eyes and and gun muzzles locked.

Outside, they were bathed in the purple light of the dying sun. Rodrigue steadied Susan on the padded gunwale, and then stepped painfully up, dragging his throbbing leg. The effort was like smothering his consciousness in a hot wet towel for an instant. Morgan could've shot him them then, but he seemed fascinated by their act.

With his left arm around her slender waist, Rodrigue lunged outward, striving for distance from the violent wash of the props. They smacked painfully on the water and went tumbling under, twisting apart.

Somehow he found her. She gasped deeply and her wide,

frightened eyes found him. "God, what a weird day I'm having," she said.

The *Abaris* was already seventy-five yards away. Rodrigue saw Morgan disappear inside the saloon just before the boat was swallowed by darkness. He looked around. The opposite horizon twinkled with lights, like a distant city on the desert. But there was no sign of the cutter.

"Here—" He had a coughing spell that left him nauseous, then he managed to put the gun into her hands. "Push . . . down . . . here. Fire when . . ."

Of course, maybe she wouldn't see a boat for hours. Even in the summer, prolonged immersion would drain her body heat dangerously. Then there was always, always, always, always, always the possibility of sharks. . . . But at least now she had a chance.

He didn't, he figured. The chokes made him feel as if he had swallowed a bath towel soaked in gasoline—and it would get worse as more and more bubbles clogged the pulmonary bed. Silently, he recited: *Oh my God, I am heartily sorry for having offended—*

There was a dull thud and they looked up in time to see a tower of flame where the *Abaris* had been. In less than a second, it was gone, and the only noise was the gentle slap of the warm black sea.

Must've found a match, Rodrigue thought dreamily. . . .

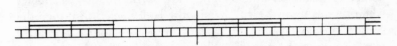

Chapter 41

When the pressure in the outer lock passed thirteen pounds per square inch, gauge, the dish-shaped inner door popped its seal. Suspiciously, Special-Agent-in-Charge Joseph Saccone pushed it open.

He was on his hands and knees like a lumbering bear.

"Crawl on in here, Joe," said Rodrigue evilly. "This'll be good for your rheumatism."

They were at the Marine Biomedical Institute in Galveston, right across the Strand from the Holiday Inn. Soileau, the Mac-Donald pilot, had flown Rodrigue in so low, he'd had to pull up to keep from leaving skid tracks in the dunes.

Earlier, the coast guard cutter *Point Baker* had fished him and Susan out of the water. Running without lights, it had been a little over a mile away when the *Abaris* blew up. The skipper homed in on the blast, then diverted to Susan's gunshots.

Saccone eased his bulk through the circular hatch into the inner lock. He drew his legs up and leaned against the curved side of the recompression chamber and looked around warily.

"She gave us the whole story," he said. "And you figured it exactly right. Morgan purposely picked up every skirt he could so

Kindler would fire him and give you a chance to move in. It also helped to hide their little love match. Morgan found the shooter when he was up in Kemah having the boat hauled. But then the shooter mistook Vandegriff for Kindler, and of course you killed him and the shit hit the fan. They never had the chance to get together again, so she decided to do it on her own and make it look like an act of terrorism this time. That was why she leaked the information about Ahlmark, so you'd have something to tell the police. Then she simply plugged up the sink and moved the drain hose over to the LP bottle for the griddle. Down in the forward stateroom—which was normally unused—she Super-Glued one of those scented candles in a glass to the wall, right down by the floor, then she just barely cracked the knob on the bottle. She figured the gas would eventually flood out of that forward bilge, which is a pretty small area, and reach the flame sometime well after her husband came aboard. But then McKenzie gave up his bunk in the port cabin to Miss Foch and, blundering around in the forward stateroom, drunk, simply blew out the candle and forgot about it until I questioned him this morning."

Saccone shook his head wonderingly. "It was a full bottle. Probably had discharged itself long before Morgan got back on the boat at the rig, filling the whole front of the boat except for whichever staterooms were closed. But then when he took off again, the angle of the boat changed and the gas flowed back up into the area where Morgan was when he lit his cigar."

"Alas, poor Morgan," Rodrigue said, using sarcasm to mask genuine regret. "What about Mrs. Kindler, she in jail?"

Saccone shook his head. "After she gave me her statement, I told her that Morgan had been the only one aboard in the end. She went into shock. She's in the hospital."

"I guess she really loved the guy."

"How did you know the boat was booby-trapped?"

"I finally recognized the smell of the gas. I had known about the hose, of course, and then I remembered some other things— like earlier she had told me not to mess around in the galley, and when I went to see her at her condo, she sort of acted like she was expecting something. It all made sense when I realized I was smelling propane."

Rodrigue also remembered that after everyone else had left the buffet, Leigh had tried to talk him out of baby-sitting the *Abaris* that night. Was it because she was afraid the boat would blow too soon and she liked him enough to want to spare him? No, more likely she was afraid he would piddle around and discover what she had done.

It didn't matter anymore. So she had been using him, so what? A man could slip in the shower and break his neck. He could choke to death on a beer nut. God did not make women for men to run and hide from.

Saccone rose to his knees and peered through the port light— the thick round Plexiglas window. The chamber operator spotted him and raised his eyebrows questioningly. Saccone waved him off and sat back down, looking at the phone receiver. "Sure this thing isn't working?"

"It's not working. You have to depress this switch here, see?" He showed the FBI man the button on the inside of the receiver handle.

"Yeah, they use 'em in secured spaces," Saccone said. "Okay, that's the way it was. It's all wrapped up and we can file it away in our private little memories. But that version has some troubling public ramifications, so there's an official version that I'm going to ask you to adhere to, do you understand?"

"Mrs. Kindler's getting off, isn't she?"

"This is how it is: Morgan made a pass, which Mrs. Kindler rejected. When Kindler and Ahlmark confronted him with it, he flew into a rage, killed them with a fish knife, and stole the yacht. The Bureau got involved when he hijacked an offshore oil installation—"

"Gas," Rodrigue said.

"What?"

"That platform produces natural gas, not oil. If you're going to be willing to sacrifice citizens over our domestic sources of energy, Joe, you at least need to know one from the other. Lignite, for example, can't be worth as many lives as West Texas Intermediate."

Saccone stared. "All right, Rodrigue. You've got a little pissing and moaning coming, I guess. It was a bad situation. Trouble is, it is still a bad situation. We have to—"

There was a loud hiss of air and Saccone jumped, bumping his head. The operator was ventilating the chamber—simultaneously twisting knobs to let air in and out, and carefully maintaining a pressure consistent with thirty feet of seawater. When occupants of a recompression chamber were breathing the air inside, ventilating was necessary to prevent carbon dioxide buildup.

Rodrigue knew what was coming next. When the hissing finally stopped, he denied the FBI agent the privilege of dictating it.

"So the message is, fuck with the domestic energy supply and the FBI'll blow you out of the water."

"That's affirmative," said Saccone.

"And we sure can't let anyone know about the CIA's future base on Jamaica, can we?"

"Al Alhmark was a successful charter-boat captain in the Bahamas, a civilian. I can't stress upon you enough how dangerous it would be for you to deviate from this cover story."

"Oh, I can keep a secret, Joe."

"We're counting on that."

"You're going to have to do a little more than that."

Saccone clicked his tongue. "This is not exactly unexpected. What's your price?"

"Let's see now . . . with Kindler dead, Mrs. Kindler indisposed, and Vandegriff in the hospital, I guess Bones McKenzie ought to be made executor of the *Abaris's* Calcutta winnings, right? I believe my cut was around a hundred thousand at last tally."

Saccone glowered at his own hands for a moment. "There are some heavy hitters in that tournament, Rodrigue. We can't let men like that be swindled."

"You can't let men like that *find out* they've been swindled. If the FBI can't keep a secret, who the fuck can?"

238

"You don't have that kind of stroke. You talk and I'll have you up on a violation of the Lacy Act for bootlegging that marlin."

"Whoop-de-do," said Rodrigue, lazily looping his index finger in the air. "Think of the shit that'll come out at my trial."

Saccone's face flushed and his eyes glittered. "Rodrigue, you've used up every inch of slack a citizen's entitled to. Your ass is right against the buzz saw. If you ever get off the straight and narrow, if you ever as much as wobble, we're going to chew you up."

"Guess this means we've got a deal, eh, Joe?"

"We do. Remember your part of it."

There was a polite tapping and a face darkened the port light. Rodrigue rose painfully and peered out. It was his nurse, a handsome black woman with a no-nonsense manner. She was holding the phone to her head. He picked up the receiver and depressed the talk switch. "Yeah?"

"Say goodbye to your guest, John. Almost time to go back on oxygen."

Because her patient had been nearly dead when they rushed him under and was now as chipper as a schoolboy, the nurse had grown fond of him. The nice thing about the chokes was that if it didn't kill a person, his chances of a complete recovery were excellent.

"Aye aye," he said into the phone. He turned to the FBI agent. "Joe, your secret is safe with me. But don't be keeping any files on me, now. They'd just come back to haunt you."

Saccone crawled backward into the outer lock, glaring at Rodrigue with nagging doubts playing across his face.

Rodrigue closed and dogged the door and listened to the pressure being slowly bled off behind it. He stretched back on the thin blue mat, at home in the tiny steel room. Some of the most peaceful hours of his life had been spent in recompression chambers.

The nurse took Saccone's place, staying in the outer lock with the door between them cracked slightly. Rodrigue fastened the oxygen mask on his face and picked up the Gideon Bible Bones had stolen from the Holiday Inn for him. This was a good time to do penance.

He read all of Matthew Chapter Five, and went on into Chapter Six, to the part about the birds of the sky and the flowers of the field.

A tapping noise interrupted him and he looked up at into Susan's large brown eyes in the port light. He closed the Bible and put his fingers to the light the way they do in prison movies.

"How are you?" she asked.

Rodrigue raised an index finger and eased the inner door shut with his bare foot for privacy.

"I'm fine," he said then.

"I had no idea you were in such a condition. You nearly *died*. I'm really grateful for what you did."

"Aah, all in a day's work."

"By the way, *Abaris* won all the marbles. Mrs. Kindler gets seven hundred fifty-nine thousand and ninety dollars, including the skim for the Jamaican Free Enterprise Foundation. And you guys—you and Bones and Vandegriff and the Japanese guy— each get a hundred and six thousand, seven hundred and forty. Before taxes, of course."

"Well, I don't begrudge her her share. She's suffered quite a loss."

"Did she, uh, trifle with your affections, Rod?"

"The old eternal trapezoid."

"Eternal pentagon. You forget about me." She was smiling in a sad way.

He shook his head. "Tell you what, I honestly wish you would write the story—and then visit me often in prison." That wasn't exactly the truth but it was close. He didn't want the secret to come between them.

"There's not going to be any story. An FBI agent who looks like a Mafia don explained the national-security imperative to me in no uncertain terms. And what's the use, anyway? Kindler's dead, and all it would do is hurt you and Bones."

"What about Shokaito? Did anyone get ahold of him?"

"Yeah, Bruce Phillips got him on the sideband and told him what happened, in so many words. He's on his way in. Oh, yeah, Shokaito said to ask you if you'd consider selling your boat. Apparently, he wants to try his hand at shrimping."

"Good. That's what it's for."

Her hair was still tousled by her exit from the helicopter that had carried her and Bones to Galveston in the wee hours that morning. She was showing her little-girl vulnerability and big girl promise all at once, and— No one but a working diver would understand it, but the feeling that spread over him was like warm urine in a wet suit, pushing back the cold in the deep and dark. Here we go again, he thought happily.

"You're not through with me yet, are you, Sue?"

She cast a furtive glance toward the chamber operator, sitting at the console with his knobs and gauges. "Not until we make love cold stone sober." She wiggled her eyebrows like Groucho Marx. "They say it's even better."

The door to the first lock creaked open, and the nurse poked her head in tentatively. "Time to surface."

"I'll be out of here in about a half an hour," he said into the phone. "Why don't you wait for me at the restaurant across the street?"

"Uh-uh. I'll be right here."

It would be too noisy for conversation as the operator carefully bled off pressure at the equivalent of a foot a minute, so Rodrigue settled back comfortably.

Hyperbaric treatment was good for all sorts of ailments, from hangovers to gangrene. It had been good for what ailed him, too; Rodrigue felt like his old self again.

He'd have to share with the pharmacist/gunman's widow and kids out in California, but he didn't need that much money, anyway. Retirement didn't suit Rodrigue the Pirate.

And Leigh? Poor Leigh. At least she'd had a damn good motive.

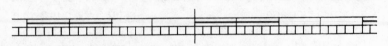

About the Author

Ken Grissom was born in Corpus Christi, Texas, in 1945. He has traveled extensively and has worked as a commercial diver and an engineer on offshore oil-field supply vessels. An outdoor writer for the Houston *Post* and a frequent contributor of articles on boating to magazines, Mr. Grissom lives in Seabrook, Texas. His first John Rodrigue novel, *Drop-Off,* was published in 1988 by St. Martin's Press. He is currently at work on his next John Rodrigue novel.